Contents

Volume II
LIST OF PAPERS

List of Contributors

Yves Berthelot is Executive Secretary of the UN Economic Commission for Europe in Geneva. He was formerly in charge of research at the Development Centre of the Organization for Economic Cooperation and Development (OECD), Director of the Centre d'Etudes Prospective et d'Information Internationales (CEPII), and President of the European Association of Development Research and Training Institutes (EADI).

Agnès Chevallier is Senior Economist at the Centre d'Etudes Prospectives et d'Informations Internationales (CEPII) in Paris. Her research interests are mainly in the economics of the Mediterranean countries.

Meine Pieter van Dijk is Professor of Economics at Erasmus University in Rotterdam. He has worked in various capacities at the ILO, the World Bank and several UN agencies.

Derseh Endale is a Research Fellow at UNU/WIDER in Helsinki. He is currently conducting research on changing employment patterns and the structure of unemployment in Africa.

José Figueiredo is an economist working at the ILO's International Institute for Labour Studies in Geneva. He has done extensive research on labour markets and poverty issues, mainly in Asia and Latin America.

Michel Fouquin is Deputy Director of the Centre d'Etudes Prospectives et d'Informations Internationales (CEPII) in Paris. He has worked in various capacities for the OECD, and his main area of research is the industrial development of Asia.

Orio Giarini is Professor of Economics at the University of Geneva. He is also a Member of the Executive Committee of the Club of Rome, and Secretary General of the Geneva Association.

Hernando Gómez Buendía is UNU/WIDER-Sasakawa Distinguished Professor holding the Chair in Development Policy, based in Helsinki. He is a former Director of the Instituto de Estudios Liberales in Bogota, and has authored many publications on the economics and politics of Latin America.

Ervin Gömbös is the Director of Studies at the International Business School in Budapest. He is Secretary-General of the UN Association of Hungary and Vice-President of the World Federation of UN Associations. He was formerly the Head of Department at the Hungarian Statistical Office.

Mogens Hasdorf is Honorary President of the World Federation of UN Associations. He worked for the Danish Industrialization Fund for Developing Countries both as Deputy Director, and then Resident Representative for Africa.

Klaus Hüfner is Professor of International Economics at the Free University in Berlin and Honorary President of the World Federation of UN Associations. He is currently working on research on the reform of the UN and financing the UN system.

Mieczyslaw Kabaj is Professor of Economics at the Institute of Labour and Social Studies in Warsaw. He is currently conducting research on labour market policies and employment in development within Poland.

Üner Kirdar is Senior Adviser to the Administrator of UNDP in New York, and Director of the Development Study Programme. He has held several senior positions within the UN and the Ministry for Foreign Affairs of Turkey.

Arvo Kuddo is a Research Fellow at UNU/WIDER, where he is conducting research on the consequences of transition in the new market economies. He was formerly the Estonian Minister for Labour and Social Affairs, and Senior Officer at the Bank of Estonia.

Ajeet Mathur is Professor of Economics at the Indian Institute of Management in Calcutta, and an adviser to the Government of India on industrial restructuring.

Valentine M. Moghadam is a Senior Research Fellow at UNU/WIDER, where she is carrying out research on gender and development issues. Born in Iran, her interests span the Middle East and North Africa; economies in transition; and the effects of global economic restructuring on women workers.

Moustafa A. Moustafa is a Research Fellow at UNU/WIDER, carrying out research on new regionalism and the international system with implications for development security.

Jouko Nätti is Director of Social Studies at the University of Jyväskylä in Finland. He is currently doing research on labour market issues, especially new forms of employment, flexible working hours, job insecurity and labour market policy evaluation.

Henk Overbeek is a Senior Lecturer in international relations at the University of Amsterdam. His areas of research include the international political economy, migration and refugee issues.

Maria de Lourdes Pintalsilgo is Chairperson of the Board of UNU/WIDER, and Deputy Chairperson of the InterAction Council in New York. She is a former Minister of Social Affairs, a former Secretary of State for Social Security, and former Acting Prime Minister of Portugal.

Jean Pisani-Ferry is Director of the Centre d'Etudes Prospective et d'Information Internationales (CEPII) in Paris.

Gerry Rodgers is Head of the Labour Institutions and Development Programme of the ILO's International Institute for Labour Studies in Geneva. He has carried out extensive research on labour markets and poverty issues, mainly within Asia and Latin America.

Tuire Santamäki-Vuori is Research Director at the Labour Institute for Economic Research in Helsinki, and also a lecturer at Helsinki University. Her areas of research include: employment, unemployment, employment mobility and wage differentials.

Mihály Simai is Director of UNU/WIDER. He has written extensively on the topics of international business, governance, transforming economies, and the role of TNCs. He was a co-founder and former Director of the Institute for World Economy of the Hungarian Academy of Sciences, where he taught and conducted research for several years. He is a Professor of the Budapest University of Economic Sciences, a former Chairman of the Council of the UNU, and is Honorary President of the World Federation of UN Associations.

Rehman Sobhan is Director-General of the Bangladesh Institute of Development Studies in Dhaka, and is a former Member of the Council for the UNU.

Arne Ström is Head of SIDA's Policy Planning Secretariat in Stockholm. He was formerly SIDA's Resident Representative in Tanzania, and has held various posts within SIDA and the Swedish Foreign Ministry dealing with development cooperation, poverty alleviation, employment generation and environmental economics.

Marja-Liisa Swantz is a Visiting Professor at UNU/WIDER. She is an anthropologist and has written extensively on Africa, and women and development. She was formerly Director of Research at the Institute of Development Studies at Helsinki University.

Alexander Tkachenko is Director of the Labour Market Policy and Population Department within the Ministry of Labour of the Russian Federation in Moscow.

Pawadee Tonguthai is with the Faculty of Economics at Thammasat University in Bangkok. She is currently working on a skills development programme for women workers in the Asian export-oriented industries. She has worked for several international organizations as a consultant within the areas of labour, migration and industrialization.

Udo Udo-Aka is the Chairman of the Applied Resources Consortium Ltd, a finance and management firm based in Lagos. He is the former Director-General of the Centre for Management Development in Lagos.

Naohiro Yashiro is a Professor of Economics at Sophia University, and the Institute for International Relations in Tokyo. His research interests are concentrated mainly on the economics of Japan.

List of Figures and Tables

Preface and Acknowledgements

The need for a new global commitment to enable all people to earn livelihoods through freely chosen productive employment, self-employment and other forms of work has become during the final stages of the twentieth century a crucial political and economic issue for all countries on our globe. The 28 chapters in these two volumes were selected from over 40 contributions to a conference organized by UNU/WIDER in June 1994 on the political and economic aspects of global employment. The conference was a contribution to the intellectual preparations for the World Summit for Social Development. It was organized in cooperation with the UN Secretariat of the Preparatory Committee for the World Summit for Social Development, the UN Economic Commission for Europe, the ILO's International Institute of Labour Studies, the European Association of Development Research and Training Institutes (EADI), and the World Federation of United Nations Associations (WFUNA). As part of the pre-Summit dialogue between academics, government experts and officials of international organizations, the conference sought to find the correct diagnoses of the new problems created by unemployment, to seek ways of generating productive employment, and to find policy responses relevant to the 1990s and beyond.

I have divided the two volumes into five parts. In the first volume, Part I (Unemployment and the Changing Labour Markets: General Issues) deals with some of the more general aspects of the economic, political and social dimensions of unemployment; factors that have been influencing employment globally and in Europe; labour market processes; differences in employment policies; and how present trends may affect the future of work. Part II (Women in the Labour Markets) analyses the gender dimension of unemployment, trends in women's employment patterns, and women's informal economic activities, from global and regional perspectives. Part III (Internationalization and Global Responses) offers perspectives on the growing internationalization and flexibilization of labour markets, the links between trade and employment, and some of the national and international policy responses to the challenge of employment creation.

In the second volume, Part I consists of Regional Studies, with a focus on sub-Saharan Africa, Eastern Europe and the former Soviet Union, the Middle East and North Africa, and Latin America. Part II (Labour Market Policies: Country Case Studies, Successes and Failures) focuses on the policies of selected countries that have been directed towards employment generation or that have tried to target growing unemployment.

This book is the product of a collective effort involving the contributors and UNU/WIDER staff. I would like to express my gratitude to the Finnish International Development Agency (FINNIDA) and the Swedish International Development Authority (SIDA) for their assistance in facilitating the conference. For their part in helping to organize the conference and edit the papers, I am grateful to my colleagues Valentine M. Moghadam and Arvo Kuddo. UNU/WIDER Senior Secretary Liisa Roponen was especially helpful in putting together the final manuscript and perfecting the tables and figures.

Mihály Simai
Director, UNU/WIDER

November 1994
Helsinki

Foreword
Unemployment: A Threat to a Humane Society

– MARIA DE LOURDES PINTASILGO –

Unemployment in a plurality of contexts

As different countries have followed different stages (even cycles) of development, unemployment and job creation cover very diverse social situations and need very different cultural means to cope with them. Unemployment and job creation have different meanings and require diversified solutions which can only be found from within each society by taking into account all the dimensions of the problems.

The overwhelming lack of job opportunities in the Southern hemisphere, coupled with a very high percentage of young people (55 per cent of the population in Africa is under 25), can be analysed in a traditional way as 'unemployment'. However, it can as well raise questions about the suitability of the concept of employment in situations where the industrialization process has not taken place in a massive way and where the contract implicit in the term 'employment' is non-existent.

Nevertheless, a small group of newly industrializing and rapidly industrializing countries (NICs) in the Southern hemisphere are thriving through industrial activity and have had several years of high economic growth. Like the northern countries at the beginning of industrialization, they have succeeded in international competition by mobilizing a labour force which does not exercise pressure for better working conditions. Unemployment, as it is known in the industrialized countries, is thus non-existent. However, as soon as industrialization dispenses with manual skill and dedication to work as the main ingredients in competition, it is likely that the pattern we see now in the Northern hemisphere will appear in the Southern hemisphere as well.

Worldwide competition, which has created new possibilities for the newly industrializing countries (NIC)s, has contributed to unemployment in the highly industrialized countries, while most of the so-called developing world has remained marginal to this new redistribution of job opportunities.

In the Northern hemisphere, unemployment, beside its obvious link with the general economic situation of every society, is at the crossroads of other social and economic factors, namely:

1   Demographic changes – which upset the traditional equilibrium between active and non-active people;

2   Increase of poverty – spread throughout the fabric of society;

3   Urban life style – growing everywhere;

4   General trend of pessimism – which discourages risk-taking by economic agents.

Structural unemployment: the industrial equation in the crossfire

The present crisis clearly shows the structural foundation of un-employment. Many causes are responsible. It is therefore important to analyse those causes in order to fight each one with adequate policies and institutions. Paradoxically, it has become clear that the problem of unemployment has no solution, at least within the framework created by the industrial revolution. Indeed, all the components of the equation that forms the basis of industrial organization have been changed. The preservation of the rate of employment in a given society, when all the other components of the industrial equation have changed, appears to be totally unrealistic. Thus, we have to analyse the different functions present in the industrial process.

The need for new economic perspectives

At the outset of any concrete policy, one guiding principle must be emphasized, namely the need to move towards a people-centred economy. For such an option statistics are not enough – an understanding of the problem at the individual level is fundamental. Nor will well-known economic recipes do – such a policy requires new economic perspectives.

One idea seems to impose itself: it is urgent to give priority to sources of growth that are able both to act as multipliers of other activities and to provide jobs. In order to do this, 'deregulation' has to be overcome. Indeed, as the examples of Central and Eastern Europe are so clearly showing, it is unthinkable to provide jobs in a totally deregulated economy. A precondition to tackling unemployment is, thus, the regulation of the deregulated economy.

Nevertheless, we must warn ourselves, the problem of combating unemployment cannot be equated with creating jobs. What is also at stake is, in the words of Jacques Delors:

> 'systems of employment' encompassing education and training, the functioning of the labour market, the management of enterprises. Therefore, true employment policy tackles at the same time the economic system and the systems of employment.[1]

Systems of employment do not speak only of universal economic conditions. They necessarily make room for the specific economic realities of different regions, for the way in which the organization of society can lead to productive work for all, and for the fundamental basis of general and specific education and training. What is needed is, then, another orientation of the package of economic/social policy, one which 'raises the possibility of employment, reinforces the qualification of people and improves competitivity'.[2]

It is most important that unemployment be dealt with as a decisive economic problem. If it is looked upon only as a social disease, a 'social welfare' approach to unemployment is unavoidable. Compulsory as it was to look at conjunctional unemployment in periods of economic growth as part of the concerns of social policy, those times are over. Earlier the rules of economy could go on unchallenged. Today, it becomes clear that social welfare in a situation of unemployment is not going to solve the problems at stake. We are then obliged to question some of the rules of the economy itself.

Two helpful ideas come from extreme situations in the diversified spectrum of development: the concept of an 'active society' in the highly industrialized countries; and the concept of the 'informal sector' in the developing countries. As all the terms of the industrial equation modify themselves in the post-industrial world, there is the need to redefine the social contract. Hence, the move in the industrialized world towards a concept that is all-embracing: the concept of an 'active society'.[3] Elaborated by the OECD, the concept of an active society provides a renewed intellectual frame for the problems at stake.

> Enhancing 'activity' goes beyond attempts to achieve full employment or increased labour participation. It means taking bold steps to encourage economic and social participation by recognising the multiple areas of activity — market and non-market – the individuals are engaged in, and acknowledging the growing interdependence between those areas of activity.[4]

At the same time, in the Southern hemisphere, we encounter what has been called the informal sector. It covers a wide range of activities, focusing on the most basic needs of people, and it provides people with the elementary goods they need. It is labour-intensive, feeds on traditional knowledge, serves the immediate market area with occasional exports to neighbouring countries, is initiated by people themselves, does not figure in the national accounts, and is equally 'invisible' in the administrative scene of the country where it develops. In its most striking examples, the informal sector is one element pertaining to the 'strategy of survival' of individuals or societies living in utter destitution.

It we want to speak about global employment, it is necessary to see where these two trends meet and where they diverge. It is a challenging task for scientists and activists alike to discover the possibilities opened by these concepts. They have the most interesting feature of being born not from the outside, but out of the functioning, or rather disfunctioning, of the economy itself.

NOTES
1 Jacques Delors, intervention at the European Parliament, December 1993.
2 *Ibid.*
3 *Shaping Structural Change: The Role of Women* (1991). Report by a high-level group of experts to the UN Secretary-General, Paris, OECD.
4 *Ibid.*

– PART I –

Unemployment and the
Changing Labour Markets:
General Issues

1

The Politics and Economics of Global Employment

– MIHÁLY SIMAI[1] –

The issues related to employment and unemployment have major political and economic importance. Research has established a link between unemployment and poverty, while historical developments and contemporary political conflicts in various parts of the world have revealed the adverse effects of rising inequalities on social cohesion. The European turmoil between the two world wars proved that socio-economic conflicts, caused to a large extent by unemployment, could destabilize and even destroy democratic regimes. At the same time, economic cooperation collapsed, the world market dissolved into competing blocs, and relations between nations turned hostile and unmanageable. Despite advances in social policies, humanity still confronts the intractability of the social problems that in the past resulted in extremism, war, and social disintegration.

The human security implications and the politics of the employment issues are linked in certain ways to the global, regional and national political changes in the post-Cold War era. In a number of countries, the Cold War and the arms race played a significant role in creating and sustaining employment based on defence orders and the needs of large armies. The armies themselves absorbed a certain part of the population from the working-age groups. Demobilization and the reduction of defence expenditures which have been necessary also have their effects on the level and patterns of employment in many countries. The world should find more humane, rational, and sustainable international incentives for employment creation than defence expenditures. It is also necessary to establish other, more efficient instruments and guarantees for human social security than systemic competition.

The politics of employment are also connected with the character of the national political forces and their configurations which sustain different models of the market economies or mixed economies. International policy recommendations, such as those which are related to the adjustment programmes, must take into account the characteristics of various political regimes, and should not destabilize democratically elected governments by creating large and unsustainable social problems for them, such as unemployment and marginalization. The structural adjustment programmes and their employment implications generate crucial problems in the developing countries and in the evolving market economies in Europe (or the transition economies).

The Report of the Secretary General of the UN to the Preparatory Committee for the World Summit for Social Development stated:

> Employment is the result of a number of interlinked factors. On the supply side, population growth, labour force participation rates, migration, and education and skills development affect the growth and pattern of employment. On the demand side, while expansion of output is, in general, the major determinant of employment creation, it is also influenced by the labour intensity of technology used, productivity increase, various structural factors and the way available work is distributed.[2]

The politics and economics of employment are difficult and highly complex areas of national decision making. They also comprise a not very well developed, and in practical terms very much constrained, area of international cooperation. The often conflicting interests of the various social groups involved, the differences in the economic philosophies of the governments and the various patterns of linkage with the global economy explain why most of the existing theories fail to provide a comprehensive explanatory framework and are consequently inadequate to guide comprehensive policies.

Employment as a global concern in the 1990s and beyond

According to the estimates of the UN, the world labour force stood at 2.8 billion people in the early 1990s. This represented about half of the total population of the globe. Out of this large reservoir of people, the number of those who were not productively employed was close to 800 million, a little over 30 per cent. The number of registered unemployed was 120 million (about one fourth of them in the industrial world). More than 700 million were underemployed.[3]

The task of employment creation has been on the agenda of international organizations in the past. The World Employment Conference in 1976 was organized within the framework of the ILO's World Employment Programme, and it projected that between 1980 and 2000 about one billion new jobs would have to be created on the global level. A number of experts disagreed and questioned the one billion figure. The economically active population grew, however, by close to 400 million during the 1980s. During the 1990s the growth of this group is expected to be about 380 million. At the same time a great number of jobs have disappeared under the influence of the recession, the transformation of the former socialist countries, and technological and structural changes. Indeed, by the end of the 1990s, the one billion new jobs requirement may not be too far from reality.

The high level of unemployment and underemployment in the mid-1990s is a signal of major structural problems and policy deficiencies in the world economy. The wasting of human resources in the forms of unemployment and underemployment is a major loss for the global community in general, and certain countries in particular. It is not just the loss of important investments made in health and education. It is a source of dissatisfaction, tension, and human suffering. Exclusion from the category of employed people is a cause of poverty and declining standards of living for hundreds of millions in large parts of the world. In Volume One, the chapter by José Figueiredo and Gerry Rodgers emphasizes the need to distinguish between poverty within and poverty outside the labour market, because it may be associated with *a priori* limited opportunities, such as those experienced by persons on the basis of gender, race, or disability.

People are employed (or unemployed) within a national economic framework. The individual governments formulate and implement their employment policies in response to the domestic political, social, and economic pressures and conditions (even though the domestic policies may have important international implications). Fundamentally, most of the world's labour force is working, or seeking employment, within the frontiers of their national labour market institutions. A macroeconomic category based on a definition of full employment, or the natural rate of unemployment (the relevance of which is a highly debated issue anyway), cannot be given and would make no sense on a global level.[4] Within countries, employment has its demographic, technological, macro- and micro-economic, political, and institutional dimensions.

The papers in these two volumes also underline the global nature and interconnectedness of the employment problems, the sources of their convergence, and the need to deal with them in a cooperative international framework. They recognize, however, the constraints and the potentially counterproductive character of globally imposed policy packages, which would not sufficiently take into account the specificities of the regions or of the countries. The differences between the factors and forces shaping the labour markets in Europe and in the United States may require different solutions. The labour market of the United States is defined by the demand of highly competitive and flexible entrepreneurship; by the symbiosis of small, medium and large firms; and by a supply of mobile and qualified workers traditionally exposed to the uncertainties and risks of a market place which may implement measures not acceptable in Europe.

The diverse labour markets in Europe have been formed by the political traditions of representative democracy, with the active participation of labour in the political process; by the intensive interactions between the different social groups and the state; and by a delicate balance of market forces and state and group interests, resulting in a relatively high level of social security and labour market rigidity. The simultaneous presence of structural and cyclical, short- and long-term causes and consequences of unemployment may require a greater diversity of policies and actions.

The approaches will have to be different in the evolving new market economies in Europe. The specificities of the employment problems in that region also have great similarities in the causes and consequences of their employment problems and unemployment. Arvo Kuddo's chapter in Volume Two explains that in the former socialist countries there was, of course, no labour market in the past. Job security was combined with low wages and a certain egalitarianism. The highly subsidized prices were important implicit components of the system of incentives. They had virtually no unemployment programmes and the phenomenon of in-house unemployment or underemployment has been a major impediment to structural changes. In the transformation process in those countries, the labour market is evolving rather slowly. Policies are characterized by short- and medium-term emergency measures. The development of new labour legislation, the bargaining process, social security measures, and the inevitable structural changes make the politics and economics of employment issues particularly important and difficult in the transition process.

In spite of a number of similarities in the 'general' socio-economic background of the employment problems, the specificities dictate increasingly different solutions in the context of the developing countries. There are a number of special cases (like the large, populous countries, or the mini-states) beyond the regional differences in the character and pressure of demographic problems; in economic development levels and patterns; in the efficiency of the institutions; and the functioning of the labour markets. The chapters that deal with regions or country-specific issues look at the differences first of all, from the perspectives of the relevance of national and international measures and the new policies needed in the upgrading of the labour force and in employment creation.

Hernando Gómez Buendía highlights some of the main features of Latin American labour markets: the specifics of the modern sectors; the extent and persistence of the urban informal sector; and the early appearance of labour legislation and social security, which, however, remains restricted to a minority of the working population. In his chapter on economic reforms and Arab labour markets, Moustafa Ahmed Moustafa draws attention to the large size of the young population, to social disparities, to attitudes and values that are influenced on one hand by the imperatives of modern industrial development and on the other hand by traditional religious values. Derseh Endale's chapter on Africa emphasizes the problems caused by a fast-growing labour force and a predominance of self-employment over modern-sector wage employment, which consists of only about 10 per cent of total employment. The informal sector accounts for more than half of the employment in the urban areas and about a quarter of total employment. Open unemployment is about 23 per cent in the economy and it is increasing particularly amongst the youth.

The chapter by Rehman Sobhan deals with some specific issues in Asia. Asia has the largest labour force in the world, and is characterized by diverse patterns of employment and unemployment. Differentiation is mainly between, on the one hand, the countries of East and Southeast Asia, such as the successful newly industrialized countries (NICs) which enjoy high growth rates and low unemployment, and the emerging second-generation NICs that are also beginning to invest in other countries in the region; and, on the other hand, the economies of West Asia and South Asia, which experience high unemployment and much poverty. It is evident also from these papers that the global character of employment problems is basically different from the global nature of capital, production, and trade.

First of all, while most dimensions of the national employment problems have their international aspects or consequences, the institutions and policies related to the labour markets are predominantly national. Second, while the intensive international economic inter-actions through trade, capital and technology flow are inter-connected with the changes in national employment and unemploy-ment trends on a historically unprecedented scale, the international mobility of labour is still rather limited. Third, there are a few specific issues in the labour markets which are of an international nature by definition, but the level of international cooperation on those issues is rather limited, or non-existent.

Is there a global employment crisis at the end of the twentieth cen-tury? Is global full employment a realistic goal for national policies and international cooperation? How could the world cope with present problems and future trends influencing the supply and demand sides of the global labour balance? To what extent and into which direction should the present policies and actions change, in specific countries and in the framework of international cooperation, in order to provide a source of sustainable livelihood even in the poorest countries? What are the realities for achieving those changes?

In the search for answers to these questions, one has to look at some of the major issues in an international and long-term perspective.

Problems and processes shaping employment in a global perspective

There are a number of reasons why employment creation, along with the reduction of unemployment, will probably be one of the most important socio-economic issues of the next 20-25 years for the majority of countries.

THE LONG RECESSION

The first half of the 1990s has experienced the most widespread and longest global recession since the Second World War. This recession has been distinctive in that its factors go beyond the 'regular' cyclical economic components; there has been, for some time, a longer trend of deceleration of output in the industrial world. The recession has been connected, or has coincided, with some long-term problems of the world economy. Certain branches of the manufacturing indus-tries in the industrial countries have been in a depressed state due to sharpening global competition and shifts in demand. There has been a deceleration and decline in the defence sector. The developing countries (with the exception of Southeast Asia) did not have any real recovery in the 1980s. The collapse of the European Communist regimes and the beginnings of the transition to the market system

resulted in a major 30–40 per cent decline in GDP and mass unemployment in those countries. In addition, there has been a certain
degree of synchronization of the recession in the industrial world.
The recession influenced the functioning of the labour markets not
only directly, by increasing unemployment and shrinking employment opportunities; it has weakened the capacity of many governments to deal with human development issues. It has diverted
resources from productive investments to unemployment benefits,
the principal macroeconomic aim of which is to block the fall of
consumption.

THE STRUCTURAL CAUSES OF UNEMPLOYMENT
The recession accentuated and deepened some of the long-term
problems which have been present in the labour markets of the
industrial countries for some time. Not only has the demand for
labour in expanding economic activities been smaller than in those
which were contracting; the emerging employment needs usually
require different qualifications as well. Both occupational and
regional mobility have become more difficult in environments of
stagnation or slow growth in many industrial countries. A number
of structural problems have emerged in the context of those who
have entered the labour market for the first time. There have been,
of course, other structural problems related to the functioning of the
economies. Referring to the industrial countries, Tuire Santamäki-
Vuori (Chapter 3) concludes that 'in the end, the principal reason for
the unsatisfactory labour market performance stems from the same
roots: the failure to innovate and adapt satisfactorily to change'.

Unemployment became a reality for many more widespread
groups in various societies. In the US in the first two years of the
recession, about 20 per cent of the labour force was temporary unemployed. This also reflected, of course, the greater mobility of
labour in the US than in other countries. Long-term unemployment
also became one of the new realities, especially in Europe. These
trends in the labour market are discussed in detail by Yves Berthelot
(Chapter 2).

Employment has also changed and there has been a growing
trend toward temporary and part-time jobs. There have been major
differences between various countries in their job-creating capabilities and in the character of jobs they can create. The high level of
unemployment together with the large number of part-time and
lower-wage jobs made a strong and durable recovery more difficult
to achieve through their impact on the consumer markets. They
reduced job security, undermined the confidence of consumers,

widened income inequalities, and increased poverty in many countries. These problems are also extremely important in the light of
future changes in the factors influencing the character of work and
future patterns of demand for labour. In his chapter in Volume One,
Orio Giarini characterizes these changes as 'probably comparable
only to the creation of a new type of civilization'.

THE TECHNOLOGICAL CHANGES AND THE DANGERS
OF JOBLESS GROWTH

A large part of long-term unemployment and the emergence of the
dangers of 'jobless recovery' are indeed connected with the new
interrelations between demand patterns, competition, production,
employment and technological changes.[5] Excessive labour market
regulations and wage rigidities have been blamed for the reluctance
of entrepreneurs to add to their workforces in Western Europe in the
1980s. Technological progress was considered a key, and still not too
well understood factor in the future changes in employment growth
and occupation patterns.

A number of important issues have been raised, including critical
statements about the simplifications and misconceptions related to
the impact of technological changes on employment and unemployment. The debate on appropriate technologies, for example, revealed
not only the employment-creating opportunities, but also the limitations concerning real choices in the modern competitive sectors. The
impact of income distribution on consumption patterns and their
employment-creating effects was also raised in the context of
experiences in the developing countries. The employment-creating
effects of international or intersectoral technology linkages have
been discussed on the basis of the South and East Asian perspectives.

It has been suggested that the employment effects of new technologies include a number of highly diverse and heterogeneous
processes in the industrial and in the developing countries, such as
influencing the kinds of jobs available and which will be available in
technical, managerial and new types of administrative occupations.
These jobs require high technological qualification as the result of
two trends: the creation of jobs in the new high-technology industries
and services and the creation of high-technology jobs in traditional
industries and services. The modernization of commerce, banking,
transport and infrastructure also changes employment needs.

The 1990s have been characterized by a new wave of rationalization of the production process. There are a number of important
characteristics of this rationalization based on technological change.
First, the technologies involved are much more labour-saving than

the earlier technologies. Second, the technological transformation is not confined to industry, but includes all sectors. The computer-based and telecommunications-related processes have revolutionized the service sectors as well, which in the past could absorb a large number of people released by industry. Third, the process is spreading to the developing countries mainly through the transnational corporations. Their investments create much fewer new jobs than earlier, when a key attraction for their investments was cheap semi-skilled labour. Low-wage competition involves increasingly skilled, low-wage labour working with highly productive technology. Fourth, there are two other areas of the technological transformation which do not receive sufficient attention at present, but already have or will have major influence on global employment. One area, which influences the global material sectors, is the more efficient use of metals, minerals, fuels, etc. and the further growth of the 'knowledge' or information content of GDP. The other is the increasing role of biotechnology in agriculture.

Technological progress is resulting in employment changes in agriculture and rural–urban linkages (especially production and consumption linkages). Due to the fact that in the mid-1990s agriculture still employs the bulk of the world's labour force, the spread of biogenetically produced plants may have a major influence on future agricultural employment. It is in this context that an important question has been raised, within the papers, particularly in relation to the developing countries: to what extent could the labour-supporting capacity of agriculture be sustained or even increased? According to historical experience, technology not only saves, but also creates new jobs. Some of those new jobs are related to the needs of producing and using the new technologies, others are the sources of the related growth of income. At this stage, however, the job-saving tasks related to the new technologies or to the reorganization of the production processes are in the centre of the research and consulting work.

THE CHANGES IN THE GENDER DIMENSION OF THE LABOUR MARKETS
These issues are often dealt with as problems related to the supply of labour. They are, however, much more complex and have to be raised in different perspectives. Valentine Moghadam's chapter deals with the various dimensions and implications of the increasing participation of women in the labour force and their position in the labour markets, in general terms and in sectoral and regional specificities. The educational level of women has increased, which boosts their productivity in employment. The lowering of the

fertility rate has increased the amount of time women have for activities outside their homes. The increasing participation rate and the share of women in the economically active population means that more jobs will have to be created in order to satisfy the increasing demand for the employment of women. Such questions have to be dealt with as: the needs of the changing labour conditions; the greater vulnerability of women; and their greater exposure to restructuring, recessions and other causes of the deteriorating economic conditions. This has been manifested very strongly, whether in the developing countries or in Central and Eastern Europe, in the early 1990s.

Urbanization has moved a large number of women from the rural informal sector to the labour market. There is also the income aspect, which forces many women to find jobs. In many developed countries in the earlier decades, women were the 'secondary participants' in the labour force with the aim of increasing the household income. In the mid-1990s, a large proportion of the working women are 'primary participants' as heads of households or independent persons. In the developed industrial countries, the participation rate of women increased from 48.3 per cent in 1973 to 60 per cent by 1990. The share of women increased to 42 per cent in the economically active population by 1990 in those countries. In the developing countries, the share of women is also growing in the economically active population beyond those sectors, like the informal sector, where the share of women has been high traditionally. In export processing zones, for example, 70–90 per cent of the labour force is accounted for by women.[6] Although the women employees of EPZs constitute a very small proportion of the total labour force in those countries, women's involvement in the industrial sector in Asian countries is known to be substantial in both the formal and informal sectors. Structural and technological changes are taking place in manufacturing, and these changes are affecting women workers throughout Asia, as discussed by Pawadee Tonguthai in her chapter.

THE LONG-TERM CONSEQUENCES OF POPULATION GROWTH

Employment problems in the long term are especially closely interrelated with the demographic issues. These interrelations are, however, rather complex. There is historical evidence from late eighteenth-century England that the interaction of population explosion and rapid technological changes could also be favourable. The population growth stimulated the demand for food, and encouraged investments in agriculture. Industrialization increased employment and demand. The post-war baby boom in the US also boosted investments, demand, and employment. Each example happened, however, within a single country. In the economy of the late twentieth century, those favourable interactions are not present in the developing countries. While the rise in industrial employment has been quite rapid in the developing countries, around 4.0 to 4.5 per cent during the past 25 years – albeit with large regional differences – it was able to absorb only 22 to 24 per cent of those in the working age group.

The diverse growth rates have resulted in major changes in the territorial and age distributions of the population throughout the many regions of the world, and their continuation will further accentuate the role of demographic factors in future employment problems.[7] Most directly, however, it is the number and proportion of people in the working age groups, those between the ages of 15 and 64, which indicate how many new jobs are or will be required globally. Naturally, not all in the working age groups are intending to enter the labour force. At the global level, the proportion of people in the working age group has increased from 57 per cent in 1970 to 62 per cent in 1990, and will reach 64 per cent by 2000. In the developed industrial countries it has remained relatively high (close to two thirds of the population), but in the developing countries it will increase from 54.4 per cent in 1970 to over 60 per cent by the year 2000. Between 1970 and 1990 about 1,140 million persons were added to this working age group, amounting to more than one billion in the developing countries.

According to the population projections of the UN, between 1990 and 2010 the number of people in the working age group will increase by 1,360 million persons (specifically, by about 620 million in the 1990s and 740 million in the first decade of the next century). Of the total increase, only 4.7 per cent will be in the developed world, with more than 95 per cent, or 1,300 million people, in the developing countries. In the developing regions, the rate of increase of people in working age groups will be the most rapid in the Middle East, South and Central America, and in certain African countries. In total numbers, the largest increment will take place in South Asia and China.

According to the available estimates, taking into account the increase in the working age groups, the level of unemployment, and the increasing participation of women, about one billion new jobs will have to be created within the next ten years.[8] This is a historically unprecedented task. It would justify coordinated policies and actions in order to increase employment. In the absence of appropriate measures, the employment issue could become a potential source of global instability.

THE SPECIFIC PROBLEMS CAUSED BY AGEING

The ageing of the population is an aspect of the interrelations between demographic trends and employment. Ageing reduces the proportion of the working age groups and of people belonging to the labour force. This factor, on one hand, reduces the pressure of job seekers on the society, and, on the other hand, due to the extension of the average age and human capabilities to work, presents new kinds of employment issues for the older part of the population. This phenomenon is characteristic of a number of developed industrial countries. In countries where the contracting working age groups represent a more serious problem, there is a push to increase productivity by innovation and by an accelerated mastery of new technology. This may impel certain countries to phase out and redeploy labour-intensive activities to other countries and concentrate instead on high value-added production and services.

The increasing number and proportion of people in the working age group (in the developing countries) reduces the demographic dependency ratios. This could be favourable from the perspective of economic and social development, but only on condition that a sufficiently large number of new jobs are created. Ageing, on the other hand, increases the dependency ratios and puts a greater burden on the working age groups.

The influence of the increasing segment of the older population increases the need for restructuring social expenditure in order to concentrate on special health and other services needed by the higher age groups. There are already countries where more than half of social and health expenditure is spent on such services. Some of these issues are addressed in relation to the Japanese labour market by Naohiro Yashiro in Volume II. He raises a number of adverse consequences of the process, including the contraction of the labour force, the increase of the dependency ratios, and the difficulties in maintaining the seniority system.

THE POSTULATES OF SUSTAINABLE DEVELOPMENT

Employment issues on both national and global levels are also directly or indirectly interconnected with efforts to achieve environmentally sustainable development. The achievement of sustainable development requires appropriate social policies to moderate poverty. Relatively stable employment and income opportunities are, however, key components of long-term conditions for environmental sustainability, by reducing the incentive for migration into areas which are already environmentally strained, by facilitating the increase of public revenues for environment conservation, and in numerous other ways.

There is another aspect of the interrelations between environmental sustainability and employment. The patterns of industrial and agricultural development, and the ways natural resources are exploited, often ignore the long-term environmental consequences, especially in the developing countries, for the achievement of short-term gains. It has never been easy, of course, to find the appropriate balance between the goals of employment and environmental policies. While in many developed industrial countries it has been understood that appropriate environmental management – the development of special services and industries for that purpose – also has job-creating potential, the trade-offs are not so clear in a number of important industries, between environmentally sound industrial patterns and job-creating or sustaining potential in the given branches.

In the majority of the middle-level economies and the developing countries the decision makers are giving greater priority to employment creation than to environmental considerations. The global-level interrelations between employment and environmental sustainability are communicated through the patterns and conditions of trade and foreign direct investments. The debate about the North American Free Trade Agreement (NAFTA) in the US revealed some of the concrete problems in this context, between the US, with stricter environmental rules, and Mexico where the environmental legislation has been more permissive.

Employment-oriented economic and social policies

As has been indicated by the above-mentioned problems, technological and structural changes and the slowdown of economic growth will increase tension in the labour market in most of the industrialized countries, in Central and Eastern Europe, and in the former Soviet Union. Such goals as employment creation, the improvement of the quality of jobs and greater job security are conditioned by complex and basically long-term socio-economic processes. Those processes include changes in the rates and patterns of economic growth and in the efficiency of the markets; as well as the quality of national governance and of the different institutions which are shaping the character of labour legislation and policies; the relevance of education and training; and the mobility of people. The political importance of those processes underlines the necessity of political commitments and initiatives in all those issue areas, including relevant policies and practical programmes of action aimed at stimulating the economy and developing new sources of employment.

There are, of course, important methodological issues to be clarified. The statistical definition of economic activities by individuals has always been ambiguous. The role and concept of domestic work with the appropriate economic calculation of the participation of women and their economic contribution comprise one aspect of the problem. The other aspect is related to the informal sector and to the frontiers between farming, unpaid domestic work and self-employment, which are far from being properly understood and established. Some sociologists and economists consider the redefinition of participation as a sufficient instrument to change the number of the unemployed. In the real world, however, people need to move out of the status of the unemployed and the underemployed through gainful employment and not merely through the redefinition of statistical categories. Statistics may be important, but they are not sufficient to induce social integration, recognition, and status.

This is especially true in the case of certain vulnerable groups which may require special attention through active employment-oriented growth and labour market policies. All the regional chapters emphasize the existence of vulnerable groups and the persistence of labour market segmentation along lines of gender, ethnicity and age, in both the North and the South.

Among the most vulnerable sections of the working population who require special attention are rural workers, the poor, the unskilled urban work force, youth and a large segment of the female labour force. Landless rural workers constitute the poorest parts of the population in the industrial and in the developing countries. They are working in a variety of employment forms, which may include temporary jobs and sharecropping. Their earnings are relatively very low. In most cases they are unorganized and exposed to different forms of additional bondage and dependency. The lowest segment of the urban work force is typically unskilled. In the developing countries, many of them are the new immigrants from the rural areas, who have very limited access to information about jobs and access to stable and regular work. They are also extremely vulnerable to unemployment.

The situation is worse for women than it is for men in the labour market. They experience discrimination in hiring, occupational sex-typing, lower wages, sexual harassment, and a greater tendency to be made redundant during periods of recession or restructuring. Especially vulnerable are female household heads, young women, and poorly educated working women. The rapidly increasing proportion of young people, especially in the poorer urban house-holds, who are neither studying nor working represent another important group, which requires special attention.

EMPLOYMENT-ORIENTED ECONOMIC POLICIES
The need to develop employment-oriented economic policies has been receiving increasing attention in international organizations and in many countries. The efforts for comprehensive labour force policies which characterized the earlier decades, especially the beginnings of development planning, have been gradually replaced by more moderate and confined goals, focusing on the issue of how to keep the unemployed off the streets. In other cases, detailed programmes have been formulated for training and employment of youth or for rural industrialization. In most countries, there has always been a gap between the goals and the available instruments, and between the rhetoric and the actual political commitments.

The success of employment creation and the reduction of un-employment must be directly related to the rate and patterns of economic growth. Policies related only to macroeconomic equili-brium are not sufficient for employment-oriented development. Factors which influence the rate and patterns of economic growth, the level of demand, investments, income distribution, linkages between urban and rural economies, and many other things must also be taken into consideration. The specific tasks of such policies must be elaborated at the level of the individual countries with a view to short- and long-term measures. Improving the capacity of economies to create new jobs implies different specific tasks in the different regions and countries. Increased efficiency of the labour markets is a limited goal even in the industrialized countries.

In general terms, a key condition for sustained employment-oriented growth is increasing productivity. This is a fundamental source of income growth. It requires more investments in research and development, in plants and equipment, in skills which promote wider applicability, in better adaptation to rapid technological changes, and in improving the quality of the educational system to make it more capable of meeting the needs of countries. It also requires the raising of the productivity of the economically active members of households, the improvement of the quality of jobs, the modernization of incentives, the stability and the higher level of earnings, and greater job satisfaction. There are heavy costs – in terms of economic efficiency and social injustice – involved in the vicious circle of low-pay, low-productivity strategy everywhere. The globally important tasks also include the retraining of unemployed persons, providing the bridge between formal education and work for first-time entrants to the labour market, and special help for women in removing those obstacles which restrict their access to better employment opportunities. The starting of emergency employment programmes must also be considered in certain countries as temporary solutions, but not as substitutes for other sources of employment.

In the industrial countries, and in a number of transition economies, the improved functioning of the labour markets in a humanized way, which must be supported by international commitments and cooperation in specific areas, should include a number of measures. Some of those measures are especially important, like sustaining and improving the instruments for the inter-sectoral and inter-territorial mobility of labour required by the structural changes in the economy, and at the same time minimizing the costs of dislocation for individuals. Innovative approaches are needed to combine the necessary rationalization with the preservation of jobs, without deterioration in the quality of employment and working conditions. This could be achieved by reduced working hours combined with part-time employment opportunities with wages calculated on a full-time job basis, well-conceived training and retraining programmes, and other measures.

CHANGES IN THE LABOUR MARKETS

The labour market, which had become acquainted with the high growth syndrome of the post-war period – full employment, the relatively many job openings that compensated for job losses connected with technological change, positive conditions for both vertical mobility (upgrading the labour force) and horizontal mobility (moving in the direction of more productive sectors) – will find that under the new economic conditions of slower growth they can only adjust at low speed. The required structural adjustment is always painful, and those who are most affected are seldom reasonably compensated.

Europe will face probably more difficult and more long-term problems than the United States with its more flexible labour market. In the US, the less regulated labour market offers employees a wide variety of combinations of working conditions, fringe benefits, and wages. They have a number of disadvantages of course, since they offer less job security and fewer mandated social services. Excessive regulations as a means of preserving employment and sustaining traditional work patterns can be extremely costly for the whole economy, however. They result in the conservation of structural patterns which are losing their competitive position and comparative advantages.

The 'lifelong' employment commitment of Japan is also endangered by the new economic realities. Naohiro Yashiro's contribution in Volume II presents the most recent experiences and future dilemmas of Japan, a country which has been considered a model for successful innovations and a high rate of stable employment, and which is now facing major new challenges. A key question is raised in the chapter: will the Japanese employment model be sustainable? And if so, under what circumstances, taking into account the fast technological changes, the structural shifts, the ageing of the population, the gender problems, and the growing pressures for greater flexibility in the labour market? He emphasizes the necessity of important policy adjustments.

Ajeet Mathur traces the context of India's experience in the development of the labour market and its institutions. He focuses on the long-term implications of the ongoing industrial restructuring within the transition to the new economic regime. He raises strong doubts on the short-term reality of full employment, not only in India, but also in a global perspective. The Indian patterns also indicate that changes in the functioning of the labour markets are very difficult everywhere, not only in the industrial countries. While it has been generally emphasized that greater scope should be given to the play of the market forces, a number of new measures are needed for building up a new consensus among entrepreneurs, employees, and governments. This should include a radical improvement in the quality and scope of retraining, the improvement of mechanisms promoting intersectoral and inter-regional mobility, and much more efficient international coordination of policies related to the development and efficient utilization of human resources.

POTENTIALS AND LIMITATIONS OF THE INFORMAL SECTOR

The problems of employment-oriented growth are much more complex and difficult in the developing countries. In the developing countries, the growth of the modern formal sector, the development of modern industries and services, and the modernization of agriculture are the key and lasting guarantees for the generation of stable employment. The informal sector can be considered an important supplementary source, but not a substitute for modern employment opportunities.

However, at this stage in many developing countries, the majority of rural households have either no land or such a small amount of land that they must contract out their labour. For these families, as well as for the majority of the urban poor, and a large segment of the female labour force, the informal sector is the only available source of income. The majority of people (about 60 per cent) in the developing countries are employed in agriculture and in low-productivity manufacturing and services, including the 'informal sector'. The informal sector is, and will be for many years, the largest employment area of last resort; unfortunately, it also preserves poverty.

The increasing importance of the informal sector is also closely connected with the character of the urbanization process which results in shanty towns. The informal sector basically serves the local population. Its upgrading, from the point of view of productivity and income, depends to a large extent on an increase in the purchasing power of the people. Still, the informal sector should not be idealized or considered a permanent panacea for unemployment or underemployment. It must be looked at in a comprehensive and complex framework of the economy of any given country. Its upgrading must also be considered a major task.

The development of small-scale industries and service firms must be considered a key instrument for upgrading the informal sector in rural areas. The increase of non-agricultural rural employment requires different measures, like improving the rural financial and transport infrastructure. Improving and upgrading the urban informal sector requires a number of important measures. Training is one of them. It should be geared to the specific needs of the people and should help to increase incomes or facilitate employment opportunities in the formal sector. Special assistance for the very small enterprises, tax incentives and special training programmes, represent another important area of support for both the rural and urban informal sectors. Upgrading the traditional and the informal sectors further requires more stable and sustainable employment, and skill-intensive production.

Investment needs for creating new jobs in the modern industrial sectors of the economy are quite large in these countries. This industrial employment situation stands in contrast to the historical patterns of the developed industrial countries, which were able to employ 40 per cent of those entering the labour market in the last century. Today, the labour needs of industries using modern technologies are much more limited.

There have been proposals that the developing countries use more labour-intensive technologies within their modern sectors. Although this alternative was rejected by those developing countries involved in modern industries, some countries have been able to combine modern technology and labour-intensive operations, achieving especially good results in employment creation.[9]

IMPROVING HUMAN CAPABILITIES

Education and the improvement of human capabilities have been considered key conditions of gainful employment, especially in an era of fast and widespread technological changes and intense competition. Several chapters emphasize that educational policies, therefore, should also be conceived as integral parts of employment-oriented economic and social policies. The relations between educational policies and economic policies have been considered especially important in four areas. One area relates to participation in the educational process: improving enrolment and reducing drop-out rates. The need for improved access to a higher quality of education was looked at as an important instrument for helping in the achievement of functional literacy (with special attention to young females). Second, the task of better harmonization of the educational system with the changing socio-economic needs and with job training measures was stressed as an indispensable condition for greater convertibility and more efficient utilization of skills. Third, qualitative improvements in the content and management of the educational system and in training and retraining have been needed as specific requirements directly related to employment creation and the upgrading of the labour force. (In the industrial countries, the interest in raising skill levels has encouraged 'competency and outcomes' approaches.) Fourth, it was emphasized that the structural adjustment measures in many countries have reduced their capabilities to provide appropriate financing for the educational sector at a period when its crucial importance has become increasingly evident from the point of view of the success of long-term adjustment measures.

In his discussion of linkages between higher education and employment, Klaus Hüfner considers this level of the educational system as especially important in increasing the capacity of countries to absorb, disseminate and develop new knowledge. He also emphasizes that the capacity of different economies to absorb people with high skill levels depends on a number of factors, including the size and structure of the modern sectors, and the attitudes of potential employees and employers. In many developing countries the labour market trends show that while, in the past, civil service employment absorbed most of the local graduates of upper secondary schools and universities, in the future the civil service requirements can absorb only a very small fraction of graduates. The 'labour queue' theory, according to which education is a critical background factor used by employers in ranking the workforce, in general and especially in case of unemployment, may be correct. The present unemployment level among university graduates in many developing countries reflects the difficulties experienced by young people in finding appropriate jobs.

THE ROLE OF DIFFERENT AGENTS AND GROUPS
Private sector
There was consensus that the private sector has an important role to play in the creation of jobs, and should be supported by governments and by the international financial institutions. However, the capabilities of the private sector in the poorer developing countries are still very limited for creating new employment opportunities. Udo Udo-Aka's chapter examines the role of the private sector in employment creation in Nigeria, the most populous country in Africa. While he concentrates on the role and capabilities of the formal private sector, he also examines its interactions with the public sector. The chapter notes some of the constraints on the private sector in job creation. The example of Nigeria proves that when the private sector has been preoccupied with the struggle for survival in a liberalized, competitive environment, its capacity for generating productive employment has not been too strong. The chapter at the same time underlines the importance of the national private sector in skill development, job training, and in the general upgrading of the labour force. His chapter emphasizes the need to increase private sector investment as a way of spurring growth and employment.

   In the context of the role of the private sector, other chapters, such as that of Pawadee Tonguthai on women in Asian manufacturing and that of Ajeet Mathur on India, also underline that it should play a greater part in active labour market policy and the broad upgrading of skills for combating unemployment and social polarization. Firms can be encouraged to train and continually upgrade the skills of their workforce, or commit a part of their wage bill to a national training fund, as is done in some European countries. This is called the 'high-skill, high-productivity strategy'. Investments in human capital can be made by the private sector (investments in research and development, for example, as well as investments in training), and not just by the state.

Transnational corporations
There is a role for transnational corporations, which have been important actors in the internationalization of the markets of goods

and of capital, although their role has been much more limited in the internationalization of labour markets and especially in employment creation. It is necessary that the TNCs should take into account the employment problems of the host countries and help them with employment creation and employment upgrading measures through the direct and indirect effects of their foreign investments.

Role of the state

There is a role for the state, especially where markets are backward or undeveloped, or entrepreneurship and the private sector are small. This will necessitate a more active role for the state in industrial development and in employment generation. The necessity of active labour market policies was also emphasized, such as increasing the labour content of public works, training, retraining, skills upgrading and employment services. The state can also contribute to ending the marginalization of the unemployed population by providing workfare, or subsidized employment, by reducing the 'mismatch between supply of the education system and demand of the employment system', and by making universities more diversified and more responsive to labour market needs. State emergency measures may include rural public works and housing construction programmes. Improving and enforcing the labour standards rather than lowering them is also an important task for governments. Other measures may include affordable child care for women workers, and other investments in female human resource development.

Role of the community

There is a role for the different voluntary organizations and especially for the local communities: with respect to the unemployed and underemployed, and concerning exclusion and other forms of job discrimination. This must be conceived and developed in a given economic and social context. Especially (but not exclusively) in the industrial countries, unemployment benefits may be accompanied by community service or other forms of voluntary activity – such as hospital work, caring for the elderly, caring for youths with special needs, park service, and so on. These unpaid jobs should be considered as possibilities for transitions to situations of employment or re-employment, so that people do not feel resentful that they are not getting paid for jobs while others are. On one hand, the broader public acknowledgement of community activities outside the traditional concept of regular, remunerated work (the socially productive tasks for the community), and on the other hand the initiatives of the local authorities, would be needed to facilitate this process.[10] The different central training and retraining programmes could also be supplemented by community initiatives. They should allow individuals, especially those who are not actively engaged in training or retraining, to take educational courses: computing; accounting; upgrading computer skills; foreign languages; courses in child development, etc. These could come in short cycles or in longer-term courses. Communities may also help in facilitating the availability of information about local job opportunities. The forms and scope of community initiatives may have different dimensions in the majority of the developing countries. In certain cases they could be combined with government-supported public works or other emergency employment programmes. The positive role of the communities in the field of employment could also be extremely important in promoting social integration. There are, of course, different levels and dimensions of social integration, but from the point of view of the individuals, the local community is the most direct and transparent level.

The consequences of the interconnectedness and internationalization of the labour market for employment

The achieved level of internationalization of the labour markets, the role of different mechanisms in the process and the consequences of it, are discussed in a number of chapters.

THE INTERNATIONALIZATION OF THE LABOUR MARKETS
The analogy of internationalization of the capital markets or the technology markets cannot be applied to the labour markets due to a number of political, social and economic factors. In spite of all the constraints, however, labour markets are more internationalized, through various direct and indirect linkages, than in the past. In Chapter 13, 'Employment and the Internationalization of the Labour Markets', it is argued that the higher degree of global inter-connectedness, which is still growing, also has a major influence on trends and patterns of employment. It influences skills, wages and labour standards. Already the present level of internationalization requires much more extensive international cooperation. The most direct factor of internationalization in the case of the labour markets is migration, which has become more of an increasingly important global social issue than an economic issue. In Europe, migration has increased public tension concerning foreigners. In this, the push

effect of the economic difficulties in the evolving market economies and the growing trend of economic refugees from the developing countries have been playing important roles. On the American continent there is the new 'migration explosion', the increasing volume and the changing patterns of migration, not only to the US but also to Argentina, Brazil and Venezuela. In Africa, migration has resulted from the influence of civil wars and instability on the mass outflow of refugees. In the Middle East, migration was increased by the consequences of the Gulf War and the shrinking revenues of the oil-exporting countries. In Asia, the new opportunities for the foreign workers created by fast economic growth brought the issues into the forefront.

Ethnic conflicts created by the influx of foreign workers, and other new political and economic aspects of migration, dictate a new comprehensive approach in the analysis of the process, beyond its economic causes and consequences. The neo-classical model, concentrating on 'expected higher income', is an irrelevant framework for explaining or even studying the process. The structural approach, which looks at the demographic, political, institutional, socio-economic, gender, urban, rural and international interactions, has been much more relevant for studying its determinants and consequences, including return flows and options for re-migration. There will be a number of problems related to the future of international migration. One is the diminishing absorptive capacity of the labour markets. As well as having legal consequences, this is reflected in the ability of the immigrants to attain the income levels of the native population – out of reach in many countries for the majority of the new immigrants.

THE NORTH–SOUTH DIMENSIONS OF THE EMPLOYMENT ISSUES
The North–South interconnectedness of the employment issues receives special attention in the chapter by Michel Fouquin, Angnès Chevallier and Jean Pisani-Ferry, and in the chapter by Rehman Sobhan. This latter underlines the importance of the fact that the evolving new developments in the international division of labour – the increasing mobility of labour, which has been also institutionalized in some parts of the world – increases the interconnectedness of the employment problems of the developed and developing countries. On this basis, much of the blame for rising unemployment in the North has been placed on the South (mainly Asian countries) whose export successes, especially in the textiles and garment industries, are linked to 'unfair' competitive advantages due to extremely cheap and exploited labour (including child labour). Even

in the growing field of teleworking, people can 'price themselves into a job'. For example, an Indian teleworker earns one tenth of a European teleworker's wage.

The extremely wide gap between wages in the industrialized North and the industrializing South is usually explained in terms of the lower productivity of the latter. Yet, assuming that world-class technology is made available through foreign direct investment or licensing agreements, there are not many reasons why productivity in the modern, export-oriented sectors should be much lower than in industrial countries, which should result in higher wages for workers in those sectors. There may also be the 'deliberate lowering of social standards by a government in an attempt to attract foreign capital'.

These problems show the necessity of finding new ways to manage increased international competition, based on wage differences, without disrupting the trading system by different protectionist measures and without undermining international efforts for the improvement of labour standards. Suggestions related to the deliberate redeployment of certain industries, based on international contractual arrangements, have not received sufficient practical support in the past. Certain institutionalized forms of mutual adjustment, however, may be the only relevant and relatively fast response.

NATIONAL EMPLOYMENT POLICIES AND MULTILATERAL COOPERATION

The ability of the economy to create jobs is also a complex institutional and structural question. The tasks include redefining and improving the efficiency of government policies and actions by the introduction of a comprehensive policy related to human resource development and more efficient international cooperation. One of the most difficult problems in the context of international cooperation in employment issues has been to define the scope and content of international public policies. Employment issues belong to the neglected dimension of international cooperation, in spite of the important international implications of national employment policies.

In a liberalizing global economy, national protectionist policies, the freedom of international trade, and foreign direct investments have been very closely related to national employment levels and patterns. The governments in many countries during the 1970s and 1980s considered the sustaining of high-level employment and the creation of employment opportunities as important components of their programmes. Practical approaches to employment problems in

UNIVERSITY OF WOLVERHAMPTON
Harrison Learning Centre

ITEMS ISSUED:

Customer ID: WPP61979317

Title: Global employment : an international
investigation into the future of work
ID: 7620920733
Due: 29/12/2016 23:59

Total items: 1
Total fines: £8.40
08/12/2016 12:38
Issued: 11
Overdue: 0

Thank you for using Self Service.
Please keep your receipt.

Overdue books are fined at 40p per day for
1 week loans, 10p per day for long loans.

national frameworks have been conditioned by the character of political power in the respective countries, and by the strength of those national groups and organizations which have considered employment creation and full employment priority issues. While many experts emphasized that this cannot be achieved and sustained any longer in an isolated national framework in an interdependent world, in practice this view was not shared by the main political groups which shaped national policies.

Workers and their unions – who in many cases want to protect the jobs, wages, and labour conditions which they have achieved within the national state framework through political struggles, bargaining, and contracts – have to come to the understanding of the internationalization of the main processes influencing employment, wages and social policies. Understanding that the intensity and character of international competition and the drive for greater competitiveness have also increased the international interconnectedness of the labour markets, and that labour standards have also been shaped by international agreements and commitments, is not sufficient for the promotion of the harmonization of national employment policies and for stimulating more meaningful and efficient international cooperation.

At this stage of global economic development, the possibility of full employment is constrained by a number of factors: political ideologies; economic theories serving as guidelines for economic policy orientation; a number of internal and international imbalances; a growing diversity of economic interests between different groups in the societies; and the limited instruments available for national investments and government policies. International competition and the degree of international interconnectedness are also important factors in making the implementation of national employment policies more difficult. Under these circumstances, there are no uniform global possibilities of, and routes to, full employment. The pressing global needs, the increasing pressure piling up in different parts of the world for increasing human security, not only justifies but demands the re-emphasizing of the moral commitment of countries, made in the UN Charter, to promote welfare and full employment. This could be a significant global guideline for national policies and future international cooperation.

NOTES
1 I would like to thank my colleague Valentine M. Moghadam for ideas and suggestions.
2 UN General Assembly, Preparatory Committee for the World Summit

for Social Development (1994) *World Summit for Social Development: An Overview. Report of the Secretary General.* A/Conf.166/PC/6, January, New York, p. 37.

3 'Expert meeting on the expansion of productive employment. Report of the expert group', Saltsjöbaden, Sweden, 8 October 1993.

4 The internationally accepted definition of unemployment (ILO) is a pool of people above a specified age, who are without work, are currently available for work and actively searching for work in the period of reference. Neither the definition, nor the method for collecting unemployment statistics, is universally accepted. There is no universally accepted definition for the 'natural rate' of unemployment either. Some experts consider the natural rate of unemployment as the full employment rate (under the assumption that there cannot be a zero rate of unemployment in an economy), others consider it as a rate which is not accelerating inflation (corresponding to macroeconomic equilibrium).

5 The terms *jobless recovery* and *jobless growth* have been spreading in the vocabulary of experts and also in the press characterizing a trend for the changing relations between growth and employment in the industrial world. While the phenomenon is not new, the widening of the gap between GDP growth and employment increase has been accelerating all over the world. According to the projections of UNDP experts, this trend will continue. See, for example, UNDP (1993) *Human Development Report*, pp. 36–7.

6 United Nations (1993) *UN Social Development Report on the World Social Situation*, pp. 202–6, New York.

7 While on a global level there has been a slowdown of population growth, and in the future growth of the world population may look like an increasingly manageable issue through different measures, the regional distribution of population growth may be a source of historically unprecedented problems and tragedies with major global implications. Long-term trends in the second half of the twentieth century suggest that 88 per cent of the increment of the global population between 1950 and 2000 will take place in the developing countries, and 62 per cent of the increment in Asia. In 1950, 54 per cent of the global population lived in Asia. In 1950 about one third of the global population lived in the developed world, more than twice as much as Africa and Latin America taken together, and in Europe alone there were almost twice as many people as in Africa. By the year 2000, there will be 50 per cent more people living in Africa than in Europe. In 1950, about two thirds of the global population lived in low-income countries; by 2000 close to 80 per cent will live in those countries. Urban population is continuing to increase about 50 per cent faster, in general, than the overall population growth. In the developing countries the difference will be almost 100 per cent till the end of the century.

8 Sources for the above data include United Nations (1989) *World Population Prospects*, New York, and UNDP (1991 and 1993) *Human Development Report, 1991*, New York.

9 Certain countries, like China for instance, have combined the development of modern high-technology industries with small-scale, labour-intensive rural and township industrialization in order to ease not only

the pressures of unemployment or underemployment, but to slow down or prevent migration to the larger cities. The small-scale rural industrial (and service) firms have simultaneously been able to produce goods and services for local demand at much lower prices. The local industrial enterprises contributed also to the increase of exports. They directed small savings into productive channels, stimulated entrepreneurial spirit and contributed to the development of different skills. The share of rural enterprises in the increase of employment was above 70 per cent in China in the period 1985–91. More than 71 million new jobs were created in this sector.

10 See, for example, OECD (1994) *Societies in Transition: The Future of Work and Leisure*, OECD Forum for the Future, Paris, OECD/GD (94-39), p.12.

2

European and General Global Issues Influencing Employment and Unemployment

– YVES BERTHELOT[1] –

The unprecedented high rates of unemployment throughout Europe reflect not only the many forces which are always at work (such as technological change, structural changes in the mix of goods and services produced and traded internationally, and so on) but also the strategic policy choices made by governments. Both in market economies and transition economies, priority has been given to fighting inflation and the level of unemployment has tended to become a residual. The present levels of unemployment have adverse social effects and risk the promotion of political instability. They also have adverse economic effects in encouraging all forms of protectionism which stand in the way of the efforts of the transition economies and developing countries to achieve integration with the global economy. Hence, there is an urgent need for a new strategy of economic development and cooperation to promote productive employment growth.

In developing countries, where there is little or no social security, attention is drawn, on one side, to workers who do not get enough income from their activity to reach a minimum standard of living and, on the other side, to supernumerary employees, mainly in the civil service or public enterprises. The first category raises the issues of poverty and of the informal sector. Training, access to credit, self-organization and the protection of rights are the main instruments used in anti-poverty policies. Restructuring, privatization, housing and reconversion are among the policies followed to deal with the second category. In the following pages, I will not address the situation of developing countries, which are better described by other participants, but will focus on the employment situation in Europe.

Labour markets in Western Europe and North America

The labour markets of Western Europe and North America are currently in severe disequilibrium, with unemployment approaching a total of 30 million people, or almost 9 per cent of the labour force. Whilst figures such as these point to an unacceptable wastage of scarce resources, they tend to mask the real depth of the social crisis in the labour markets, evident in the very high levels of un-employment among young people; the large number of workers who have been without a job for at least one year; and the rising incidence of 'discouraged' workers, who have left the labour force altogether.

The dismal state of Western labour markets is a reflection of the combined effects of both cyclical and structural factors, the relative importance of each varying from country to country. In the United States, the recovery has continued to strengthen and labour markets have started to improve accordingly, but this is in sharp contrast to many countries in Western Europe, where the pace of recovery remains weak and a further deterioration in labour markets is expected this year.

Whilst the cyclical component of unemployment in Western Europe is likely to moderate as countries emerge from recession and move progressively into recovery, the problem of structural unemployment may prove to be intractable, even in the medium term. Indeed, structural unemployment appears to be on a long-run rising trend in many West European countries, a trend which began after the first oil shock in the early 1970s. A large part of this structural unemployment may actually be accumulated cyclical unemployment, which would explain the tendency for unemploy-ment to ratchet upwards from cycle to cycle.

Much of the structural unemployment seems to be accounted for by unskilled male workers, the demand for which has fallen relative to the demand for skilled workers. The tendency for the rise in labour costs to outpace productivity growth over the long term has led to capital–labour substitution, which has been accentuated by technological progress. Another factor is the increasing competition from developing countries and, more recently, from the transition economies, in the area of low-skilled, standardized tradeable goods. Given the sizeable wage differentials, it seems unlikely that Western Europe can defend its competitiveness in this area. Nor is it in the longer-term interests of the Western industrialized countries to erect protectionist barriers against these changes in the pattern of comparative advantage.

Increasingly, employment conditions will be influenced by economic globalization, which allows capital to seek cheap and productive labour anywhere in the world. Traditionally home-based manufacturing capacity will tend to migrate. For example, German luxury car producers are currently planning new factories in Mexico and India, and are considering opportunities for investment in Southeast Asia. The impact of globalization on employment may have been insignificant to date, but it is a factor which is perceived to be important to future developments in the labour markets of the Western industrialized countries.

The re-emergence of unemployment as a central focus of concern among economic policy makers has prompted debate about the appropriateness of different policy instruments to address the problem. Whilst there is agreement that cyclical unemployment is likely to moderate as countries emerge from recession and move progressively into recovery, the strength of any increase in the demand for labour will depend crucially on whether there is sustained growth in output, and on the outcome of collective bargaining rounds, particularly in respect to wage restraint. Furthermore, there is a lack of consensus on the policy mix required to tackle the complex foundation of structural unemployment, with the argument split along broadly ideological lines. On one hand, there is support for a strategy of more deregulated labour markets, which could involve a less generous social security net and possibly more decentralized wage bargaining procedures. This approach is exemplified by the labour market reforms introduced in the United Kingdom in the 1980s, and is characteristic of labour markets in the United States. On the other hand, there is the more consensual approach of social partnership, which has evolved in continental Western Europe since the Second World War, and which is embodied in the Social Chapter of the Maastricht Treaty.

The priority currently afforded to labour market problems is evident in the number of high profile meetings which have been convened since the end of 1993: EU heads of government met in December 1993 to consider a White Paper on employment, growth and competitiveness; G-7 ministers discussed employment problems in March 1994; and later an OECD presentation was made to ministers of a synthesis report of its new Jobs Study.

The analytical conclusion of this study is that the root cause of the unemployment crisis in the Western industrialized countries has been their inability to adapt to change. The policy conclusions which follow are a mix of supply-side structural measures, with macro-economic policy relegated to a somewhat passive role: in the short term, to limit cyclical fluctuations in output and employment; in the longer term, to provide a framework, based on sound public finances and price stability, to ensure that growth of output and employment is sustainable.[2] Similarly, the EU White Paper envisages an essentially limited macroeconomic framework, with budgetary policy constrained by the convergence criteria of the Maastricht Treaty, and interest rate reductions linked to inflation targets of 2 to 3 per cent.[3]

The policy prescriptions of these recent studies focus mainly on the classical component of unemployment and largely ignore the Keynesian deficient demand component and the mechanism by which the latter may be transformed into the former. Yet tight macroeconomic policy is currently holding back output and employment growth in Western Europe. Not enough attention has been given to the evolution of producer and consumer behaviour in the course of the 1980s, which may explain why the current recovery has occurred in the United States and Europe without inflation and why, if sustained, it would allow for a more active macroeconomic policy. Given international interdependencies, a joint, coordinated macroeconomic initiative by the G-7 countries would make national policies more effective.[4]

Unemployment in transition countries

One of the major costs of the reforms in Eastern Europe and the former Soviet Union has been surging unemployment which did not exist, at least officially, under central planning, with the main exception of the former Yugoslavia. Open unemployment reacted slowly to the introduction of reforms, the collapse of the Council for Mutual Economic Assistance (CMEA), and the severe decline in output. However, since 1991 unemployment has risen sharply and is now a major economic and social problem in the transition economies.

Assessing the real magnitude of labour market developments in the transition economies remains difficult due to the limited and often varying coverage of available statistics. Nevertheless, the general tendencies dominating the labour markets are rather clear.

In Eastern Europe there were 7.5 million registered unemployed at the end of 1993, nearly a threefold increase since the end of 1990. As a proportion of the labour force, the average unemployment rate is around 14 per cent, although individual rates range from 3.5 per cent in the Czech Republic[5] to 30 per cent in the FYR of Macedonia.

In the former Soviet Union, official unemployment rates are still exceptionally low given the large falls in output – although unemployment has started to increase sharply in the Baltic states. These low levels of official unemployment, which range between 0.2 and 1.3 per cent in the Commonwealth of Independent States (except in Armenia where the rate is 6.2 per cent), reflect the slow rate of structural change in many parts of the former Soviet Union, but there are grounds for believing that the statistics are greatly distorted. In Russia the unemployment rate at the end of 1993, based on the number of people classified as 'having the official status of being unemployed', was 1.1 per cent of the labour force, but on the ILO definition of unemployment (those out of work and actively seeking employment) it was just over 5 per cent. If the count is extended to include partial unemployment and workers on 'unpaid leave', the estimate of the unemployment rate increases to over 10.4 per cent.[6]

Unemployment on the present scale in Eastern Europe would be a serious problem in any country, but it is particularly disturbing when previous experience of it is virtually non-existent and where governments are still without an effective strategy for industrial and labour market restructuring. At the same time, governments are being forced to reduce the social protection given to the unemployed because of the macroeconomic pressures to reduce overall spending. Not only has unemployment benefit as a proportion of the average wage fallen considerably in all the transition economies since 1991, but the proportion of the unemployed actually entitled to benefit has also been sharply reduced. Rough estimates for six East European countries suggest that, on average, only about 30–40 per cent of the unemployed are entitled to a benefit which is equivalent to about one third of the average wage.[7] In Russia the unemployment benefit is equivalent to about 30 per cent of the official minimum subsistence income. This helps to explain why workers are prepared to accept periods of unpaid leave, since they remain attached to the labour force and retain access to the social support system of the enterprise, and why the government is reluctant to face the social consequences of a more rapid restructuring of the large state-owned enterprises. Notwithstanding, a striking feature of these countries is the high level of excess labour apparent in their deficient productivity performances. This implies that extensive labour shedding is likely when restructuring gathers pace in the large state-owned enterprises. Another feature of the transition economies is that there is substantial labour 'churning', with workers moving from job to job without going through the pool of the unemployed, which increases the duration of unemployment significantly.

The trade-off between social justice and economic efficiency, the formula offered by the recent OECD jobs study in order to increase the job creation ability of the Western economies to adapt to change, is difficult to recommend in the immediate future to the transition countries, where suitable labour market institutions are not yet established and unemployment-related poverty and reform fatigue have reached critical levels. At best, the nine structural policy measures prescribed by OECD, stressing a passive role for macro-economic policy, can be used as a frame of reference for formulating longer-term labour market policies and mid-term incomes policies in the transition economies. In the short run, to avoid further increase in mass unemployment, extensive cost-cutting, increases in competitiveness and restructuring can be achieved by using scarce, non-labour resources more efficiently. Given the extremely low level of wages, labour is not the most costly resource in these countries and hence labour shedding should not be *the* priority measure in the restructuring process. This is particularly important for large state-owned enterprises, which are not only economic entities but also perform a number of social welfare functions which in the West are taken care of by the state.

Active labour market measures are extremely important, par-ticularly for encouraging the acquisition of the new skills required by changes in the pattern and quality of production. However, such measures are expensive, and to organize training for the un-employed without actual jobs being available may lead to a waste of resources. Hence, the only way to reduce unemployment (both open and hidden) and lower social tension and political risks is to increase the demand for labour simultaneously with productivity gains. In other words, the key elements on which the main efforts should be concentrated are growth in output and capital investment.

Having said that, we can consider the main bottlenecks to be faced and the main policy issues involved in reaching this objective of sustainable output growth and employment creation. Here I will highlight the main views of the Secretariat of the United Nations Economic Commission for Europe as reflected in the most recent Economic Survey of Europe.[8]

Nearly four and a half years after the collapse of the communist regimes in Eastern Europe and the former Soviet Union, most of the region is still in a deep economic depression. Even the 'advanced' group (namely the Czech Republic, Hungary, Poland and Slovenia), where recovery is gradually emerging, face considerable problems in the areas of macroeconomic stabilization, privatization, and the reform of the banking systems. Trade and supply shocks after the collapse of the CMEA and the disintegration of the Soviet Union, together with privatization and the liberalization of prices, led to sharp disequilibria in product, capital and labour markets. Not only has the level of demand collapsed but its structure has also changed drastically due to large changes in relative prices. Even though the reform process is still in its early stages, significant parts of the capital stock have been rendered obsolete by considerable changes in the structure of output dictated both by domestic and foreign demand. On the other side, the rapid expansion of output and employment in the services sector in Eastern Europe is one of the most conspicuous breaks with the former centrally planned regime. This expansion of services took place not only in the form of small-scale enterprise (retail trade, restaurants, and so on) due to privatization, but also in newly established financial, legal and business services, which are required for the functioning of the new market economies.

Gross fixed capital investment in new plants and equipment is a fundamental requirement for the long-run restructuring of the transition economies and for creating the basis for a sustained expansion in economic activity. For most of the transition economies, however, fixed investment has remained in a deep slump since 1989. This weakness of fixed investment is both a reflection and a cause of many of the rigidities which are holding back or slowing down the transition process. Without a strong recovery in fixed investment it will not be possible to achieve the extensive restructuring of the supply side of the economies which is essential for a sustained reduction of inflation to rates broadly comparable with those in Western Europe. At the same time, investment and the expansion of new activities is essential for creating new jobs to replace those destroyed in the course of restructuring uncompetitive, state-owned enterprises.

Given the very low savings ratio, the lack of clarity about property rights and political instability, together with very high real interest rates and scarce bank credits, private sector investments are at very inadequate levels for the reforms to be considered to be giving concrete results. Between 1989 and 1993 gross fixed investment fell by 40 per cent in Eastern Europe, nearly 60 per cent in Russia and the Ukraine, and some 80 per cent in the Baltic states. Furthermore, these countries are not only desperately in need of a high level of gross fixed capital investment to increase productivity and create new jobs; they also need human capital investment, in the training of managers, for example, for the optimal exploitation of new technologies in a competitive market setting. Investment demand could be increased via an expansion of public expenditure on infra-structure (roads, railways, telecommunications, the environment) which is in need of considerable improvement in all the transition economies and which is currently a source of major bottlenecks to private investment (both domestic and foreign) and economic activity in general. However, this way forward is also heavily cir-cumscribed because of pressures to reduce government budget deficits. One major obstacle to a faster reform process is the underdeveloped tax collection systems and widespread tax evasion which inhibit the increase in budget revenues. On the other hand, cutting expenditure presents governments with painful dilemmas: public infrastructure investment is already very low and further cuts would reduce the contribution of the international development banks' expenditure in this area; reducing social security benefits at a time of sharply rising unemployment is politically dangerous; and a sharp cut in subsidies to ailing state-owned enterprises will lead to a large increase in unemployment with further demands for unemployment benefit and the risk of social instability, particularly in the CIS countries where enterprises have traditionally played a paternalistic role by providing not only jobs, but also health care, child care, education and social contacts in the often isolated towns built around the enterprises.

One of the initial assumptions made by Western governments and some international institutions was that private foreign direct investment (FDI) would play a key role in the transition process and that this would obviate the need for official assistance on, say, the scale of the Marshall Plan. So far this has not proved to be the case. The net inflow of FDI into Eastern Europe has been much less than was expected – or hoped for – by both Western and Eastern governments. The total for 1993 was estimated to have been some US$3.5 billion, and since 1990 the total inflow has been under US$10 billion (for nine countries). Moreover most of the investment is concentrated in just a few countries: the four 'advanced' transition economies have received over 90 per cent of the total since 1990, with most (80 per cent) of it going to Hungary and the Czech Republic. Negligible amounts, if any, have gone to other transition economies in the former Soviet Union. Foreign investors are deterred from entering these markets for much the same reasons as are holding back investment in general. The most appropriate encouragement for FDI flows is to create the essential infrastructure of the market economy, including an appropriate, non-discriminatory legal frame-work for foreign investment.

In the absence of a significant boost to domestic fixed investment from FDI, it might be expected that official assistance and development bank lending would step in to fill the gap. Official multilateral flows of new finance to the transition economies have in fact been generally larger than private capital since 1990, although private funds to Eastern Europe last year were much larger than official funds. In the four years since 1990, the development banks' lending to Eastern Europe has totalled some US$5 billion, to which some US$5.4 billion of official grants from Western governments can be added. Just over 70 per cent of development bank commitments to Eastern Europe were to the four 'advanced' transition economies, with Poland receiving the largest share. Very few resources have gone to the countries of the former Soviet Union. In other words, the countries that have achieved most progress in the transition process have succeeded in not only attracting most of the private foreign investment but also most of the official funds as well. However, the needs of the less well-off countries are just as urgent and much less likely to be met by private investment. If one rejects the argument that their difficulties in getting an effective transition programme under way only reflect a lack of political will or determination, then a review of the scale and distribution of official assistance is urgently needed.

To sum up this very important and urgent issue, it is my judgement that both the volume and the coordination of international assistance for the transition economies have not been commensurate with the scale and complexity of the problems to be overcome. The perception of a growing gap between the rhetoric of assistance and its reality is a source of disillusionment for much of the population in many of the transition countries and provides useful ammunition to the various groups opposed to the transition process itself.

The transition countries' access to foreign markets has been greatly improved since 1989, although many products of significance to the transition economies are still hedged by restrictions and the threat of contingent protection. However, economic recovery has recently started in the West and this may help to weaken the protectionist pressures. In addition, the conclusion of the Uruguay Round promises a strengthening of GATT rules and authority, and this too will benefit the transition economies, especially if this leads to much stricter control of anti-dumping procedures and other forms of contingent protection

In short, the current difficulties of the majority of the transition economies suggest the need for a coordinated strategy incorporating: a clear, depoliticized policy towards enterprise and industrial restructuring, including specific measures to reduce the burden of accumulated enterprise debt; a programme to recapitalize and privatize the banks; and a significant increase in infrastructure spending, particularly on transport and communications. Since most of the transition economies would need outside help to pursue these objectives, necessary for a socially and politically feasible transition, they effectively constitute a set of priorities for revised programmes of official assistance. The challenge for both domestic and international policy makers is thus to find ways of spreading the burden of adjustment among a wider range of policy instruments and of easing the resolution of some of these dilemmas. This would be greatly helped by a greater and more coordinated level of commitment on the part of the developed market economies of the West.

I conclude this Euro-focused chapter with a few general remarks. First, the call I have just made for active support by Western economies for the transition process in Eastern European countries applies *mutatis mutandis* to support for the structural adjustment process in developing countries. I do not consider that financial and technical support provided to the East is detrimental to the South, since the resumption of growth in transition economies will open their markets to Third World countries, as well as increasing world security and stability, which are positive elements of development. Among the questions to be addressed are the need to increase the volume of soft loans and grants and, for a given amount of resources, how to allocate them between the most needy countries of East and South.

Second, the globalization process goes hand in hand with the harmonization of norms, standards, rules and practices from one country to another. This facilitates trade and foreign investment, and at the same time limits the margin of manoeuvrability of governments in the design of their economic policies, in particular to stimulate or to protect employment. Non-harmonization opens the door to new trade disputes: differences, for instance, in norms related to the environment may increase the competitiveness of those countries which have the softest environmental standards. An appropriate balance will have to be struck between the advantages of harmonization and the necessity of difference to take care of different situations and needs or, more fundamentally, because diversity is inherent to life itself.

NOTES
1 I would like to thank my colleagues Handan Del Pozzo and Jean Salmon for their help in preparing this paper.
2 OECD (1994), *The OECD Jobs Study: Facts, Analysis, Strategies*, 44, Paris. The nine recommendations of the programme of action are developed under the following headings: appropriate macroeconomic policy; the creation and diffusion of technical know-how; work-time flexibility; the entrepreneurial climate; wage and labour cost flexibility; reform of employment security provisions; enhancement of labour market policies; improvement of labour force skills; and reform of the system of unemployment and related benefits.
3 Commission of the European Communities (1993), 'Growth, competitiveness and employment: the challenges and ways forward into the 21st century', White Paper, *Bulletin of the European Communities*, Supplement 6/93, Luxembourg.
4 For a fuller discussion see G. D. N. Worswick (1992), 'The scope for macroeconomic policy to alleviate unemployment in western Europe', United Nations Economic Commission for Europe, *Discussion Papers*, Vol. 2, No. 3, New York.
5 The low rate of Czech registered unemployment, given the fall in aggregate output, continues to intrigue observers, but no one has yet provided a fully satisfactory explanation. Among the factors suggested are: a loss of jobs among a large number of workers already above retirement age, who then left the labour force rather than joining the unemployment register; very tight eligibility rules for unemployment benefit, as well as the introduction of youth training schemes, which have also kept down the numbers on the unemployment register; low real wages and the slow rate of restructuring large SOEs which have encouraged enterprises to retain labour; and a substantial increase of output and employment in small private enterprises (in services, tourism, etc.) which may not be fully reflected in the official employment statistics.
6 RF Goskomstat started publishing all three estimates in November 1993.
7 Although not strictly comparable, this latter figure is considerably lower than the replacement ratios (of unemployment benefit to previous disposable income) to be found in the countries of Western Europe and North America. See Economic Commission for Europe (1983), 'The cost of unemployment, 1972–1982', *Economic Bulletin for Europe*, Pergamon Press for the United Nations, Vol. 35, No. 3, pp. 289–306, Table 3.1.
8 United Nations Economic Commission for Europe (1994), *Economic Survey of Europe in 1993-1994*, New York and Geneva, United Nations.

3

Fighting Unemployment and Polarization: Investments in Adaptive Capacity Through Broad Upgrading in Skills

– TUIRE SANTAMÄKI-VUORI –

In most regions of the world, unemployment and underemployment are rising rapidly. In Western Europe, too, the percentage of recorded unemployment rose continuously between the early 1970s and the mid-1980s, with a new surge in the early 1990s. The average unemployment rate in European OECD countries rose from about 3 per cent in 1970 to over 10 per cent in 1993. This overall picture certainly conceals considerable national variation. In this respect Finland exhibits the most striking example with a relatively impressive labour market performance during the preceding two decades and a huge surge in unemployment during the deep economic depression in the early 1990s.

The persistently high rate of unemployment has become Europe's most pressing economic problem. On the economic policy agendas of both individual governments and international bodies, however, quite inadequate importance has been attached to policies for combating unemployment. In recent times, fortunately, new discussion of the priorities of macroeconomic policy and the scope of joint action in Europe has arisen. (For a fuller discussion, see Yves Berthelot in the previous chapter.) In spite of the disappointing experiences from the last two decades, one must remember that mass unemployment was a major problem in the inter-war world economy, too. If mass unemployment was defeated in the past, there is no obvious excuse for fatalism now.

The Flexible labour market: is it an alternative?

The alternative policy strategies for growth and for tackling unemployment may differ, however, in terms of economic efficiency and equity, especially in the long run. Given the severity of long-term unemployment, the heavy concentration of unemployment on

41

unskilled workers, and the increasing importance of human capital for the process of structural change and economic performance generally, the important question arises whether it is possible to promote the achievement of both efficiency and equity objectives simultaneously.

In this context, the question has been raised whether it is the more flexible, unregulated labour market that has made possible superior job creation in the US. Yet in this debate insufficient attention has been paid to differences in the evolution of the factors of production across the countries concerned. If these differences are taken into account, it is – in the spirit of economic growth theory – more appropriate to put the question in another way. Why has the US not achieved a faster economic growth although the increase in the size of the labour force there has been manifold compared to that in Europe – more than 60 per cent compared to 5 to 10 per cent in Germany and the UK?

The answer is to be found in the economic strategy that has led to very low productivity growth in the US. The low productivity growth has not made room for major increases in welfare, either through higher real wages or cuts in working time (that is, increases in leisure time). In 1985, real wages were just 13 per cent higher than a quarter of century earlier. Since 1969, real average weekly earnings in the US have fallen by more than 12 per cent.[1] Moreover, this burden has been shared unequally. The incomes of the top 30 per cent of earners increased while those of the other 70 per cent spiralled downward. Hence, as a dark side of the favourable job growth, there has been a change towards a poorer and a more unequal society.

Also, as pointed out by Nolan, the adverse comparisons drawn between the allegedly rigid structures pervasive in Europe and the more flexible unregulated markets of the US tend to be misleading in some other respects.[2] First, the employment gains associated with the union density decline in the US tend to be overstated; and second, the considerable diversity of labour market institutions, and their associated employment impacts within and between the countries of Europe, are often understated. Yet the policy response to the rise in unemployment in Europe has been labour market deregulation, most vigorously pursued in the UK since 1979.

Analogously to the impacts of a greater resort to protectionism, in the deregulation strategy short-run results are sought at the expense of technological dynamism and greater industrial efficiency in the longer run.[3] An economy which is based on low pay is essentially an economy with limited incentives. Firms are provided with fewer incentives to compete through innovation in production methods or to seek new markets. Instead of revenue-enhancing strategies to boost profits, competition is then based on cost reduction by further reliance on low pay and casualized employment as the only means of survival.

In this respect, the findings of a survey on the perceived skills gap and employment needs among American employers were quite startling.[4] First, only 5 per cent of the employers felt that education and skill requirements were increasing significantly. Therefore, little evidence of a far-reaching desire for a more educated workforce was found. Second, more than 80 per cent of the employers expressed concern about skills shortages, but they generally meant a good work ethic and social skills. Third, employers who thought that education levels were insufficient usually referred to illiteracy and a lack of basic mathematical skills. And finally, only 15 per cent of employers reported difficulty finding workers with the appropriate occupational skills. These shortages were generally in chronically underpaid women's occupations and traditional craft trades.

Similar evidence from the UK suggests that in the low pay segments of the labour market, there is a relatively greater degree of unsatisfied demand for labour, meaning that, compared to other sectors, wages are too low.[5] Rather than low pay being an answer to unemployment, high levels of joblessness are a precondition for many people to accept low-paying jobs. Consequently, investment in training shows poor return for both employer and employee. Slow growth of productivity and income, combined with an increasing dependence on social security, makes it difficult to attain a reasonable degree of fiscal balance, too. In all, there are heavy costs – in terms of economic efficiency and social injustice – involved in the vicious circle of low-pay, low-productivity strategy.

Moreover, a very different picture of Europe's comparative record emerges when Japan rather than the US is chosen as the reference point. Japan has been able to combine a very high productivity growth with a low rate of unemployment. Given the very different labour market institutions in Japan, the question arises about the appropriate contents of adaptive capacity. As Kenney and Florida argued, it may be innovation, not flexibility, that is the crucial variable.[6] If flexibility is to be a real factor in global and national economies, it must be enmeshed within relatively stable social institutions that bind production and innovation together, giving rise to structural flexibility. Without such structure, flexibility can be economically disruptive, a sign of weakness rather than strength.

Strikingly enough, in the Group of Seven job summit in Detroit, in March 1994, more moderate views than usual were put forth

concerning the limits and preconditions of pursuing greater flexibility. Japan warned against too much emphasis on labour flexibility, since excessive mobility of workers discourages incentives to
enhance human resource development by enterprises. The US, in
turn, warned that countries which pursue structural improvements,
without taking steps to increase aggregate demand, will see little or
no return for their efforts.[7]

Even within Europe there seem to be different strategies of
seeking flexibility. The form of restructuring in Germany offers a
striking contrast to the deregulation in the UK. In Germany flexibility and sustainable productivity gains have been sought in a
labour market context supportive of job security and high wages.
The relatively high labour costs and social charges in Germany are
largely offset, however, by high productivity without the competitive position being harmed. Table 3.1 indicates that while the
total labour costs in Germany in 1987 were about 22 per cent above
the EU average, unit labour costs were only marginally above the
average. The contrast was most striking with the UK, where the
labour costs were less than 80 per cent of the EU average, yet unit
labour costs exceeded those of Germany. The difference in cost
structures is accounted for by the fact that Germany has sought to

TABLE 3.1

Labour costs and unit labour costs in the European Union:
1987 (whole economy)

Country	Labour cost per employee (as a percentage of the EU average)	Unit labour cost (as a percentage of the EU average)
Belgium	114.9	105.9
Denmark	114.7	109.6
Germany	122.1	104.0
Greece	44.0	75.4
Spain	73.7	88.8
France	118.5	102.8
Ireland	89.2	104.4
Luxembourg	115.7	122.5
Netherlands	127.6	104.0
Portugal	26.6	86.7
UK	77.0	107.3

Source: Marsden, D. and J. J. Silvestre (1992), 'Pay and European integration' in Marsden, D. (ed.)
Pay and Employment in the New Europe, Edward Elgar, Aldershot.
Note: Labour cost includes gross wages and salaries, employers' social security contributions, and
imputed social contributions; unit labour costs are calculated as labour costs per 1,000 Ecu GDP.

compete on the basis of high wages and high productivity, rather than emulate Britain's low-wage, low-productivity route.[8]

Also, Streeck argued that the high-quality, high value-added production system emerged in Germany precisely because of the existence of powerful institutional constraints. According to Streeck, by blocking 'quick-fix' solutions, the framework of rules and institutions induced a virtuous circle of upmarket industrial restructuring and compelled management to embark on more demanding strategies.[9] As Nolan concludes, the key point to emerge is not that Germany bucked the European trend towards higher unemployment, but rather that it is less severely constrained by trade and supply-side weaknesses, and hence more able to expand output and employment in the event of the resumption of growth in Europe.[10]

Consequently the lessons from recent comparative analyses suggest that, in the end, the principle reason for the unsatisfactory labour market performance in OECD countries stems from the same root cause: the failure to innovate and adapt satisfactorily to change.[11] As stated by Schwanse, the bottom line is to adopt a broad-based strategy to invest in adaptive and creative capacity in a more effective and more equitable way than before.[12]

Labour market policy measures to tackle long-term unemployment

Given the fact that long-term unemployment accounts for a very large share – often the majority – of total unemployment in many European countries, it is obvious that tackling long-term unemployment is a precondition for reducing markedly total unemployment. In considering policy initiatives, it is useful to distinguish two aspects of the long-term unemployment problem: a flow dimension and a stock dimension. As economic conditions improve, one can expect that fewer short-term unemployed will become long-term unemployed (flow). The stock problem arises when the flow out of this group is small, even in the context of negligible inflow rates. A quick solution to the flow problem might not be offered by the revival of economic growth, since, according to earlier experiences, a significant proportion of any net addition to jobs is filled, not by the unemployed as officially recorded, but by people who were previously inactive. The chances are even worse for the long-term unemployed to find a job on their own. As a result, special measures will be required if the stock problem is to be addressed because long-term unemployment is to some extent irreversible. Removing the causes that led to unemployment is not sufficient to improve the chances of those people finding a new job after a long period of joblessness.[13]

Indeed, from a growing amount of economic literature on hysteresis and unemployment theory[14] a central message has emerged: the most effective way of reducing unemployment is to target the policy measures for the long-term unemployed. Apart from considerations of efficiency, these policies are often motivated by the welfare losses associated with long-term unemployment. Another motivation frequently cited – for which, however, the evidence is rather shaky[15] – is that targeted policies have little if any side-effects in terms of higher inflation.

An analysis of labour market policy budgets shows that policy emphasis has shifted virtually everywhere in Europe, since 1985, towards more targeted measures aiming to mobilize labour supply for productive work.[16] Such measures include five sub-categories of targeted programmes: training for unemployed adults and those at risk; measures for unemployed and disadvantaged youth; subsidies for regular employment in the private sector; subsidies for un-employed persons starting enterprises; and finally, rehabilitation of the disabled. Apart from some exceptions, direct job creation (public or non-profit) has been scaled down.

Passive income maintenance, however, still dominates: it costs more money to governments than all active measures together. In the late 1980s active labour market measures accounted for about 40 per cent of total spending on labour market programmes (active measures + income maintenance) in the OECD countries. The national differences were substantial, labour market policy being the most active in Sweden and the most passive in Spain (Figure 3.1). A striking thing is that, with the economic depression, the Finnish position has deteriorated drastically.

Even without putting a greater volume of public resources into labour market policies, there remains a considerable scope for switching resources from passive income support to active measures. The shift of emphasis would be well placed on grounds both of social welfare and economic efficiency. Higher public spending on active measures may foster wage moderation by strengthening the ability of so-called outsiders, particularly the long-term unemployed, to compete more effectively for jobs, thereby contributing to a reduction of structural unemployment.

Many lessons have been learnt about the design of special measures and policies for tackling unemployment and improving the functioning of the labour market. There has been a shift away

FIGURE 3.1
Public expenditure on active labour market measures
% of total spending on labour market programmes

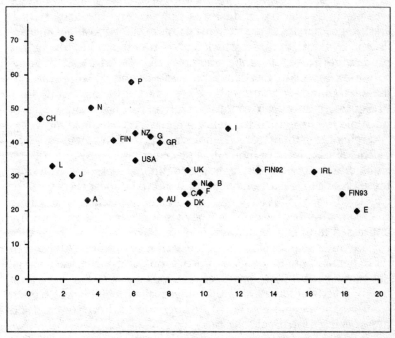

Source: Data from OECD (1992), pp. 91–103; and OECD (1993) 'Active labour market policies: assessing macroeconomic and microeconomic effects', in *Employment Outlook*, pp. 73–8. The figure for Finland in 1993 (FIN93) is based on data from the Ministry of Labour.

Note: A = Austria, AU = Australia, B = Belgium, CA = Canada, CH = Switzerland, DK = Denmark, E = Spain, F = France, FIN = Finland, G = Germany, GR = Greece, I = Italy, IRL = Ireland, J = Japan, L = Luxembourg, N = Norway, NL = Netherlands, NZ = New Zealand, P = Portugal, S = Sweden, UK = United Kingdom and USA = United States.

from measures to create jobs for the long-term unemployed – public work programmes, enterprise creation and wage subsidies – towards training and other measures designed to fit the long-term unemployed to existing job vacancies. This change in the late 1980s was partly a reflection of the increasing demand for labour which encouraged a move away from measures designed to alleviate mass unemployment to those which concentrated on improving the productive potential of the unemployed. Nevertheless, in some countries, especially Sweden, France and Denmark, large-scale off-the-job training programmes have been part of the policy for years. In Southern European countries with particularly high rates of unemployment, in turn, the policy emphasis has changed much less and reliance is still placed on employment creation schemes.[17]

The development of innovative placement measures, such as job clubs, offers a low-cost alternative to traditional measures. However, these types of measures have been found to be most successful for clients who are 'job-ready', and in local labour markets where there is a ready supply of vacancies. They are much less effective in very depressed local labour markets and for clients who are in need of considerable help. In fact, one of the challenges of the 1990s is much more demanding on the government employment services: that is, developing sensitive forms of counselling for the long-term unemployed, with regard for the wider social problems which often confront the people concerned, in order to find appropriate and more lasting individual solutions.

Given that the persons concerned have potentially a long career in the labour market ahead, the measures should be viewed as investments in human capital. The benefits of successful manpower policy measures – as well as the costs of current shortcomings – will therefore be evident for a long period of time. In the short run, the measures should be judged by their ability to ensure that un-employed people can be helped to keep in touch with the labour market, and to compete effectively within it, rather than by their effectiveness in reducing the overall level of unemployment.

It is important to realize, too, that any success of manpower policy measures may be critically dependent on their presenting reasonable prospects for the participants in the future. Schemes that acquire a reputation for disguising unemployment, creating new forms of cheap labour or for failing to provide adequate training will merely have a downgrading effect on the participants, in labour market terms. Individuals then become unwilling to participate in the programmes, because of the knowledge that the time and effort spent is wasted. The better the measures are tailored to meet the

individual needs, the smaller the risk of disappointment of participants and the smaller the amount of wasted resources.

Especially in regions with high unemployment persisting for
years or even decades, being unskilled may simply be part of a much
wider set of social disadvantages which need to be overcome in
equipping a person for a job. The circumstances which deprived
some of the chance to acquire skills may already have begun to be
passed on to the next generation. Moreover, the interrupted work
and contribution records resulting from unemployment or various
abnormally practised schemes, such as working without an employment contract and entitlement to social security, may turn the long-
term unemployed into the 'new poor' in the forthcoming decades
when they get old. Policies aimed at addressing the structural factors
which create and transmit disadvantage, rather than ones which are
primarily palliative, should therefore be emphasized. Indeed, in
many countries there is an increasing political worry about the links
between joblessness and deprivation, with dangerous consequences
for social cohesion and political stability: developed countries
cannot afford to ignore the non-employed.

The scope of improved education and training in preventing polarization

Over the last decade or two, virtually all sectors of the economy have
been pervaded by new technologies, particularly the new information technologies. Many of the consequences of the new information
technologies are yet to be seen – under circumstances of intense international competition and the increasing ease with which production
locations change. Experience in the most successful countries
suggests, however, that the best route is to take a forward-looking
policy stance by embracing rather than resisting structural change –
to invest in adaptive and creative capacity. Knowledge, in its broad
sense, is therefore recognized as a key element in determining a
country's competitive advantage.

Such a perspective reinforces the need to focus policy efforts on
ensuring that all members of the society are kept well informed.
Otherwise we risk producing a society extremely polarized in terms
of incomes, skills and job opportunities. The important task is
therefore to engage in large-scale efforts to upgrade the qualifications of the whole workforce – both the employed, the unemployed
and those who have yet to enter the labour market.

Sound initial education is the essential base for acquiring higher-order skills. At the moment, the educational level varies widely across countries, even among Western countries. This is reflected, for instance, in figures for the proportion of persons who actually stay on in education once it becomes optional to continue. In the late 1980s, the educational enrolment of 17-year-olds in the OECD countries ranged from a low of 34 per cent in Turkey to a high of 93 per cent in Belgium.[18] In most countries, there is a trend towards an increased attainment level of education. This is reflected in the fact that, in many but not all countries, younger people have sharply higher educational attainment than older people.

It may be of some interest to consider the exceptions to this cohort rule. In Greece, for instance, the enrolment rates of 17-year-olds decreased between the years 1975 and 1986, and in Spain, over half the men aged 55 and over, but well under a quarter of those aged 20–24, have the minimum level of education.[19] Both of these are countries where the unemployment rate of those with the highest educational attainment is greater than the rate of those with the lowest educational attainment. A high level of education is then no guarantee of gaining employment, if the adopted national strategy does not encourage demand for those skills in the labour market.

Even though the initial conditions exhibit a great disparity, many Western countries seem to be well placed to succeed with the high-skill strategy. Everywhere, however, education should become an ongoing process that allows workers to adapt to changing industrial structures, as well as changes in technology which may lead to a faster depreciation of human capital. By increasing adult education and encouraging employed persons to engage in systematic retraining, it would be possible to promote job rotation and provide job opportunities for a larger number of people. Rather than rationing gainful employment and concealing and diverting unemployment into a more even layer of hidden unemployment as is the case with enforced work sharing, these kinds of work-sharing measures would serve the primary need of enhancing human resources in the long run.

Basic human capital models view the pattern of investment in training as endogenously determined by individual maximization of the discounted value of lifetime earnings. In its simplest formulation, the human capital theory suggests that general training (useful to many employers) should be financed exclusively by employees, who have the right incentives to invest in training since they are able to recoup their investments when it raises their productivity and hence their wages. The costs of specific training (useful only to a specific employer) should be shared by employers and employees, so that employees internalize the cost to their employers of quitting and employers in turn internalize the cost to their trained employees of dismissal. In either pure case, employers and employees are compensated for the training and there are no market failures. In practice, however, there are various reasons why private market-based decisions by firms and individuals will lead to less than socially optimum training. These reasons are related to imperfect competition for labour, poaching, production externalities, complementarities between labour and capital, and interactions between skills and product quality and/or innovative performance.[20] The high-skill, high-productivity economy then requires government intervention to correct market failures and to provide sufficient incentives for acquisition of skills.

A substantial literature exists on comparative national education and training systems. The consensus view in the literature is that, if higher education is set aside, Germany, Japan and Sweden have effective educational and training systems, while the United States and the United Kingdom do not. As Soskice convincingly argued, the educational and training policy followed with such success in the former countries has ultimately served to relax the trade balance constraint on the economic activity.[21] By enabling firms to compete more effectively in the world market, such a policy will reduce overall unemployment in equilibrium by reducing the trade deficit (or increasing the trade surplus) at any given level of unemployment with stable inflation. In the process, mismatch is reduced both in the bridge from school to employment and in the retraining of skilled workers within companies to meet changing skill needs.

Yet there are new problems of mismatch which arise in these schemes. First, the success of these countries in providing generally high-quality goods and services has exposed them to competition in product innovation, where preservation of market shares requires more and more highly-qualified professionals. Second, if the unemployment rate for unskilled workers is high, it is more difficult for these systems to reduce it. This is primarily because high wage coordination is needed to reduce poaching and to provide overall wage constraint in the interests of maintaining international competitiveness. Therefore, there is less potential for widening wage differentials.

Strikingly enough, the structures of incentives both for companies and for workers have important similarities within the various patterns of education and training systems. According to Soskice, an understanding of these similarities lies in the power of employer coordination and employer–government links, and to a lesser extent in the role of unions and of financial institutions. And, most importantly, besides financial incentives a great many other elements related to wage determination, employment security and industrial relations are involved to reduce risks associated with training investments in order to form an integrated whole of an educational and training system. At the level of work organizations, arrangements to create commitment and cooperation are highly emphasized to materialize the gains in terms of high-productivity work performance.

In every case, the goal of the national system is to encourage companies to train, to spread costs and ultimately to create a self-perpetuating programme for continually upgrading the skills of the adult workforce. Yet much more research is needed on the impact of various forms of government-based involvement on enterprise incentives to engage in training. They are not independent of the scope of labour market training schemes implemented by governments as a way of easing labour force adjustments. If the training of the unemployed is mainly financed by governments, substitution and dead-weight effects will without doubt play a role. The same problems certainly arise, perhaps in a more acute form, in the case of subsidized in-plant training.[22]

This chapter discussed the scope of active labour market policy and the broad upgrading of skills for combating unemployment and social polarization. The framework for considering policy strategies was characterized by two particular features: first, the current severity of long-term unemployment in Europe; and second, the ever increasing demand for cognitive skills and multi-skilled qualifications as a result of the advance of computer-based technologies in the future. The alternative strategies for growth and for tackling unemployment will certainly differ in terms of economic efficiency and equity, especially in the long run. In Europe, a great emphasis is being put on promoting labour market deregulation in an attempt to combat unemployment. The economic and social effects of deregulation include a widening of pay differentials and a lowering of labour standards in large areas of the market. This process itself occurs highly unevenly, raising obvious questions of equity, but as convincingly argued by a variety of analysts, deregulation strategy also induces substantial risks of inefficiency, entrenching the long-run dependence of the economy upon low pay as a means of competitive survival. The bottom line message of this chapter is to underline the importance of averting this vicious circle by investing in the adaptive capacity of the whole workforce. Corresponding to the idea of a virtuous circle of economic development, extensive and high-quality training bring about high productivity, process and product innovation and higher profitability of production. Profitability funds additional investments in human resources which, in turn, improve economic performance.

All too little is known about the ways of pursuing this high-skill, high-productivity strategy. Yet a few general lessons seem to emerge from comparative studies and experiences. First, the success of the manpower policy measures to tackle long-term unemployment seems to be critically dependent on their offering reasonable prospects for the participants. The better the measures are tailored to meet the individual needs and the circumstances of local labour markets, the smaller the amount of wasted resources. Second, the high-skill, high-productivity economy requires government intervention to correct market failure and to provide sufficient incentives for acquisition of skills. The most important challenge concerns the development of a successful system for enterprise-related training. Besides financial incentives, a great many other elements related to wage determination, employment security and industrial relations seem to be involved in reducing the risks associated with training investments in order to form an integrated training system. And finally, it is important to disentangle the ways that skills combine with work organization to determine productivity, job content and technological redundancy. As discussed by Knuth, the change of the trade union approach in Germany from humanizing to shaping work and technology signalled a marked shift.[23] A reactive approach was replaced by a pro-active one where work was not conceived merely as technologically determined. Vigorous attempts should be made to combine self-confident mastery of new successful technology with identification of alternative organizational and technological choices that decrease the number of unemployed and those whose work changes adversely, or that reduce the impact of job loss.

NOTES
1 National Center on Education and the Economy (1990), *America's Choice: High Skills or Low Wages!*, Report of the Commission on the Skills of the American Workforce, Rochester, New York, p. 19.
2 Nolan, P. (1994) 'Labour market institutions, industrial restructuring and unemployment in Europe', in Michie, J. and J.G. Smith (eds), *Unemployment in Europe*, Academic Press, London, pp. 62–3.
3 Harrison, B. and B. Bluestone (1990) 'Wage polarization in the US and the "flexibility" debate', *Cambridge Journal of Economics*, Vol. 14, No. 3, pp. 351–73.
4 National Center on Education and the Economy (1990) pp. 24–6.

5 Michie, J. and F. Wilkinson (1994) 'The growth of unemployment in the 1980s', in Michie, J. and J. G. Smith (eds), pp. 19–20.
6 Kenney, M. and R. Florida (1988) 'Beyond mass production: production and the labour process in Japan', *Politics and Society*, Vol. 16, No. 1, pp. 121–58.
7 *Financial Times*, 14 March 1994, p. 4.
8 Nolan (1994) p. 69.
9 Streeck, W. (1991) 'On the institutional conditions of diversified quality production', in Matzner, E. and W. Streeck (eds), *Beyond Keynesianism: The Socioeconomics of Production and Full Employment*, Edward Elgar, Aldershot, p. 54.
10 Nolan (1994) p. 70.
11 Cf. Berthelot in this volume.
12 Schwanse, P. (1993) 'OECD unemployment: some policy options', paper prepared for the Conference on Technology, Innovation Policy and Employment, 7–9 October, Helsinki.
13 OECD (1993,) 'Long-term unemployment: selected causes and remedies', *Employment Outlook*, Paris, p. 112.
14 See Nickell, S. (1990) 'Unemployment: a survey', *Economic Journal*, Vol. 100, No. 401, pp. 391–439.
15 Holmlund, B. (1991) *Unemployment Persistence and Insider–Outsider Forces in Wage Determination*, OECD Economics and Statistics Department, Working Paper No. 92, Paris.
16 OECD (1992) 'Monitoring labour market developments', *Employment Outlook*, Paris, p. 86.
17 Commission of the European Communities (1991) 'The complex problem of persistent unemployment', *Employment in Europe*, Luxembourg, pp. 58–9.
18 OECD (1992) p. 58.
19 *Ibid*. p. 59.
20 See references in OECD (1991) 'Enterprise-related training', *Employment Outlook*, Paris, pp. 136–7.
21 Soskice, D. (1991) 'Skill mismatch, training systems and equilibrium unemployment: a comparative institutional analysis', in Schioppa, F.P. (ed.), *Mismatch and Labour Mobility*, Centre for Economic Policy Review, Cambridge University Press, pp. 386–400.
22 Standing, G. (1991) 'Structural adjustment and labour market policies: towards social adjustment?', in Standing, G. and V. Tokman (eds) *Towards Social Adjustment, Labour Market Issues in Structural Adjustment*, ILO, Geneva, pp. 42–4.
23 Knuth, M. (1992) 'Shaping work and technology: West German trade unions, the quality of work and industrial relations', International Contributions to Labour Studies, Vol. 2, pp. 45–59.

4

Higher Education
and Employment

– KLAUS HÜFNER –

Higher education in both industrial and developing countries is in crisis. The optimistic view that higher education investments are important for economic growth, which is in turn a critical prerequisite for sustained poverty reduction, has lost its former attraction. What has been true for industrial countries during the 1960s is not necessarily true for the developing countries; what has been true in earlier periods is not necessarily true for the 1990s. Today, a search for new strategies and policies regarding higher education can be observed in order to solve the present higher education crisis.

It is a crisis both in quantitative and qualitative terms; it relates to structural and functional components. Everywhere, discussions take place concerning measures in order to increase both the internal and the external efficiency of higher education systems, the latter referring to their relationships with employment systems.

A world-wide analysis of linkages between higher education and employment necessarily implies the highest level of analytical aggregation. Even the attempt at a North–South differentiation will not take into due account the specific features and problems of regions, sub-regions and individual countries. Therefore, the following analysis of the problems within and between the systems of higher education and employment will be restricted to overall issues.

The world-wide expansion of higher education

Over the last two decades quantitative expansion of higher education continued dramatically. As reported in UNESCO's World Education Report 1991, third-level education has been expanded from 28.2 million students in 1970 to 47.5 million in 1980 and 58.4 million in 1988. In other words, over the last two decades the number of students has more than doubled. It is in the developing countries that the increases have been particularly high. Whereas in the 1970s there was explosive growth with the numbers quadrupling in sub-Saharan Africa, East Asia and Oceania, and trebling in the Arab states and in Latin America and the Caribbean, the increases in third-level enrolments in North America, Europe and the former USSR were around 50 per cent. In the 1980s, educational growth slowed down in all regions, but it remained generally higher in developing countries than in industrial countries.[1]

These educational growth rates need careful interpretation, however. It must be taken into account that the growth in developing countries took place from a very low initial base. Furthermore, the picture looks very different when one takes into account the differences in population growth. When looking at the numbers of students per 100,000 inhabitants or at gross enrolment ratios, namely total enrolment in third-level education regardless of age, expressed as a percentage of the population in the five-year age group following the secondary school leaving age, considerable inequalities of access to this level can be shown among the various regions (cf. Table 4.1).

As shown in UNESCO's most recent *World Education Report, 1993*, the greatest differences between countries do not occur in primary or secondary education, but in tertiary education. In 1990, higher education enrolment per 100,000 inhabitants ranged from 5,591 in the United States and 5,102 in Canada to 21 in the United Republic of Tanzania and 16 in Mozambique (cf. Table 4.1). 'Over the past decade', the Report noted, 'there has been only a slight decline in inter-country inequalities in opportunities for higher education.'[2]

UNESCO developed a typology consisting of six groups:[3] *Group A* includes the United States and Canada. Both countries have high income levels and virtually unrestricted access to higher education.

Group B includes most of the OECD countries. They have relatively high incomes of more than US$10,000 per capita and relatively large numbers of students of over 2,000 per 100,000 inhabitants. Since completion of secondary education does not necessarily ensure admission to higher education, access in these countries is generally more restricted. It is impossible to find a causal correlation between income level and enrolment level in higher education among these countries. Although Switzerland, Japan and Sweden have income levels about double those of New Zealand, Spain, and Ireland, they have lower enrolment levels in higher education, whereas Norway and Finland have the same income levels, but have much higher enrolment levels.

Group C includes mostly the Arab Gulf states which have somewhat lower enrolment levels than the OECD group because their higher education systems are still at a relatively early stage of development and they have many students studying abroad.

TABLE 4.1
Number of students in higher education (selected countries): 1990

	Students per 100,000 inhabitants	Gross enrolment ratio
Africa		
Algeria	1,146	10.9
Burkina Faso	60	0.7
Chad	70	0.8
Egypt	1,698	18.4
Mozambique	16	0.2
United Republic of Tanzania	21	0.3
North America		
Canada	5,102	71.2
Honduras	854	8.3
Jamaica	662	5.9
United States	5,591	72.2
South America		
Argentina	3,293	39.9
Guyana	588	5.1
Paraguay	769	8.1
Uruguay	2,315	30.1
Asia		
Bangladesh	382	3.4
China	186	1.7
Israel	2,790	32.3
Japan	2,328	28.7
Korea, Republic of	3,899	37.7
Laos People's Dem. Rep.	116	1.2
Myanmar	516	4.8
Pakistan	266	2.6
Europe		
Albania	679	7.0
Belgium	2,725	37.8
Finland	3,326	48.2
Hungary	970	14.5
Romania	711	8.6
Switzerland	2,048	27.4
Oceania		
Australia	2,839	35.0
Fiji	1,080	12.0
New Zealand	3,287	44.5

Source: UNESCO, *World Education Report 1993*, pp. 144–7.

Group D includes countries with low and middle incomes, generally less than US$6,000. They have enrolment levels in the same range as the OECD countries. The majority of these countries are in Latin America, the others are the Republic of Korea, the Philippines, Jordan, Bulgaria, and two OECD countries, namely Greece and Portugal. It is important to note that the Republic of Korea, Peru, Argentina, Venezuela, and the Philippines all have higher enrolment levels than the majority of OECD countries.

Group E includes countries with low and middle incomes, generally less than US$3,500, with enrolment levels between the range of Groups B and D.

Group F includes most sub-Saharan African countries plus several other very poor countries from other regions (all with incomes below US$500).The UNESCO authors concluded that the outstanding higher education gap is between sub-Saharan Africa and the rest of the world.

> In other regions it appears to be almost random whether countries have a high enrolment level or not, doubtless because there are so many historical, cultural and other factors involved, as well as differences as regards enrolment in 'open university' and part-time courses. In Latin America, the Arab states, East Asia, the OECD group and Eastern Europe some countries have high enrolments while others with similar or higher incomes have lower enrolment levels. The United States and Canada, with very similar income levels to other OECD countries, have largely unrestricted access to higher education. Switzerland, with the highest income level of all, has an enrolment level lower than Bulgaria – one reason being the latter's large enrolment in evening and correspondence courses. In sub-Saharan Africa and a handful of other very poor countries there seems to be no choice: they all have lower enrolment levels.[4]

Higher education, employment and economic growth in the 1980s

When Philip H. Coombs published his *Future Critical World Issues in Education* in 1981 he made the following observations for the 1980s:

1 There exists in the industrial countries a large latent demand of potential 'unconventional' students who have not been served by most higher education institutions and deserve much greater attention in the 1980s;

2 Qualitative dimensions, 'judged not simply by traditional "quality standards" but by what is actually being taught and learned today and how well it fits the present and future needs of the

particular students and society' (p. 25), will have to be recognized during the 1980s.[5]

He therefore demanded that higher education systems, especially in Western Europe, should become more diversified – taking into account the model of the United States. In his outlook for the developing countries, he anticipated that they will have an even larger task than the industrial countries – that of adapting their universities and other higher education institutions, which have been modelled after foreign institutions, 'to better their own needs, conditions and cultures and their very limited resources'.[6] Again, he argued for more diversification of higher education systems.

With respect to linkages between higher education and employment, he reminded us of the phenomenon of the 'educated unemployed' (already well known in India, Egypt, and the Philippines during the 1960s) and the problems of traditional rigid linkages between specific educational credentials and specific job openings, especially in government and in the educational system itself. Coombs did not dare to predict future developments in the employment system which will depend on economic growth rates as well as technological, social, and economic structural changes. Nevertheless,

> One thing seems quite clear, however: few if any countries are likely again to experience the burgeoning demand for graduates that prevailed almost everywhere in the 1950s and 1960s – when war-torn industrial nations were rebuilding their economies, making major technological strides, and rapidly expanding their educational systems; when newly independent nations were freshly building and staffing their new governmental, educational, economic and other infrastructures; and when economic growth rates in most of the world were running at unusually high levels.[7]

Coombs also anticipated a growing financial squeeze in the 1980s which would certainly be most acute in the developing countries, but showed up in OECD countries even during the late 1970s, forcing higher education institutions to make painful cuts in their budgets, programmes, and staffs. He predicted that in industrial countries the squeeze would tighten further in the 1980s:

> Higher education institutions in developing countries, unlike those in developed countries, will continue to be besieged by powerful pressures to expand, but their ability to do so without seriously eroding quality and without further distorting the whole educational structure will be extremely restricted in most cases by overall national budgetary stringencies.[8]

In retrospect, Coombs was right in his cautious predictions. However, the squeeze became worse than anticipated. In both industrial and developing countries higher education systems did not receive more public resources in order to absorb the effects of the rapid enrolment increases. On the contrary, as a result of the decline of economic outputs and necessary structural adjustment measures in many developing countries ('the 1980s as the lost decade') public resources for higher education institutions had to be reduced considerably. This, in turn, led to a decline in the quality of teaching and research caused by, among other things, inadequate staffing, deteriorating physical facilities, insufficient equipment and poor library resources. In sub-Saharan Africa, for example, between one third and two thirds of the initial entrants to higher education failed to complete their studies or completed them behind schedule. In other words: the internal efficiency of many higher education systems – primarily, but not only in the developing countries – is extremely low.

Also, their external efficiency – their relationship with the labour market – is increasingly questioned. Many countries are confronted with the structural problems of graduate unemployment and under-employment, a problem caused not only by economic recession, but also by dramatic structural changes in the employment system.

Today, many parts of the world experience a new phenomenon: jobless growth. The cover design of UNDP's *Human Development Report 1993* reflected this disturbing development by comparing GDP growth to employment growth, both weighted by region, between 1975 and 1990 and its projected trend until the year 2000. Since 1975, employment growth has consistently lagged behind output growth. This gap is likely to widen during the decade of the 1990s.

Whereas unemployment in the European countries of OECD increased from 3 per cent in the mid-1970s to about 10 per cent in 1992, the situation in the developing countries is much worse.

In Sub-Saharan Africa not a single country had single-digit unemployment figures throughout this period.... And in Asia, countries like India and Pakistan, despite respectable GDP growth rates (more than 6 per cent a year), had unemployment rates above 15 per cent.[9]

In the industrial countries, the output growth came from productivity increases as a result of labour-saving technology advancement (encouraged by labour shortages in the 1960s and relative high labour costs later on). Unemployment levels remained high or even increased. Recently, an OECD study argued that around 35 million people, or 8.5 per cent of the workforce, are out of work in the 24 member states covered in the report. Worse still, the long-term unemployed, namely those who have been out of work for more than a year, account for a high proportion ranging from about one third of total unemployment in Australia, France, Germany, and the United Kingdom to almost 60 per cent in Belgium and Italy. According to the OECD report, this 'represents an enormous waste of human resources, reflects an important amount of inefficiency in economic systems, and causes a disturbing degree of social distress'. Moreover: 'It brings with it unravelling of the social fabric, including a loss of authority of the democratic system and it risks resulting in the disintegration of the international trading system'.

In the developing countries, the rapid population growth plus the number of un- or underemployed increases the demand for new jobs for the 1990s to around one billion; this would imply an annual increase of total employment by more than 4 per cent – a rather unrealistic assumption.

UNDP's *Human Development Report 1993* also mentioned that in developing countries 'many remain unemployed despite, or because of, their high level of education'.[10] In India, the unemployment rate in 1989 for university graduates was 12 per cent (cf. Table 4.2). 'In Bangladesh, about 40 per cent of people with a master's degree are either unemployed or underemployed. In Thailand during 1973–83, unemployment rates among university graduates ranged from 20 per cent to 35 per cent.'[11] The Report expects that graduate unemployment in Africa, which is not yet as high as in some Asian countries, will rise in the coming years because of cuts in recruitment to government service.

The fundamental problem in both industrial and developing countries is an increasing mismatch between supply of the higher education system and demand of the employment system. Publicity

Table 4.2
Unemployment in selected countries by educational levels

Country	Year	No education	Primary education	Secondary education	Tertiary education
Algeria	1989	9.2	24.2	28.9	5.8
Tunisia	1989	11.2	20.4	17.4	5.2
Ghana	1988	3.4	7.6	13.5	14.7
Kenya	1986	13.5	15.6	22.2	5.4
Zimbabwe	1987	1.6	6.8	11.6	0
Malaysia	1985	4.7	22.9	30.6	3.9
India	1989	2.0	3.0	9.0	12.0
Indonesia	1985	0.6	1.5	7.5	5.3
Sri Lanka	1981	4.5	14.5	15.1	4.2
Côte d'Ivoire	1985	1.0	5.2	21.7	13.7

Source: UNDP, *Human Development Report 1993*, p. 38.

is highest in the case of academic unemployment although, in absolute figures, it represents only a small part. This obscures the fact that there exists a much larger 'youth unemployment' problem of those with lower formal educational qualifications or none at all.

Furthermore, Table 4.2 indicates that there exists no clear trend claiming higher educational level corresponds to a higher percentage of unemployment. In some cases, such as Ghana in 1988 and India in 1989, it is true; in other cases, secondary school leavers showed the highest percentage of unemployment (Algeria in 1989, Egypt in 1989–91, Kenya in 1986, Malaysia in 1985, Uganda in 1989–91 and Côte d'Ivoire in 1985).

Finally, it should be stressed that the actual unemployment rates among graduates in most industrial countries were generally much lower than among those with lesser formal educational qualifications. The worst that happened to them was that they finally had to take jobs below their qualification level – at least temporarily. This resulted in a displacement process which implied an unemployment impact down to the next qualification level with the result that those at the bottom with the least education were left really unemployed.

This process of upgrading the educational requirements for various types of occupation, or of devaluation of credentials, has been going on for generations in all industrial countries. The problem which occurred during the last two decades was the sudden acceleration of this former gradual adjustment process which led to a growing gap between the graduates' expectations and the new realities of the employment system. A similar development can be expected for the developing countries.

Many open questions remain to be answered: if there really is a mismatch between the output of the higher education system and the demand of the employment system, how can the external efficiency of higher education systems be improved? Is only the short-term unemployment of highly qualified new entrants into the labour market to be interpreted as a natural 'job-searching process'? Will there be long-term unemployment of higher education graduates? If so, what are the necessary measures on both sides, the higher education system and the employment system, in order to prevent such a development?

Higher education and the labour market – some theoretical considerations

The linkages between higher education and employment can be

analysed with the help of two market models. One is the 'higher education market' where the demand of higher education meets the supply of higher education institutions in terms of number of study places; the other is the 'labour market for highly qualified personnel' where the supply of the higher education institutions in terms of graduates meets the demand of the economy (private enterprises, public and private service sector).

In economic terms, the rising demand for higher education must be seen from two angles:

1 As a precondition for future economic development (human capital formation as an important production factor);

2 As a consequence of economic development (as living standards rise with continued economic growth, the 'social' demand for higher education increases).

Two other factors will influence this trend, especially in developing countries:

1 The expansion of democracy is closely linked to the equality of educational opportunity aspect and will also increase the demand for greater access to higher education;

2 Given the hierarchical interdependence of the overall education system, basic education for all will lead to tremendous increases in the demand for secondary education which will, in turn, increase the demand for higher education (structural effect).

In the past, centrally planned economies applied a rigid concept of the manpower requirements approach: the planning of higher education became an integral part of central overall economic planning. In other words: the higher education market was fully controlled by the labour market in terms of numbers of entrants for different subjects of study and graduates for different jobs. Because of this rigid linkage of the intake and output of higher education to the requirements of the employment system as laid down in national five-year plans, the manpower requirements approach was the most often used programming technique in former socialist countries.

The market economies of Western industrialized countries preferred other approaches in the planning of higher education. In Western Europe, the social demand approach was dominant, which postulated increasing enrolment ratios and offered the corresponding supply of study places. The application of this approach did not cause any major problems in the 1960s when the demand of the economy, mainly due to high rates of economic growth, absorbed the increasing number of graduates without major problems. Later on, due at first to economic recessions, the higher education systems served as a waiting room for future employment. Finally, a decoupling of the two systems was proclaimed: the right to higher education was delinked from the right to work. In other words: given increasing and permanent unemployment, graduates from higher education institutions could no longer claim corresponding jobs in the economy.

In the United States and Canada, the human capital approach reflecting neo-classical theory through the application of the rate-of-return approach became the most popular approach. Rate-of-return analyses in higher education link the two systems and offer private and social signals for decision making by individuals and governments. Private rates of return are the result of comparing additional, private educational costs (including opportunity costs – earnings sacrificed in order to attend higher education institutions) with additional future lifetime income which the person expects after graduation. Social rates of return are based on public costs for higher education compared with more or less crude estimates of social needs and benefits, on manpower studies, and/or on sophisticated cost-benefit analyses. If all elements on the cost side as well as on the return side are commensurate – quantifiable – the result will be calculated rates of return which can be compared with each other (private vs social rates of return from higher education investments) or rates which can be compared with alternative investment opportunities (for example, returns from capital investments or assets). If social rates are lower than private rates of return, then the government is asked to influence the components of private rates of return, either by increasing the costs of higher education or by decreasing the expected returns on the labour market.

A mismatch in the linkages between higher education and employment (more graduates, fewer employment opportunities) indicates that either the rate of expansion at higher education institutions should be reduced or more employment opportunities should be created. This creates a policy dilemma not only in terms of responsibilities, which are generally shared by different ministries, but also in terms of government responsiveness. Since governments generally respond first to so-called imminent dangers, they are inclined to react to the pressures of the private demand for higher education. Evidence on educational expansion in many developing countries is consistent with this hypothesis of political behaviour. Only when growing unemployment emerges – much later – as a political threat, will the challenge of employment creation be given priority.

In most developing countries, the private rate of return of higher education exceeds the social rate of return because education-related wage differentials are excessive and the beneficiaries of higher education are publicly subsidized. In order to narrow the gap between private and social signals, and thus reduce excessive private demand for higher education, basic policies are required concerning:

1 The revision of the allocation of educational costs;

2 The revision of the role of private institutions of higher education; and

3 The revision of the determination of wages.

In developing countries high, in some cases accelerating, rural–urban migration, in the face of rising levels of urban unemployment, can be observed. When analysing differential rates of migration by educational level, individuals with higher levels of formal education are more likely to migrate than those with less formal education. The major reasons are:

1 The expected larger urban–rural increase differentials, and

2 The expected probability of obtaining a lucrative, urban job in the modern sector of the economy.

Furthermore, the widespread 'certification' phenomenon, characteristic of labour markets in the developing countries, offers highly qualified persons a greater chance of finding higher-paying urban jobs than those with less formal education because governments and private employers, faced with more applicants than openings, tend to select individuals on the basis of their formal educational certificates.

When urban labour supply is higher than demand, the already mentioned displacement process is set in motion. On the demand side, jobs which were formerly filled by secondary school graduates now require a higher education certificate. On the supply side, job aspirants now seek extra years of formal education which leads to an increase in the demand for higher education to meet the new qualification standards. This process leads to a vicious circle: rapidly increasing private demand for higher education; expansion of public higher education facilities due to strong political pressures, even though the social rate of return on such investments is likely to be considerably lower than the private rate of return. In order to break this cycle of accelerated rural–urban migration and rising urban unemployment, the current system of economic incentives must be changed. In the higher education system the private cost must be increased, for example through the introduction of fees and the privatization of former publicly financed cost components, in order to decrease the private rate of return. However, this does not seem to be sufficient; therefore, fundamental changes in the system of economic incentives outside the higher education system are necessary, such as raising rural incomes while holding down urban wage increases. This requires a reallocation of public funds not only from higher education to the employment system, but also within the employment system; from the civil service and capital-intensive industrial and agricultural enterprises to rural infrastructure, small farmers and small-scale industrial and service activities.

Rate-of-return calculations can be a useful planning tool for public authorities if applied with caution and not in isolation. Those calculations represent signals and serve as an information tool in order to influence market behaviour. It should always be kept in mind, however, that they fail to allow for changing conditions in the employment system. They may prove seriously misleading because rates of return are always calculated on the basis of expected earning differentials which cannot be equated with existing differentials. Therefore, governments are well advised to use them as one additional information tool in the decision-making process.

Towards more diversity in systems of higher education

In order to clarify the relationship between the higher education system and the employment system, a working definition of what is meant by higher education is necessary. Generally, there exists an implicit assumption that higher education refers only to universities. This notion is misleading in both structural and functional terms. Many higher education systems around the world consist not only of universities, but also of other post-secondary or tertiary institutions which include clearly defined elements of technical and vocational education.

Such a comprehensive definition of higher education is necessary when the relationships between the higher education system and the employment system are to be analysed. In both developing and industrialized countries, there exists an urgent need for a skilled and highly qualified workforce – a task which cannot be fulfilled by a mere expansion of university institutions.

Higher education cannot and should not be equated with university education. In the past, traditional universities have shown a unique capacity to resist innovation. They are, as a prominent sociologist once said, even more conservative than the Catholic Church and the army. Universities have demonstrated great difficulties in responding to new types of education and training needs caused through social, economic, and technological developments. Issues such as tenure, assessment, and accountability demonstrate quite well the conservative nature of universities as ivory towers existing in splendid isolation. Therefore, one of the great challenges in higher education is the functional reintegration of universities.

The expansion of higher education systems leading to mass higher education is a phenomenon which can be observed in many industrial countries and can be anticipated in many developing countries. Given the rising demand, the policy makers are confronted with the following questions:

1 What is the appropriate balance between different forms of post-secondary education, taking into due account both the individual demand for higher education and the economy's need for highly qualified personnel?

2 What are the appropriate strategies for influencing higher education system management in order to improve: the funding base; equity of access; system flexibility and competitiveness through open learning and distance education; the mobility within the system through credit transfer options within and between different sectors; and the quality of higher education provisions?

Talking about the three functions of higher education systems, namely research, teaching, and service, does not necessarily imply that all institutions should perform all three functions. On the contrary, the demand for diversification implies a division of labour among institutions as well as among individuals within institutions. The claim of the complementary nature of research and teaching is a well-known argument in many university circles because of the fact that the teaching function can be much better controlled by an institutional administration than can the research function. Also, different types of research must be taken into account, ranging from basic to applied research and that demanding different degrees of academic sophistication. In other words, more diversified systems of higher education might quite well include institutions where little or no research will be conducted and mass instruction will be the main task.

In order to meet the needs of the employment system, the higher education system must develop flexible strategies which are more client- and individual-oriented. In this connection, distance education – which allows flexible arrangements for students by overcoming the barriers of time and space and thereby allows increased access to higher education – should be mentioned. Learning systems outside traditional timetables and campuses offer economies of scale through a better allocation of scarce resources; they are also at the forefront of educational application of new technologies.

The use of new technologies in improving efficiency and also improving access to teaching and learning is an often debated issue, but conservative resistance is widespread in higher education, especially in universities around the world. However, the technological revolution, in particular the ever-increasing application of the electronic computer, will have an important impact on higher education, especially in its mode of delivery. In the near future, it can be expected that computer-assisted instruction will become the dominant method of teaching and learning. Institutions of higher education will be forced to abandon the traditional model of classroom organization in favour of computer-assisted instruction where information can be continuously updated and delivered to students according to individual programme requirements. In economic terms, this development means that higher education becomes less labour-intensive. The future role of open and distance learning, integrated into systems of higher education, will also hopefully affect the traditional teaching/learning programmes of universities. It can be anticipated that the most recent development in the merging of communication technologies into integrated services ('electronic superhighways') will change higher education systems radically.

Towards more flexibility in employment systems

As mentioned above, governments have failed to solve the problem of unemployment. According to the ILO's most recent *World Labour Report*, the downward trend in employment conditions persisted in much of the world:

> Outside East and South-East Asia, to the extent that employment levels were sustained, it was usually at the price of falling wages. Where employment deteriorated, the risk of job loss persisted, young people found it more and more difficult to get jobs, and more people became self-employed in urban areas. At the same time more women entered the job market. The 'informalization' of employment patterns in urban areas continued, sometimes very rapidly. In sub-Saharan Africa, for example, informal sector employment levels in some cases exceeded three-fifths of the urban labour force. But similar situations were found in Latin America and Asia and, albeit to a much lesser extent, even in the economies in transition and in the developed countries.[12]

According to the most recent ILO labour force estimates and projections, an average of over 43 million job-seekers, most of them in the developing countries, are being added annually to the worldwide labour force. This development for the 1990s has to be seen against a backdrop of already extremely high levels of un- and underemployment.

In OECD countries, unemployment averaged 2–3 per cent of the labour force during the 1950s and 1960s and increased to an average of 8.5 per cent in the early 1990s. Whereas the current jobless rate in the United States of about 7 per cent is slightly higher than in 1980, the average unemployment rate in the European Union rose from 6 per cent in 1980 to almost 12 per cent in 1993. Yet all is not well in the United States, with a far less regulated labour market and a less generous welfare system, because the success in employment creation has been bought at the price of creating an underclass of working poor: wage inequalities between skilled and unskilled labour have widened sharply.

For the time being, governments fail to create jobs. They are confronted with both cyclical and structural unemployment. In European OECD countries, present discussion centres on existing rigidities of the labour market. The *OECD Jobs Study*, therefore, proposes, among other things, measures to:[13]

1 Increase working time flexibility through changes in labour legislation and the extension of part-time work to the public sector;

2 Reform employment security provisions which would prevent dismissals on unfair grounds but allow firings, if needed, on economic grounds;

3 Increase wage and labour cost flexibility (among other things, minimum wages if existing should be indexed to prices rather than average earnings, non-wage labour costs should be reduced by cutting taxes on labour); and

4 Reform unemployment and related benefits (for example, the restriction of unemployment insurance benefit entitlements to the period of intense job search; employers should pay some of the cost of lay-offs; benefit fraud should be attacked).

Conclusions

The linkages between higher education and employment have to be seen from both angles. On one hand, the higher education system as a societal sub-system cannot be treated in isolation. The notion of external efficiency of higher education already indicates the responsibility of ministries of education to attach great importance to the future careers of graduates of higher education. One of the most difficult and politically sensitive policy issues facing governments is that of preventing a high rate of unemployment among graduates from rapidly expanding higher education systems.

Since public and private employers are more likely to recruit people with higher levels of education in periods of rising educational attainment and/or decreasing demands of the employment system, even when the job content does not necessarily become more complex, more formal education has on average always reduced the probability of remaining unemployed. Since we can assume that the demand for higher education will continue to grow and the necessity to increase the responsiveness to the needs of the employment system will become more important than ever before, the axiom of increasing diversity and flexibility in higher education systems is of utmost importance. Institutional diversity in higher education means the introduction of private and public polytechnics, short-cycle professional and technical institutes, community colleges, and open university programmes as cost-effective alternatives to traditional university programmes. Only the existence of competitive higher education markets can guarantee the necessary modernization processes in higher education systems.

In most countries of the world, national governments have traditionally played a dominant role in the provision, financing, and control of higher education systems. Since political and economic circumstances have changed radically, national governments are forced to reassess their future role in higher education. This does not imply a move from one extreme to another. The notion of an essentially institution-less competitive world in the neo-classical sense will not be the answer to present problems in and between the systems of higher education and employment. However 'more market' under public control in both systems, thereby allowing choice between institutional alternatives which guarantee more diversity and flexibility, might be a good alternative to present arrangements.

The structural adjustment processes, not only in developing countries, but also in industrial countries, put a lot of pressure on reducing public expenditures. This leads to a fall of wages as well as job opportunities in the government sector for graduates from higher education. It can be expected that government employment growth will continue to decline. This implies that the future employment system for higher education graduates will be primarily the private sector of the economy.

Increasing employment prospects also imply the improvement of labour force skills. In order to improve the transition from higher education to work, measures could include: a greater partnership between industry and higher education systems; effective career guidance, already existing within the higher education system through the counselling and placement of graduates; a better balance between academic, technical, and vocational studies in higher education; and – last, but not least – alternative combinations of careers with continuing and distant education.

In order to improve the linkages between the systems of higher education and employment in terms of increased highly-qualified employment prospects for graduates in the labour market, both systems must interact more closely than in the past. This also implies changes in both systems towards more diversity and flexibility and less rigid structures. Finally, it demands closer cooperation and joint effort from the responsible ministries at the government level.

NOTES
1 UNESCO (1991) *World Education Report 1991*, UNESCO, Paris.
2 UNESCO (1993) *World Education Report 1993*, UNESCO, Paris, p. 35.
3 *Ibid.*, pp. 35–7.
4 *Ibid.*, p. 37.
5 Coombs, P. H. (1981) *Future Critical World Issues in Education: A Provisional Report of Findings*, ICED, Essex.
6 *Ibid.*, p. 31.
7 *Ibid.*, p. 39.
8 *Ibid.*, pp. 41–2.
9 UNDP (1993) *Human Development Report 1993*, Oxford University Press, New York, p. 35.
10 *Ibid.*, p. 38.
11 *Ibid.*
12 ILO (1994) *World Labour Report*, ILO, Geneva, p. 1.
13 OECD (1994) *The OECD Jobs Study*, OECD, Paris.

5

Patterns of Vulnerable Labour Situations and Deprivation

– JOSÉ B. DE FIGUEIREDO –
– AND GERRY RODGERS –

This chapter summarizes recent work carried out at the International Institute of Labour Studies of the International Labour Organization on the functioning of urban labour markets in developing countries and its relationship to deprivation. The text deals first with the most relevant structural aspects of such markets and with the main components and characteristics of poverty. It then considers the ways these two phenomena interact and provides some evidence on the patterns of such interactions and how they relate to the concept of labour vulnerability. The final section provides a few concluding and policy-oriented remarks.

The literature on both poverty and labour markets is substantial, that on their interrelationships distinctly less so. Of course, much research on poverty looks at employment patterns and their effects on income and living standards, but the sources of these employment patterns in labour market mechanisms are addressed more rarely. Nor has much labour market analysis examined the effects of precarious living conditions on employment and labour productivity. The reasons are to a large extent historical. The labour market, in low income settings at least, has mainly been regarded as a means to promote development. Most attention has been paid to formal labour market structures and institutions and their effects on the efficiency of resource allocation. In developing this perspective, analysts have faced a series of challenges as the limitations of traditional market-based theories, in explaining wage and employment structure and dynamics, have become more apparent. While some of the responses to these challenges – subsistence or efficiency wage models, for instance – are directly related to poverty in obvious ways, this theme has not been a priority in the literature. At the same time, poverty analysis has been dominated by studies of the identification of the poor and their characteristics. The measurement of poverty has become more sophisticated, with a shift from simple poverty lines to more multifaceted and multi-disciplinary frame-works which could better deal with the variety of situations and dimensions of poor communities. But policy to reduce poverty has remained concentrated largely on direct intervention to raise incomes or provide goods and services to the poor: in so far as the labour market is involved, it is mainly as an instrument supporting employment creation programmes.

And yet a strong case can be made not only that poverty does affect the way labour markets operate, but – more important – that policy initiatives to reduce or eliminate poverty are likely to be much more effective if they are rooted in analysis of how labour markets produce or reproduce poverty. For this purpose, it is important not to take too narrow a definition of the term labour market: informal employment, self-employment and even family work should be taken into account, if only because these different types of labour usually occur in situations where there is also wage work, so that self-employment in the informal sector, say, will interact with or depend on wage labour because of indirect relationships on the supply or demand sides. But even if we restrict the term to wage labour, it is clear that the labour market is an important transmission mechanism which links overall economic performance to poverty. For instance, it is widely recognized that the effects of economic restructuring and stabilization programmes on the poor have to a large extent been channelled through the labour market. More generally, employment levels, which have been described as the iron link between economic development and poverty, should be seen not as a simple product of macroeconomic mechanisms, but as an outcome of both aggregate factors and the labour market mechanisms which convert these into jobs and distribute them among different population groups.

Relevant features of the labour market

Many aspects of labour market analysis have a direct or indirect bearing on poverty, but there are a number of topics which are of particular importance, especially those concerned with inequalities in access to jobs, with the stratification of jobs, and with the factors which generate particular labour market features and mechanisms at low income levels.

UNEMPLOYMENT AND UNDEREMPLOYMENT
A major feature of industrialization in most countries – the main exceptions are found in East Asia – has been that even during

periods of economic expansion, insufficient jobs have been created to absorb the increase in labour supply resulting from migration and population growth. Since it was generally assumed that the poor could not survive unemployment, excess labour supply was thought to manifest itself above all in underemployment in the informal sector. The empirical evidence does not support this model: open unemployment has been rising rapidly in some parts of the world (urban Africa, for example) and is probably becoming a widespread source of extreme poverty. What is more, there are signs that employment elasticities are declining, so that economic growth generates fewer and fewer jobs, in developing and industrialized countries alike. There are mechanisms at work here which are not well understood – the creation of jobs involves social and institutional relationships, and not just economic and technological ones, and it is urgent to understand these processes better. In any case, it seems that the volume of employment is bound up with the types of jobs that are being created, and who gets them, so that there is a complex relationship between the growth of employment and of unemployment. Underemployment, in its various forms, also arises out of these relationships. Unemployment and underemployment, then, are not just the result of excess labour supply, but rather reflect important mechanisms linking labour markets and poverty.

WAGE DETERMINATION IN LOW-INCOME SETTINGS
Even market models of wage determination have to recognize that there is a floor to the price of labour because of the need for subsistence. Early models of dualistic development took subsistence in the rural sector as the reference point (so that wages remained constantly close to subsistence level until excess labour supply was exhausted). Efficiency wage models subsequently explored the relationship between wages and productivity. In low-income settings the basic assumption is that there is a physical relationship between food intake and work capacity. It can be shown that in such circumstances there is a wage below which it is not in the employer's interest to reduce wages further, because efficiency losses outweigh cost reductions. So various economic mechanisms may lead to there being a floor below which wages will not fall. But wage fixing also depends on a series of institutional factors which may generate a floor to wages: for instance, there may be a powerful social notion of what constitutes a fair wage, leading to resistance if attempts are made to lower the wage beyond this point.[1] On the other hand, the relative power of different groups in the labour market will also lead to wage differentials, so that the level of the wage floor will not be

the same for all groups. The existence of a wage floor may lead to growth in parallel, marginal self-employment at lower income levels if it restricts demand for labour.

There are a number of other specific factors involved in wage setting at low income levels. On the whole, the working poor are less well organized than others and this undermines their attempts to gain improved wages and working conditions. Irregular and casual employment also affect the way wages are set and paid. Discrimination may be important in creating groups of workers who are particularly vulnerable to low wages.

HETEROGENEITY

Industrialization is accompanied by a process of heterogenization of the labour market which goes far beyond the dualistic model. This process implies that there develop not one or two but several markets or segments of the labour market which are characterized by differences in type of jobs, rules of access and remuneration. The development of research along these lines has suggested that a distinction between horizontal and vertical segmentation is needed in order to obtain reasonably homogeneous analytical categories – vertical segmentation referring to different types of labour market contributing to a single process of production, horizontal to distinct processes of production and labour use coexisting within the same economy.

A variety of theoretical models exist which try to explain heterogeneity in the labour market. The human capital model attributes wage disparities to productivity differentials between workers, not to segmentation. Models of discrimination interpret labour market heterogeneity in terms of the way societies offer different life chances to different groups among their members. More structural models treat segmentation as essentially determined by technology, or designed to weaken solidarity among different groups of workers. Finally there are two opposed views, one proposing that segmentation is the result of the malfunctioning of the market and that it would disappear provided corrective policies were applied. The other states that segmentation is the result of the confrontation of social actors, in society in general and in the labour market in particular, who have very distinct objectives and conflicting interests as well as very different organization and representation, negotiating capabilities and power.

The importance of these issues for poverty lies in the tendency of labour market heterogeneity to give rise to strata of low-paid, poorly protected, irregular jobs. Segmentation as a concept is particularly relevant because it implies that there is little mobility between different parts of the labour market, so that the poor become trapped in these low-income segments. So understanding the processes underlying stratification is important for understanding the sources of poverty. Some of the key elements are regularity, protection and autonomy of jobs, and a series of studies has been carried out which tries to capture the structuring of the labour market into different types of jobs in terms of factors such as these.

THE INSTITUTIONAL FRAMEWORK

Labour market institutions are diverse, and include not only the formal instruments such as collective bargaining systems and labour legislation but also a range of informal institutions and socially determined patterns of behaviour. While the formal labour market institutions relevant for poverty may be more visible (minimum wage legislation, for example), many informal institutions also have a major impact on the poor, among other reasons because they affect all three topics discussed above (unemployment, wages and heterogeneity). A particularly important issue concerns the institutions for access to the labour market. While formal institutions involving schooling and training, competition and other codified selection procedures may be important in some parts of the labour market, for many jobs particularistic mechanisms such as interpersonal networks and contacts will dominate. These informal institutions may in turn reflect underlying social rules about the rights of different members of the society, the hierarchy of status and opportunity, the transmission of welfare within kin and community networks, and the like.

Poverty

There are also a number of aspects of poverty which are of particular relevance to analysing the relationship with the labour market.

COMPLEXITY

There are both simple and complex notions of poverty. The simplest, involving falling below a subsistence threshold, is most appealing and most widespread. But there are good reasons for trying to go further. There are considerable diversities in needs, and in the means by which they are met, and they generate a complex pattern of inequalities in deprivation and satisfaction. This results not only from the interrelationships between different demographic, cultural and economic characteristics, but also from the different ways families establish their priorities, and from the patterns of discrimination, inclusion or exclusion to which they are subject. As Streeten[2] points out, 'unfortunately' it is likely that the use of even *a priori* strongly correlated indicators, such as income, calorie intake and percentage expenditure on food, will identify different population groups as poor. Even in 'ultra-poverty' situations, where nutritional inadequacy is widespread, the link between income and nutrition is only strong in some areas – like South and Southeast Asia – but not in others, such as Africa. One explanation lies in differences in the social environment of different groups: differences in culture, in access to education and to information systems, in health conditions and access to other social services. But this pattern is also closely bound up with the heterogeneity of production systems, notably in the informal sector, from where many of the poor derive a large proportion of their earnings. Thus complexity in the labour market and complexity in the pattern of poverty are interrelated.[3]

RIGHTS, ENTITLEMENTS AND DEPRIVATION
Poverty is often considered in an absolute sense: those falling below a specified standard are poor. But a persistent theme in the poverty literature relates poverty directly to social rather than absolute standards. Societal institutions or the state define a set of rights and entitlements, and particularly insofar as these involve command over consumption goods the poor are identified as those who are unable to exercise these rights. There is an important link with labour market issues here in that employment may itself belong to the set of rights, and provide both social legitimacy and income. Deprivation concerns not only food and clothing but also deprivation of a social position provided by work. There may also be specific deprivations associated with work, in terms of security (duration of work, safety nets in the absence of employment) and in terms of the quality of employment. Entitlements, in the sense developed by Sen, also involve labour market mechanisms, for the value of entitlements depends on a process of exchange which may be modified over time (catastrophically in the case of famines).[4]

INCOME-SHARING ARRANGEMENTS
The ways in which income from work is shared are crucial for determining poverty. In most societies, households of one sort or another provide the basic income-sharing unit. Since households vary greatly in their income-earning power, both between different households and over time, this alone implies both differences in incidence of poverty and differences in labour market strategy. But there are also solidarity mechanisms at community level and broader social security

systems at a more general level. These different levels involve different types of links with the labour market, particularly those between labour market obligations and income entitlements.

DYNAMICS

Dynamic aspects of poverty provide another source of heterogeneity. There are important movements in and out of situations of deprivation, as individuals gain and lose access to the labour market, as households pass through different parts of the life cycle, as individual fortunes change. In the United States, for example, but also in a number of Latin American countries, it has been observed that a significant proportion of people who moved below the poverty line did so at the time their family structure changed – for example, when a female-headed household was formed as a result of the break-up of a nuclear family. New economic phenomena may also create new forms of poverty, and new groups among the poor, and these downwardly mobile groups may be quite different from the long-term deprived. So it is important to distinguish between the permanent as opposed to the transient poor, and also between the recent poor and the long-term poor, whose needs, behaviour patterns and economic characteristics are likely to be very different.

REPRESENTATION

Poverty also stems from and is aggravated by the lack of organization and, more particularly, of representation of the poor. An ongoing International Institute of Labour Studies (IILS) project on social exclusion provides much evidence on this issue.[5] It highlights the importance of the non-material dimensions of poverty, such as those associated with the absence of or the exclusion from popular associations, solidarity schemes, labour markets or forms of representation, and the way these are linked to and often precede situations of material deprivation. The UNDP project on Sustainable Human Development could also be most relevant for the analysis of such aspects of poverty.[6] Although it is concerned with the reconstruction of the social fabric at large, it actually proposes an approach based on the notion of social capital which could easily be reinterpreted so as to cover more specific concerns related to the organization (and representation) capabilities or limited capabilities of the destitute. This lack of representation and organization is also partly explained by the diversity of the poor – in which labour market segmentation plays a role, since different groups among the poor develop different and sometimes competing interests. Looking at the labour market segments where the more deprived are found, it can be seen that they are also marginalized with respect to access to institutions which provide basic information and skill formation. Moreover, the mainstream labour organizations tend to focus on the core group of workers and less on situations in which the poor are over-represented, such as physically distant out-workers or the unemployed. Non-governmental organizations aimed at representing the poor face the problem that not only do they have limited resources but they tend to be managed by the non-poor on behalf of the poor, a situation which is untenable in the long term.[7] Even the functioning of new and more adequate institutional mechanisms which were created to monitor specific social initiatives have proved not to be a sufficient condition to reach the poor, at least not the more deprived among them.[8]

The labour market and poverty

Poverty has causes which go far beyond the labour market, and in particular depends on the overall levels of production and productivity. And within the labour market, the poor do not constitute an identifiable group: there are greater or lesser degrees of poverty in different labour market categories. But many labour market mechanisms and patterns are closely associated with poverty, and give insights into the pattern and intensity of poverty, and into the factors concentrating poverty among particular groups. At the same time, the labour market is an important economic mechanism through which poverty is reduced. Recent research at the IILS and elsewhere has identified a number of specific relationships which seem to merit more careful attention in future research.

It seems important in the first instance to distinguish between poverty within and poverty outside the labour market; in other words, is poverty associated with the nature of employment and the levels of income which it generates, or is it due to exclusion from access to jobs? Exclusion from regular income opportunities may appear as open unemployment, or as marginality in one form or another – including low-productivity street activities, crime or begging. But it may also be hidden, if particular groups do not appear on the labour market because their opportunities are limited – this is often true of women, for example, and of potential migrants. Exclusion from the labour market may be associated with personal characteristics – disability, for instance, or race. The degree to which labour market exclusion is directly linked to poverty depends on the extent to which state or community safety nets or solidarity networks exist, or whether it affects particular members (women, younger workers) of households where there is another income source. But the process of exclusion itself, in so far as it is concentrated on particular groups, is often wider than the labour market alone, so that exclusion from the labour market may be correlated with exclusion from the safety nets. Exclusion also operates within the labour market, with respect to access to the more desirable jobs – this we comment on below.

At the opposite extreme there is the phenomenon of overemployment: excessive work, because low productivity or low wages imply that very long hours have to be worked to achieve a subsistence income. This is no doubt the most frequent situation of the poor, and among the self-employed it is likely to be associated with inadequate use of human or physical resources – which is often regarded as a form of underemployment in the literature (in a productivity, rather than a time sense); so underemployment and overemployment coincide. Overemployment may also involve labour force participation by groups for which it is undesirable – child labour, for instance, or work while unfit – with subsequent consequences for personal development or health.

A more classic case concerns the abuse of the position of particular groups of workers, who are vulnerable to manipulation or exploitation. Bonded labour is an obvious example, but the position of temporary migrants may be little better.[9] More generally, low-skilled and unorganized workers may be unable to obtain decent working conditions and remuneration from employers in the absence of social legislation or in the absence of its effective enforcement.

But the more general issue, which emerges from the preceding sections, concerns the heterogeneity of both poverty and labour markets. How does differentiation in the labour market affect the overall level of poverty and its incidence?

All labour markets exhibit inequality, of course. Productivity differences between occupations, or between individuals with different skill or education levels, lead to differences in returns to labour which may be regarded as efficient in conventional economic models. This is not true, however, of differences in rewards to individuals with similar abilities and qualifications, as a result of discrimination; nor is it true of differences in rewards to labour which arise out of constraints on entry to particular jobs or sectors. These factors may give rise to poverty because of the emergence of labour market segments in which jobs are irregular, insecure and low-paid. These characteristics themselves lead to poverty, which then persists because individuals are trapped in these segments.

Mobility between different labour market segments is difficult, because of the credentials, contacts, capital or skills required to move up; many groups are excluded from regular, protected jobs. So entry to low-end jobs virtually precludes subsequent career development. Because of the insecure and irregular nature of the work, workers in these segments are also particularly vulnerable to unemployment. Such patterns can be observed in high-income and in low-income economies alike. In industrialized countries they appear in short-term or casual work, in home work and in some types of self-employment – categories of labour which appear to have increased their share of all jobs over the last 10 to 15 years. In developing countries they show up in the casualization of employment relationships, in marginal self-employment and in various types of unprotected wage employment. That rather similar patterns can be observed in low- and high-income environments suggests that at least this aspect of poverty has its roots in labour market structure – increasing aggregate production and average incomes would not be sufficient for its elimination.

On the supply side of the labour market, because of their hetero-geneity and the lack of representation in and access to social institutions, the poor have very diverse labour strategies, although the latter must, as a common feature, be aimed at neutralizing the intrinsic vulnerability of the poor. Another common characteristic is that such strategies are dominated by a context of extreme need. This forces unemployed family members to search for and accept poorly remunerated jobs or to produce low-quality goods or services for sale. It also undermines the ability to invest in the acquisition of qualifications and skills, so reinforcing the inability of the poor to escape from labour market vulnerability.

The ways in which these relationships affect poverty depend on a series of additional factors. First, labour market outcomes (usually) refer to individuals, and the link with poverty depends on the pattern of earning and dependency in the income-sharing unit. Larger households with single earners are more vulnerable to poverty regardless of labour market characteristics. But there is a tendency for the most adverse labour market situations to be faced by first-time entrants, many of them in households with additional income sources. Secondly, relative deprivation may be closely related to labour market patterns: labour market inequality may be a primary element in felt deprivation, as some attain social integra-tion and regular income through the labour market, while others survive in casual, precarious employment. If poverty is defined in relation to what societies regard as decent minima for all their citizens, then the labour market situation is likely to be an important element in the definition of poverty.

Some evidence

Some of these patterns have been explored in recent work at the IILS, although much remains to be done. On the whole, the relationship between labour market patterns and poverty is not easy to study with existing data, because the surveys which collect information at the household level on welfare and consumption usually have insufficient data on labour market patterns for each household member, while labour force surveys often have rich information on individuals but little on the households to which they belong. Even in Western Europe, where the data base is otherwise extensive, it is difficult to study the relationship between non-standard work and poverty because the main data sources do not permit it. Research in this area therefore has to rely heavily on fresh data collection. With this in mind, there have been studies based on small-scale surveys in India (Coimbatore),[10] in several African countries (summarized in Lachaud)[11] and (on a larger scale) in Brazil (São Paulo).[12] These studies concentrated exclusively on urban areas. Some of the relevant results are presented, in a highly summarized form, in Table 5.1. The table includes results from Cameroon (Yaoundé) and Burkina Faso (Ouagadougou), as two rather different examples among the several cities studied in this sub-region of Africa. The figures for poverty incidence in the four cities (44 per cent for São Paulo, 42 per cent for Coimbatore,[13] 44 per cent for Ouagadougou and 17 per cent for Yaoundé) of course cannot be directly compared with each other; in particular, the poverty threshold in São Paulo was distinctly higher in real terms than in the other three cities. This is normal; poverty is defined in relation to the perceptions and needs of each society.

On the basis of such surveys, regression models have been estimated for the cities of São Paulo, Coimbatore and several African capitals. These models were attempts to verify and evaluate the importance of the various labour status variables – relative to demographic and educational variables – in explaining the pattern of income distribution and the household standard of living. A major finding was that in spite of the differences in the overall social and economic contexts, similar structural relations did prevail. Such relations indicated that labour status does not in itself fully explain the pattern of income distribution. But it is the single most relevant variable to describe it. In the case of São Paulo it was also possible to

TABLE 5.1
Poverty and the labour market: some evidence

In %	São Paulo 1990	Coimbatore 1987	Ouagadougou 1992	Yaoundé 1990–1
Unemployment				
Total	9.4	13.1	25.0	29.3
Among the poor	15.5	18.2	31.9	47.5
Poverty incidence				
excl. unemployment	44.3	42.0	44.1	16.6
Poverty incidence in				
vulnerable labour status groups	68.6	67.0	65.0	35.6
Share of vulnerable labour status				
groups in total employment	33.9	29.6	51.0	41.9
Share of vulnerable labour status				
groups among the employed poor	52.4	47.2	75.1	90.0

Sources: São Paulo: SEADE (1992) 'Pesquisa de Condições de Vida', Labour market and Income volumes, São Paulo. Coimbatore: Harriss, Kannan and Rodgers (1990) 'Urban labour market structure and job access in India: a study of Coimbatore', Research Series No. 92, IILS, Geneva. Ouagadougou and Yaoundé: Lachaud, J. P. (1993) 'Poverty and urban labour market in sub-Saharan Africa: a comparative analysis', Discussion Paper No. 55, IILS, Geneva.
Notes

São Paulo
1 All variables (except unemployment) refer to households. 'Household labour status' is defined on the basis of a combination of the head's and another selected household member's status in the labour market;
2 Unemployment: open unemployment (Labour Market vol., Table 20);
3 Poverty threshold: Household monthly income of 2 minimum wages *per capita* (Income vol., Table 20);
4 Vulnerable labour status groups are households where: the head and the other household member have a vulnerable labour status (either being a dependent or having an irregular and low-income job); the head has a vulnerable labour status and the other member a non-vulnerable one and; the head has a non-vulnerable status and the other member a vulnerable one (Labour Market vol., Table 20).

Coimbatore
1 Unemployment: open unemployment last year (Table 50);
2 Poverty threshold: household weekly income of Rs. 60 per adult equivalent (Table 48); to be consistent with the labour status rates, the unemployed have been excluded from the poverty incidence rate.

Ouagadougou and Yaoundé
1 Unemployment: open unemployment (Table E);
2 Poverty threshold: household weekly income of FCFA 2222 (Ouagadougou) and FCFA 2880 (Yaoundé) per adult equivalent (Table B); to be consistent with the labour status rates, the unemployed have been excluded from the poverty incidence rate;
3 Vulnerable labour status groups are composed of heads of households who are in unprotected or irregular jobs, or marginal self-employed workers (Table C).

verify that such relationships vary significantly across social strata and that labour status is increasingly important when moving down in the social hierarchy. The opposite is true for the level of education. In this same case study, complementary models of statistical analysis have confirmed that to move from the lowest to the next social level, the most important factor would be to upgrade the labour status of active family members, while the access to the upper class depends mostly on the improvement of their level of education.

In the next sections, we will overview the main results of our studies by addressing four issues: unemployment; segmentation; household structure; and heterogeneity.

UNEMPLOYMENT

There is a strong association between unemployment and poverty in all three studies. The unemployment rate in deprived households is up to double the average rate, and up to three times the rate for the non-poor. While this is contrary to the popular perception of some years ago that unemployment in low-income countries is mainly a middle-class phenomenon, it is consistent with evidence from elsewhere that open unemployment is a substantial source of poverty.[14] The ratio between the number of unemployed persons and the number of income earners tends to be larger – up to twice as large – in poor households as in non-poor ones. But even among the poor, unemployment affects different individuals in different ways. It is, for example, far more pronounced for secondary workers than for heads of households (5 to 10 times higher) and also higher among the young and the more educated. These patterns, of course, affect the relationship with poverty. The relatively high level of unemployment among the more educated suggests that the unemployment figures include some extended job search among the relatively well off, but this is swamped in the aggregate figures by the larger proportion of unemployment linked to poverty. Survival in such situations, in the absence of effective systems of unemployment insurance, depends on intra-family or intra-community transfers, on days of work interspersed with days of unemployment, on the sale of assets, on indebtedness, or on unrecorded marginal work. Of course, survival rates are also certainly lower among the unemployed, although this is something on which there is only anecdotal evidence.

SEGMENTATION

In all four studies, attempts were made to understand the pattern of labour market segmentation in terms such as those discussed above.

In the Indian city, seven main categories of jobs (categories of labour status) were identified, taking into account the distinction between wage work and self-employment, the degree of effective protection of workers through the application of labour legislation or union organization, the regularity of work, its duration, and (in the case of the self-employed) the amount of capital used. Mobility between these categories of labour status was low, suggesting that they gave a good approximation to the pattern of labour market segmentation. The Yaoundé study worked with five major labour statuses: protected wage workers, unprotected regular wage workers, irregular wage workers, self-employed with capital and marginal self-employed. The São Paulo study combined similar labour market categories to those in the previously mentioned studies and derived a labour status for the household as a whole, on the basis of the labour market situation of selected household members. It also used an alternative to the poverty line approach, in which the population was classified in four distinct social groups on the basis of a multi-variate analysis based on dwelling, education, income and labour status indicators.

Despite the very distinct economic and social contexts, the three studies all suggest that the identification of vulnerable labour status groups contributes powerfully to the analysis of poverty. Poverty rates in these groups are much higher than in the population at large. Detailed analysis in India using different poverty lines shows that the most vulnerable labour status categories (unprotected irregular wage employment, independent wage work and marginal self-employment – to a lesser extent also short-term regular wage work) systematically have the highest poverty incidence. Results for São Paulo for instance show that labour status is the single most important factor explaining differences in poverty between households, while education plays a more limited role. The household sample surveys carried out in Yaoundé, Ouagadougou and in other Francophone African capital cities also indicate a close relationship between the more precarious labour status of individuals, as defined by irregularity of work and lack of protection and capital, unemployment and poverty. A large majority of irregular and marginal self-employed, and to a lesser extent non-protected wage-earners, belong to poor households. For the non-protected wage-earner group, almost one in every two workers is from a poor household. An important issue is whether the head of the household has a vulnerable labour market status; poverty is particularly widespread in households headed by irregular and marginal self-employed workers. This evidence is not conclusive, since it is based on small samples – except in the case of São Paulo – but the similarity in patterns in very different urban situations strongly suggests that more attention to labour market segmentation is needed in future research on poverty.

HOUSEHOLD POSITION

Much research has been devoted to and has shown the importance of personal characteristics such as age, sex, household type and migrant status for assessing deprivation and the quality of insertion into the labour market. Results from the studies referred to above confirm the importance of these issues. They show, for instance, that much variation in poverty between households can be traced to dependency, and the vulnerability to poverty of households with a high proportion of women (especially if the head is a woman) is found here as in many other studies. But it has also been shown that for such components to explain deprivation, they need to be evaluated in relation to labour market conditions. The adverse position of female-headed households, for instance, can be traced in part to the way in which women are over-represented in vulnerable labour market segments.

HETEROGENEITY

As well as exhibiting the same kind of structural relationships between labour and poverty as in the other cases, the São Paulo exercise also documented heterogeneity in ways which merit further attention. When households were classified in relation to the four welfare indicators included in the study – housing, education, income and labour status – it was found that only 11 per cent of the families accumulate deficiencies with respect to all four indicators. Similar results were found in India – deprivation in one dimension did not necessarily imply deprivation in all. Moreover, it was found that income measures alone seem to be quite incomplete as indicators; the São Paulo survey indicated, for instance, that the richest families from the least favoured group, in terms of social indicators, had earnings similar to the average of the socially most favoured group. This survey also illustrated how different socio-economic components have varying importance and meanings for the different groups. For example, education plays a very significant role for the better-off households while for the most deprived it is the labour status which is the predominant component.

Policy implications

There is quite strong evidence here for a widespread structural relationship between labour market status – and in particular vulnerable labour situations and unemployment – and poverty. The heterogeneity of both labour market and poverty situations implies that such relationships are not uniform but on the contrary have different meanings and patterns according to the various types and levels of labour market vulnerability, of unemployment situation and of household structure. Models of labour market segmentation can make sense of this complexity by distinguishing different types of jobs which both help to explain labour market functioning and have a direct bearing on the extent and incidence of poverty. But this is not the only aspect of the labour market which is relevant, for it is important to understand the labour institutions which include some in regular employment and exclude others, and the strategies of labour market behaviour which they induce among the poor.

More attention needs to be paid to labour market heterogeneity and its causes. But this is only a part of the story: a longer list of relationships between labour market functioning and poverty was outlined earlier, and suggests some elements for a research agenda. This is not to say that labour market forces are necessarily the primary causes of poverty, nor that labour market intervention is the most effective form of anti-poverty policy. But it does seem likely that there will be fairly high returns on further research in this area.

These issues are important not only for research, but also for policy. Targeted action against poverty may well be more effective if vulnerable groups can be identified in terms of detailed labour market position. Intervention in the labour market with a view to reducing poverty also needs to take account of these structural features. If the aim is to reduce poverty by widening employment opportunities, then labour market segmentation, and more generally the ways in which jobs are created and access to them controlled, will be important determinants of success or failure. More specifically, one could propose that on the basis of the interrelationships which have been identified and the evidence on the most critical features of destitute families – high unemployment (and dependency) rates and low levels of skill – two major and intertwined sets of active labour market policies should be emphasized. The first would be aimed at increasing the supply of jobs to the members of such families. Among other ways, this could be achieved through specific and massive programmes of information on the availability of employment opportunities, notably in microfirms, a sector which has a potential for growth and demand for low-skilled workers. The second would concentrate on programmes to increase the quality of this workforce. This could be done not only through conventional training courses but also through a transfer of knowledge on the ways people can increase their social capital and reinforce their capacity to organize, to collaborate and to build systems of representation.

NOTES
1 See, for instance, Solow, R. (1990) *The Labour Market as a Social Institution*, Basil Blackwell, Oxford.
2 Streeten, P. (1990) 'Poverty concepts and measurement', *The Bangladesh Development Studies*, Vol. 18, No. 3 (September).
3 Several attempts have been made to address this question of complexity. For example, one could mention the sensitivity and dominance analysis proposed by Ravallion (1992) to test the consistency of patterns of poverty, both on a cross-section and over-time basis.
4 Sen, Amartya K. (1981) *Poverty and Famines: An Essay on Entitlement and Deprivation*. Clarendon Press, Oxford.
5 Wolfe, M. (1994) 'Some paradoxes of social exclusion'. Discussion Paper No. 63, IILS, Geneva; and Silver, H. (1994) 'From poverty to exclusion: reconceptualizing social disadvantage, reconstructing social integration', to be published in the Discussion Papers series, IILS, Geneva.
6 Banuri, T. *et al.* (1994) 'Defining and operationalizing sustainable human development', discussion paper, UNDP/BPPE, New York (April).
7 Lewis, Primila (1991) *Social Action and the Labouring Poor*, Vistaar Publications, New Delhi.
8 Danziger, S. and D. Weinberg (eds) (1986) *Fighting Poverty: What Works and What Doesn't*, Harvard University Press; and Infante, Ricardo (ed.) (1993) *Deuda social. Desafío de la equidad*. OIT/PREALC, Santiago de Chile.
9 Bremen, Jan (1985) *Of Peasants, Migrants and Paupers: Rural Labour Circulation and Capitalist Production in West India*, Oxford University Press, Delhi.
10 Harris, J., K. P. Kannan and G. Rodgers (1990) *Urban Labour Market Structure and Job Access in India: a Study of Coimbatore*, Research Series No. 92. IILS, Geneva.
11 Lachaud, J. P. (1993) 'Poverty and the urban labour market in sub-Saharan Africa: a comparative analysis', Discussion Paper No. 55. IILS, Geneva (in French).
12 SEADE (1992) *Pesquisa de condições de vida na grande São Paulo: principais resultados*, São Paulo.
13 This figure includes some groups considered above the poverty line in the original study, where 27 per cent of households were found to fall below a poverty line similar to the one used in most official poverty estimates in India.
14 Rodgers, Gerry (ed.) (1989) *Urban Poverty and the Labour Market*, IILS/ILO, Geneva.

6

Some Considerations
on the Future of Work:
Redefining Productive Work

– ORIO GIARINI –

A first paradox: structural economic crises as the result of our greatly improved capacity to produce wealth

The economic crisis of 1929 essentially originated from the explosive developments in producing goods. We entered the era of mass production and mass consumption, but historical common sense was saying at that time that we were living in a world of scarcity and that only a very small minority could benefit from a large and wide consumption pattern. The elasticity of supply, to speak in economic terms, had constantly been underestimated since the beginning of the industrial revolution. The result was that overproduction could not find a market. Therefore, prices fell at the moment of the cycle downturn, factories had to close, and employment had to be diminished because of inadequate consumption. However, it was a solvable problem of (monetarized and monetized) consumption.

John Maynard Keynes developed an elaborated economic theory to justify, on one side, government intervention for investments and, on the other side, social policies (including the legalization of trade unions) which as a consequence reinforced demand. The news seemed too good to be true and the industrial world went through a deep crisis before opening the dams which precluded demand from benefiting from the new possibilities of mass production.

Although science was considered as very serious and technology as very useful, their effects on the elasticity of supply were clearly underestimated and this attitude, in fact, was dominant until the 1950s. From the end of the Second World War until 1973, the industrial world experienced unique economic growth, unheard of in economic history. This process went on for about 25 years at the rate, on average, of 6 per cent per annum (whereas the normal rate of growth during the whole industrial revolution has been around 2 to 3 per cent).

Since 1973, economic growth, on average, has been developing at a rate which is close to that for the whole industrial revolution. The 25 golden years look like a mirage and the industrial world has had to fight for the last 20 years; first against inflation and then against unemployment. How is it that we have become so accustomed to talk about economic crisis and these days consider high unemployment almost inevitable? How is it possible, in a period where the potential for production of any sort of goods and services is higher than ever, when the average level of education of most people in the industrial countries is much better than it was 100 years ago, when our life expectancy has never been so high, that we have developed a strange feeling of impotence?

A visitor from outer space would say that on earth there has never been such a great possibility to develop the wealth of nations and to increase the well-being of people, even if they are increasing in number. Are we perhaps facing another unseen or underestimated economic, cultural or social factor which makes it so difficult to build a bridge between the potentialities and the results?

My contention is that we should reconsider the way things were done in 1929 and the following years, reconsider the profound changes in the nature of supply, or if you wish, of the production function. We would then, hopefully, be able to propose a new global strategy of full employment.

The overcoming of the 1929 crisis was based essentially on the exploitation of an extremely high level of elasticity of supply. Eliminating all sorts of national, international, cultural, and economic obstacles to the utilization of this supply was the key to developing flourishing economies and full employment. Today the question is to understand what are the conditions for the production of the wealth of nations. Shouldn't we start by considering this issue, in order to discover the path for a new era of full employment?

What is the unthought-of factor now, which by analogy to the unthought-of factor of the Great Depression era, is the clue to a qualitative and quantitative jump in developing the wealth of nations? My bet is that the essence or the answer lies in the best possible re-evaluation and thus understanding of the typical production function operating in our economies. Is there anything that has changed dramatically in this function and which – by not being correctly understood – bars the way to a new era of economic development and full employment?

It would seem obvious that before starting any discussion on how to employ all sorts of resources (be they capital, human capital or other) the analysis of the production function should be the starting point for any employment policy. My contention is that the production function, in modern economies, embarked at least 20 years ago on a profound modification linked to a fundamental phenomenon of which everybody is aware, but on which we have probably not concentrated enough of our attention. This phenomenon is the key role played by services, both at the qualitative and at the quantitative level, in the process of producing wealth.

We all know about services in the same way as we all look at the sun rising in the morning. We say 'rising' as if it is the sun which is turning around the earth and not vice versa. It might well be that there is an inadequate perception of service functions in our economic system which could well be very similar to the inadequate perception of supply elasticity in the manufacturing industry 70 years ago. After all, it is service functions, technology and research, which are at the core of the industrial revolution. It is a service function, capital formation, which has been essential for the development of the industrial revolution. Also, there are many more service functions which are today decisive both for modern agriculture and, above all, for modern manufacturing systems. It has developed to such a point that these very same service functions represent 70–80 per cent of labour employment and investments through the spectrum of all the sectors of the economy.

Is it the idea that services are somewhat secondary, as we have learned in the classical textbooks of economics, which still prevents us from adequately understanding such big changes in the production function? We can wonder if even today, in most cases, when we acknowledge the importance of services in the modern economy, we are not in the end saying, as we do for the sun, that it is 'rising'. If services have become the major part of activities and 'production' within any large or small industrial company, shouldn't we think of what this implies in the way in which wealth is actually produced and used?

I suggest that we could well find here the starting point for following this new *fil d'Ariane*, to find the thread leading to where there is a link between potentials and results in engendering a new upper level in the history of the building of the wealth of nations. If we admit that there have been fundamental changes going on in the production function for at least 20 years, couldn't we try to reconsider the role of productive work and productive activities within this new framework?

The growth of the service sector

Figure 6.1 illustrates, for Germany since 1980, not only how the so-called tertiary sector *per se* has grown, but how far service functions have become dominant within the secondary sector itself.

FIGURE 6.1
Service functions in German industry

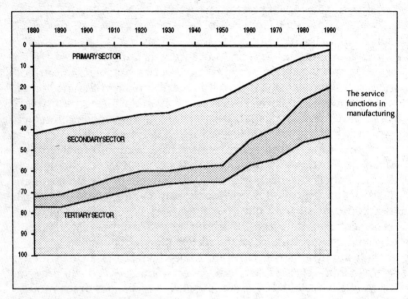

Source: From Wolfram Grühler (1990) *Dienstleistungsbestimmter Strukturwandeln in Deutschen Industrieunternehmen,* Deutscher Institutsverlag, Köln.

Some remarks about Figure 6.1:

1 I would add that for the primary sector a consistent part of its output is linked to service functions too;

2 On the other hand, a part of the so-called tertiary sector has also, in some cases, adopted procedures and processes which could be defined as 'manufacturing-like'.

The real points therefore are:

1 To accept the idea that services are spread over all sectors and therefore that the theory of the three sectors is somewhat obsolete;

2 The fact that advanced manufacturing industry is essentially an industry which has developed the most and the best performing

services – therefore dismissing the old idea that services are a kind of secondary or even backward part of the economy;

3 We should not be misled by the pre-industrial services which justify the contempt in which they are held by the economists of the industrial revolution, but instead concentrate our attention on those services which are the consequence of a mature industrial society benefiting from newer and more efficient technologies.

For the purpose of better understanding the analysis of the possibilities for a better use of human capital presented in the following three sections, let us briefly state some other key characteristics of the service economy, which I have dealt with in more detail elsewhere.

Service functions, which normally represent 70–80 per cent of production costs in most manufacturing companies, can be described as belonging to five categories:

1 Before manufacturing (research, financing);
2 During manufacturing (financing, quality control, safety, etc.);
3 Selling (logistics, distribution networks, etc.);
4 During product and system utilization (maintenance, leasing, etc.);
5 After product and system utilization (waste management, recycling, etc.).

In a graphic form, these services can be drawn as in Figure 6.2:

FIGURE 6. 2
Service functions

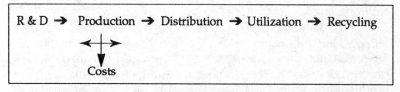

Whereas traditionally costs could normally be considered as belonging essentially to the production phase, costs related to all the other four phases have increased constantly up to the point where they have become dominant.

1 The consumer (the demand), instead of representing a totally separate activity from the production function, is always a part of this global production system, particularly at the level of distribution, and above all, in utilization and finally recycling. Alvin Toffler has described this phenomenon as the 'prosumer';
2 In terms of economic value, this is not only related to the existence

of a material product (traditionally limited to the phase of material production), but is extended over the performance of the system, whereas the utility really depends on the utilization of the product or system;[2]

3 The notion of utilization requires a time reference (duration), which can only be defined as a probability;

4 Costs and benefits, therefore, cannot be analysed adequately in a static system of reference (the general equilibrium theory), but have to refer to an economic system which optimizes different levels of uncertainty.

The growth of service functions – a first approach to the employment problem

When statistics today are provided by official institutions on service jobs and employment, they clearly indicate that most 'industrialized' nations already employ 70–80 per cent of the active population in services (inside and outside industry). For the last 20 years, the growth of jobs in the service activities has been spectacular in the United States, for example. The figure is in the tens of millions. Official figures also show a stable, but more often a declining number of jobs in pure manufacturing activities or companies. Services have also been recognized as flexible, adaptable to various conditions of production and to different social and cultural environments.

A great debate has taken place on the notion of productivity of services, but this is blurred by the fact that the performance of a service is not the same as the performance of a manufactured product. Increasing the number of automobiles produced in a production line does not have the same results as increasing the number of patients visited by a doctor or the number of students who can be crammed into a classroom. In the first case, the result has to do with a total number of automobiles produced in a unit of time; in the other cases, good results can only be measured by the level of health achieved by the patients or the level of education achieved by the students. In theoretical terms, this represents the need for a shift from measuring flows (added values) to measuring stocks (levels or end results).

In this debate, it would seem obvious to consider the notion of measuring quality in results as the key for measuring the real level of productivity in a service economy. Optimizing quality (in performance) is the proper reference for measuring productivity in services. A very fundamental question concerns the effects of technological development on services, service performance and the development of employment.

1   It would seem adequate to say that technological developments, until now, have increased the number of jobs in a powerful way for all sorts of service activities.

2   The great question today is to find out if technology, by increasing its efficiency, is starting to create possibilities of rationalization in many service activities to the point that the number of jobs available from services would decline at a faster rate than new jobs are created by new service activities. Recent studies show that traditional service activities, such as banking and insurance, even if they are expanding at an important rate, might be at the beginning of a phase of drastically reducing the possibility for creating new jobs. This question is critical, crucial, and needs very deep and detailed research efforts.[3]

Whatever the situation, it is in any case probably clear that:

1   Any developing country (and this includes the new 'tigers' of the world such as East Asia, and also Eastern Europe and Latin America) will be well advised, as a priority, to stimulate and develop adequate forms of services for their modern industrialization;

2   Services, in any case, will be a key element in the future of employment and, because there is a major difference between a worker in a production line or in a mine and a service activity, once again employment policies can benefit and exploit this situation of potential flexibility in a positive way;

3   It is also clear that most services require an adequate level of education and even of recurring education over the life cycle of individuals in all branches of activities. Hence an adequate fine tuning of the educational system is required.

In any case, we are facing a tremendous increase in our capacity to produce wealth, which needs to be organized and stimulated in the most proper way. There is a lot to be done in this area, but the question remains: will it really be possible to avoid unemployment and to offer to all able human beings, during their increasing lifetimes, the chance to fulfil their capabilities as prosumers and, above all, to achieve a higher level of human dignity by being able to use their potential in producing their part of wealth?

I must admit here a philosophical prejudice – we are much more what we produce than what we consume. Even consumption, in a Veblenian sense, is just a way to produce an image of ourselves. The majority of people, I believe, are conscious that their value is very much linked to their level of self-esteem and usefulness in society. I definitely support the idea that we consume and need to consume in order to produce (for ourselves and for society) rather than the other way around; and, again, the technical and material possibilities to produce today are more immense than they have ever been. However, we should probably also accept the idea that, in the present situation, the first essential step – to centre economic development around services – might be inadequate to provide employment for all. I would therefore propose to enquire into a second complementary strategy.

This second strategy has to do with what is often referred to as the necessity to stimulate activities which are important for individuals and for society, even if they are outside the market or the conventional economy. There appears to be a lot of consensus on this idea, which is normally accepted on moral grounds, but often proposed on unrealistic ones. The problem is that this perspective of developing non-economic activities is often relegated to the marginal realm of the things done in the name of goodwill. My contention is that we should try to find out if many of the non-economic activities are in fact a complementary and inevitable part of the general economic system, and as such represent much more than a simple secondary issue in traditional economic terms.

The effects of the notion and practice of employment through the monetarization process in the industrial revolution

Up to the beginning of the industrial revolution, the majority of resources (basically agricultural) which were produced and consumed were related to a system of self-production and self-consumption (a *non-monetarized* system). The industrial revolution accelerated the process of specialization and, therefore, of exchange. The process of exchange is what we call the process of a monetarized economy, where the value of goods exchanged is either implicit (non-*monetized*) or explicit (monetized) with reference to the value of what we call money. Keeping these distinctions in mind (between non-monetized and non-monetarized, in particular), an essentially agricultural society can be defined as a non-monetarized one, whereas when commercial exchanges take place, only a part – at least at the beginning of the process – is specifically monetized.

The fundamental importance of money in the economy is relatively new. The *history* of money has very ancient origins. Obviously, different forms of money have existed since prehistoric times, but they were far from dominant in the economic process. It was with the development of the industrial revolution that money became the essential tool to organize the new production system. It was necessary to have a developed commercial system functioning (as in the case of eighteenth-century England), so that part of the flow of money could be saved, and transformed into capital for investment. This was absolutely necessary because the new production tools, which were more and more important and costly, needed investment.

Observing the flourishing commerce around him and the birth of many manufacturing activities, in 1776 Adam Smith wrote his famous book on the wealth of nations. His genius was to detect the fact that, although the major part of the production of goods around him was still based on the traditional agricultural system, what at his time many of his contemporaries still considered as a marginal phenomenon was in fact the key and the most dynamic tool to develop the wealth of nations: he clearly perceived that the manufacturing system was based on investment and therefore linked to monetarization, and even more to the monetization of the economy. He precisely understood where the priority was and on this basis he created the foundation for a new discipline, economics, although his specific discipline of reference was moral philosophy (for the 'good of humanity').

Keeping this priority in mind, a large part of economic literature up to the beginning of the twentieth century concentrated on productive employment which was essentially linked to remunerated activity within the framework of the industrial production system. This was the main road to progress. Everything else, in particular services and all the systems of self-production and self-consumption, was considered socially legitimate and honourable, but obviously secondary to the main purpose. Therefore, since Adam Smith and up to the 1970s, notions such as trade, savings, investment and (remunerated) employment have become the fundamental paradigms of political economy and/or economics.

This vision of a genius of the new reality of production has helped in a powerful way to create the modern world: where, despite all the terrible crises and setbacks, a substantial step forward has been made for the wealth of nations; where the increase of life expectancy of each individual on earth has made indisputable and impressive progress. The moral ambition of Adam Smith has proved illuminating for creating those material products, food, shelter, and clothing which, with time, have revolutionized human history in the deepest sense. Also it was in the pursuit of this fundamental problem of increasing the material wealth of people that Adam Smith, in particular, laid the basis for the notion of economic value, which has since been, of course, improved, developed, and complemented in various ways. Even if in our century mainstream economics has shifted the notion of value from a supply to a demand side perspective, the notion of productive employment, in fact the notion of employment itself, is still linked essentially to this process of monetarization.

However, a legitimate question today could be: how far are all these basic assumptions valid in a situation in which services have become the key and greatest part of the production function itself? The success of the development of productivity and industrial production has created a paradoxical situation.

We can start by observing that where service activities are the key issue, the monetarization and/or the monetization system does not necessarily always produce the net positive results which were obvious in the classical period of the industrial revolution. Take the case of health costs: the developments in the capacity of drugs, doctors and instruments to ameliorate health (which is also possible thanks to the industrial revolution and to the monetarized systems) has undoubtedly brought decisive advantages. On the other side, when today the high costs of hospital treatments stimulate policies to persuade patients to stay at home, it is obvious that the non-monetarized, as well as the non-monetized, system is called upon to rescue the monetarized system from an implicit level of inefficiency. It is clear that women's work is a social victory, but it is also clear today that the problem of the care of children can be solved either by developing (with money) a system of kindergartens and/or through the mobilization of grandmothers or grandfathers who can do the equivalent job for free, where the conditions of the family allow such solutions. Why is the work done by specialized people in the kindergartens considered productive work, which adds to GNP, whereas the equivalent work of the grandmothers or grandfathers is not? It would seem that, in many areas, the non-monetarized is called to come to the rescue of what seem to be the limits of efficiency (in some cases) of the monetarized organization of the economy.

Can we therefore still separate the notion of productive employment, which belongs to the official monetarized and monetized economy, from the performance of activities, which can be defined as productive from a social, and even from an indirect financial, point of view, but which are not recognized as productive employment?

In the service economy, it would appear that the link between monetarized and non-monetarized activities is one of interdependence and that a growing part of these non-monetarized activities are forms of productive work in the sense of contributing to the wealth of nations and in some cases contributing even as essential elements in the functioning of the monetarized world itself. There is probably a question of optimum equilibrium of the monetarized and non-monetarized activities, where their synergy is more and more important.

Developing productive work in non-monetarized and non-monetized activities

Before enquiring into the importance for a modern economy of including in its strategy for developing the wealth of nations non-monetarized and non-monetized activities and work, it is important to avoid any misunderstanding of the value and social importance of money. There is no question of going back to the old utopia of the last century or on to a new one dreaming of a money-less society. Money has been one of the essential creations of civilization for making real progress possible. Of course human shortcomings are such that money, like religions or medical drugs, instead of being used for good, can be and are too often misused for evil.

However, it should also be clear that the old utopia of a money-less society of the past was, in a positive sense, a subconscious alternative to escape modern realities and possibilities, and simply reflected resistance to new possible improvements. A Robinson Crusoe type of society, or any similar myth, particularly in a situation of massive human interdependence, is impracticable and will most likely lead to disaster. Therefore, any sort of employment policy, keeping in mind the necessity of developing productive types of jobs, must aim at least at the availability of and access to money. It is a first step to personal freedom. By private, and when necessary, by public means everybody should have access to a necessary minimum amount of money from productive work.

In our utopia for the year 2018 (see the next section), I therefore suggest the possibility of stimulating, at the public level if necessary, the availability of at least part-time remunerated work. It is only on this function that social policy should concentrate. This is even more important, not only because of the growth of the population, but also because of the longer active life cycle from which mankind is now benefiting and which will also benefit all those in developing countries. This means a potential productive life starting at the age of about 18 and likely to last for about 60 years.

It is interesting to note that the problems arising from persistent, long-term and high unemployment in many countries are creating a kind of consensus, among both right-wing and left-wing parties, for transforming unemployment benefits (used too often for doing nothing) into some sort of compensation for socially useful and productive work. It is essential to consider all those activities which are socially and personally useful and with which the market systems alone cannot cope.

There is another very fundamental misunderstanding to be avoided here. The development of a public policy aiming to guarantee a minimum part-time job (roughly of about 20 hours per week or 1000 hours per year) is *not to be conceived* as a substitute for private initiative. Quite the opposite: the limited time of work (and the relative compensation) does not preclude, for those who might need to benefit from it, the addition of a second activity which would be entirely linked to their own initiative or, in any case, to a private type of production. I believe that it should be a goal of a modern society to eliminate the anxiety of remaining without any sort of employment and this would reinforce the possibilities for private initiative above, or in the place of, this guaranteed first layer of work.

One important psychological aspect of this first layer of work would be the effect of uncoupling the definition of the personality of an individual from the specific level or function of the person's type of job. After all, there are in our society a lot of people who perform socially beneficial or prestigious activities – when they serve in the military or in a social service activity, for example – without feeling they are in some way socially downgraded. Quite the contrary: individuals would have the freedom and even the stimulus to define themselves in terms of their own image and of society in activities which they deploy *beyond* this first level (layer) of activity.

There should also be no question of introducing such a scheme by force. The bet is that present trends in the world will go in the direction of the development of part-time jobs. It is a question of accompanying the movement and maybe one day reaching the situation in which this movement is completed and public authorities make it compulsory – as for instance in Switzerland, where about 85 per cent of the population is already involved in some sort of second pillar (privately managed social security scheme based on capitalization) to complement the first layer of governmental social security. With time, too, this trend towards private jobs should increasingly fit the interests of those doing them (students at university, married women with children, people over 60 who have 20 years of life expectancy, unemployed people who need to keep in touch with an active life, and the like).

It is therefore essential to consider this first layer of work as progress, socially and individually desirable, and to eliminate over time the ancient negative perception and realities of part-time jobs. Many functions related to this first layer of work will probably fall into the category of those productive activities which are now outside the market, as in the case of those grandmothers and grand-fathers I have already mentioned, who exist by the millions and take care of the development and education of young children. Existing social and informal structures will probably, in the future, be more and more used and supported financially. They will particularly progress in those areas in which they present an alternative – a cheaper solution – to those activities of public interest which by their more formal organization and institutionalization are more expensive.

It is again a matter of recognizing the productive value of activities which contribute to the overall wealth, even when they do not appear, or only partially appear, in the statistics of the present national accounting systems. Another key issue is the very way in which value is built into the service economy. Utility is built and is dependent on the performance of products and systems over time. I have already stressed how the quality of a performance contributes to ameliorating, over a period of time, the cost–benefit ratio.

In addition, the more the consumer becomes a prosumer, we rediscover that the proper utilization of systems has to do with an increasing amount of self-production and self-consumption activity (which is totally non-monetarized). It is here, at this level, that we rediscover the economic value of what the classical industrial revolution has by necessity eliminated, that is the economic importance of non-monetarized activities. Learning how to use a computer or any other modern tool for ourselves, or any other sort of educational or practical activity which is developed in a self-production and self-consumption system, could be seen as a complementary tool to mobilize human creativity. Economic optimization methods (taken in a larger sense) should be capable of finding a better type of equilibrium between the two worlds of the monetarized and the non-monetarized systems. The upgrading of large sectors of our social life, such as education and health, is an important growth area in this direction. The explosion of costs will probably be the main motivation to at least explore this issue and the possible solutions. As I stated at the beginning, we live in a world of human and material resources which are plentiful, and it would be a scandal in the long term if, because of societal and organizational short-comings, we continue to look at the future as something dangerous and menacing. The future is by definition uncertain, but this uncertainty should give way to new, reasonable and productive solutions. From a general economic point of view, it seems, therefore, very important to revisit in depth the notion of productive work.

The new social policy: results after 20 years of experience as recorded on 2 December 2018 [4]

Given the tremendous changes which have taken place in the last 25 years concerning social policies in most countries of the world, there is a great need for an overall analysis of the main trends and events which will pave the way of the future. Let us recapitulate the key events and changes which we have experienced over this period.

The total world population has now increased to just over the seven billion mark. It has been only in the last ten years that the birth rate has achieved, almost throughout the world, a level of stability, through diminishing birth rates in Africa, Asia and Latin America and slightly increasing birth rates in other parts of the world. This situation has been achieved while absorbing three major shocks:

1 The increased death rate during the last decade of the second millennium due to AIDS, which has since come under almost complete control;

2 The appearance of a new plague known by the name of CDS (Crazy DNA Syndrome), which has hit two continents during the first decade of our millennium;

3 The accidental atomic upheaval which devastated half a continent in the year 2005 and which led to the creation of the supra-national NCWCA (Nuclear Catastrophic Weapons Control Agency). We can hope that this type of event can really be limited to true accidents and circumscribed to very limited zones, thanks to the preventive interventions of the Agency, under the control of the United Nations Governing Council.

In the year 2018, the number of people in the world over 60 years of age has reached the level of 850 million. That is the same number of people on spaceship Earth as the total world population at the beginning of the industrial revolution, 250 years ago. The mark of one billion will be reached within the next decade.

During the last quarter of a century, the industrial revolution, which fuelled economic development during the nineteenth and twentieth centuries, has completely transmuted – as I have already stressed – into a service economy. In economic terms, the most significant event and change has been the world-wide recognition and agreement on a system of accounting of wealth based on:

1 The net value-added indicators (where the negative impacts of some economic activities are deducted). The first significant change in this direction was started by the World Bank in 1993, measuring GNP with reference to the real purchasing power of local currencies;

2 The wealth production indicators related to non-monetary activities and performances.

From an economic and social point of view, the most important factors in the new service economy have been the profound changes in the quality of work and of productive activities which have completely innovated the ancient rules and definitions concerning the notions of productive work and employment.

It was, by the way, only at the end of the last decade that the unit of full employment in most countries became fixed at 1,000 hours per year (called BFEI = Basic Full Employment and Income). It is at this level that governments, in more and more countries of the world, are now concentrating their economic and social security policies. This happens in many cases, although there are still many variations on some key measures. The notion of basic employment and income is based on what, 25 years ago, was considered to be a part-time job.[5] This part of the total productive activities of a person has today become accepted as a guarantee of the minimum basic needs. Full employment policies of governments are now concentrated on guaranteeing this first basic layer of employment. The notion of unemployment is also defined in relation to this first basic layer.

The means of attaining full employment still vary in many countries according to compulsory, semi-compulsory and totally free rules. In some countries, the government specially creates employment at this basic level, and offers it to those unable to find a job within this layer. All entitlements to unemployment benefits are normally denied to those unwilling to accept a job unless their total mental and/or physical incapacity related to the jobs to be performed is proved. This measure only became possible when the jobs in question were part-time units. Whereas this first layer of employment tends to be highly socially organized and promoted, the second layer of activity, in addition and above the first layer, is

almost everywhere totally open to individual initiative. In some
countries, there is a possibility for individuals not to take any job at
the first layer, by totally or partially abandoning the economic or
social rights linked to a first layer of activity (in some cases by paying
a specific tax).

The first layer of activity today covers generally the period of life
from 18 to 20 years of age (before entering a university or higher
education level) to the age of about 78. This has allowed the great
majority of the young population to extend and self-finance their
higher education right after high school and in parallel have
practical experience. For those continuing in an academic career, the
second layer of employment normally coincides with research and
teaching activities within the universities (as well as in many other
institutions of higher education, both private and public). This
development has facilitated the integration of the vocation of the
higher educational institutions with the function of continuing
education and updating in all fields.

Governments have played an active role in promoting these new
models with laws and civil service practice. On the one hand, they
have increased their efficiency in providing a minimum employment level for everybody in need and, on the other hand, they have
considerably reduced their direct intervention in the economy. They
have spent billions of dollars, ecus or 'yes' (yens-ecus-dollars) on
promoting programmes for retraining. It is only recently that there
is universal consensus that all workers should expect to learn new
skills over the course of their entire (work) lives. Since people work
longer and do not necessarily receive higher wages (top remuneration is to be found in the 40–50 years bracket), pension financing is
now more balanced than it has been at any time over the last forty
years. However, health expenses have increased constantly, in spite
of different cost-saving programmes (almost 25 per cent of GNP, of
which 40 per cent is managed through institutions derived from the
old HMOs). The major burden derives from the care of very old
people over 80 and of those who suffer from long-term diseases or
incapacities, which affect around 5 per cent of our population.

A fundamental change which has taken place in the social,
psychological and even the biological sector concerns the limit of
productivity and ageing. Nowadays, taking into consideration the
quality of work available, the minimum level of productivity
required for full employment, and the physical and mental health
conditions of the overall population, the age of total retirement (in
the old sense used in the last century and where it still exists)
oscillates according to different countries between the ages of 72 and

78 (three countries still maintain the age of 70, and two go as far as 80). No differentiation is considered any longer between men and women as to these limits (with few exceptions, including two countries with a higher limit for women). In fact, the notion of compulsory retirement at a given age has almost disappeared, except for very specific jobs.

Before the limit, the number of people unable physically, culturally or mentally to be productive does show limited variations throughout society and throughout the age group 18 to 78. It still oscillates at a level (between 3 and 8 per cent) in various parts of the world at any age group, excluding the last year of life of each individual. The notion of invalidity has become more flexible: people are productive again in a few months or years, since they are retrained for an activity they can accomplish, given the technological possibilities.

We must remember that this evolution is also the result of the great political movement which started during the 1990s in favour of a better integration of people over 60 years of age as productive individuals within society, and following the impossibility of the younger generations to support the financial burden of those over 60 and 65.

All social policies, and in particular those related to the pension, life insurance and savings schemes, are now derived from the Four Pillars strategy, which was first defined in a working paper in Geneva as early as 1985. We can recall that it was this strategy that helped to save the ancient pension system in many countries from the 'Pension Crash'. It has also helped to generate a number of services which were disappearing 20 years ago (round-the-corner restaurants, grandparent nurseries, do-it-yourself centres, good neighbour centres, gardeners, various health, entertainment and educational services). To put it briefly, there is a better integration of all those over 60 years of age as productive individuals in the society.

These changes have been accompanied throughout our world by an increasing overall participation of women at work, although this specific development has shown substantial differences in the rate of change in different countries and continents. In North America, for example, more than 80 per cent of women work and their professional structure is closer and closer to that of men. The number of stay-at-home jobs is still increasing, around 25 per cent of all jobs, two thirds of them being held by women.

Although nowadays there is a great diversity of models, one can say that on average families now have more children – at least in North America and Europe (where the average is almost 3). Women and men, working fewer hours on average at a remunerated job than in the past, find time and energy to combine their professional and family roles in a more harmonious way. The four generation family living under the same roof or within very short distances is something one encounters more and more these days, combining couples in various ways who, in half of the cases, have had more than one marriage or marriage-like experience.

There has also been a great renewal of community life. After decades of leisure spent in travels and sports, people devote more time and abilities to meeting and improving all aspects of community life, even when they go abroad. In this area also, people over 60 are among the most active and there is a revival of quite a few traditions which have almost been lost, and are now reinvented or just newly invented.

Concerning the general orientation of what at the end of the last millennium was called the pension system, we have now reached a level of consolidation of the Four Pillars System, based on:

1 The public guarantee of a first layer of financial resources for those excluded from any productive activity for reasons of incapacity. This pillar is almost always based on a pay-as-you-go system and in many countries is fully integrated into the fiscal system. It is also most often managed at the public level in full complementarity to the first layer of employment. Two countries have even integrated all these functions in a Ministry for Social Affairs and Full (first layer) Employment;

2 The resources are collected and managed by private institutions on a capitalization basis, within the framework of collective arrangements or legal prescriptions;

3 Private savings, managed directly by individuals (who benefit in various ways from specific incentives, but not always systematically);

4 The resources derived from productive activities. The fine tuning of this pillar together with the three others on the fiscal level has taken many years to reach its present satisfactory equilibrium and public consensus;

5 The changes which have started in the last two decades are probably of a dimension comparable only to the creation of a new type of civilization. Today, we are just at the beginning of experimenting with our new solutions and of trying, by experience and testing, to make this new system work.

It is important to underline that these types of issues and problems concerning employment, productive work, activities and social policies have become similar, for the first time in history, all over the world – a world in which the key mission is to provide a minimum economic support system and efficiency, so to enhance human freedom and dignity and, at the same time, provide a vision to integrate various age classes. With the notion of the planetary service economy, the idea of progress has achieved a new credibility and the world a new hope for advancing its civilization's potential.

NOTES
1 Giarini, Orio (1980) *Dialogue on Wealth and Welfare*, Pergamon Press, Oxford; Giarini, Orio and W. Stahel (1993)*The Limits to Certainty*, Kluwer Academic Publishers, Dordrecht and Boston.
2 This notion of performance, which is now being used more and more often in an economic sense, is quite similar to other notions, such as 'functional activity', which are emerging in different circles.
3 Some recent studies seem to indicate that the spread of new technologies, like the use of computers, has a very long lead-time linked to the problems of adequately learning how to use these new tools in a massive way. By reference, these studies indicate that the introduction of electricity in the manufacturing system, at the beginning of the century, took over 20 years before giving any sign of increasing productivity. We might therefore expect that after a long time (10, 20 or even more years) we could face in the coming decade a massive increase in productivity which, until now, has frustrated those who have been looking for global positive indicators in this area at the general economic scale.
4 A longer version of this text was presented at the General Assembly of the Club of Rome in Hanover on 2 December 1993.
5 Historically, it is important to remember that it was in 1994 that the European Union started recognizing the importance of a policy concerning part-time employment. It was at that time that decisions started to be taken concerning the adequate remuneration of part-time jobs in comparison with full-time employment.

- PART II -

Women
in the Labour Markets

7

Gender Aspects of Employment
and Unemployment
in a Global Perspective

– VALENTINE M. MOGHADAM –

Among the significant developments of the 1970s and 1980s was the
rise in female labour force participation rates caused by an increase
in the supply of job-seeking women and the demand for female
labour in white-collar and blue-collar occupations alike. East and
Southeast Asia saw the most spectacular increases in levels of female
employment (around 40 per cent of the labour force in 1990); in
Eastern Europe and the former Soviet Union half the labour force
consisted of women in full-time employment; and Western Europe
and North America saw a trend in the labour force attachment of
women, including that of married women with children. Even
regions where cultural restrictions and economic structures
inhibited female employment – the Middle East, North Africa, and
South Asia – saw increases in female labour force participation and
in the female share of the formal sector labour force.

More recently, however, the growth in the female labour force has
been undercut by economic recession, while the quality of employment has been affected by restructuring and flexibility. In Africa,
severe economic conditions have forced the growth in the female
labour force to fall well behind population growth. Women make up
the larger share of the unemployed population in Latin America and
the Caribbean, many of the non-NIC Asian countries, most of the
OECD countries, and East Central Europe and Russia. In the latter,
women's higher unemployment rates are a function of traditional
gender bias and a perception of women as more 'expensive labour'
due to the generous social benefits of the past. As a UN study aptly
notes: 'Women generally continue to be the last to benefit from job
expansion and the first to suffer from job contraction....'[1]

This chapter provides an overview of some gender aspects of
employment and unemployment in a global perspective, and is
guided theoretically by several premises: rising unemployment is a
function of the downturn of the world economy that began in the

mid-1970s; social and economic polarization and income inequalities have been increasing since the 1980s in all regions; and,
within countries, labour market processes differ significantly by
race, class and gender. In this chapter, gender differences will be
emphasized.[2] Many of the current socio-economic problems and
inequalities are systemic in nature, but this chapter will nonetheless
highlight issues relevant for policy and feasible for immediate
action. In the first section we examine the relationship between
gainful employment for women, the status of women, and national
development. We then consider the implications for women workers
of global economic restructuring. The major part of the chapter
reviews patterns and trends in employment and unemployment of
women across regions in the global economy. In the concluding
section we consider the broad policy implications of these developments and argue for a strategy emphasizing human resources, with
special attention to the female labour force.

Employment, the economic status of women, and national development

Gainful employment, as opposed to unpaid housework, can substantially improve the economic situation and social position of
women. An increase in income enhances a woman's status within
the home and may lead to shifts in the allocation of household
resources among expenditures or among household members.
When outside employment takes the form of jobs with some security
and legal protection, the economic position of women is much less
vulnerable in the household and in the society.

Many studies have identified a positive association between
female labour force participation and economic development. An
increase in the wages that women can potentially earn increases the
probability that they will enter the labour force; rising real wages for
workers in the course of development induce more women to work
for pay. Educational attainment by women and the shift from a
goods-producing to a service economy tend to have similar effects
because they increase the potential wage that women can earn in the
market. Female labour force participation is negatively related to the
number of children present; as birth rates decline at higher levels of
development, female labour force participation tends to increase.
(The causality runs in both directions.) Government policies also
play a role in encouraging or discouraging female employment. In a
progressive tax system, women married to men with high incomes

have more incentive to enter the labour market when the husband and wife are taxed as individuals (so that the tax rate of each is not influenced by the earnings of the other) than when they are taxed as a couple. Similarly, when child care is government-subsidized, mothers of young children are more likely to seek employment. On the other hand, governments that wish to maintain traditional gender relations and the sexual division of labour may bar women's entry into certain occupations and professions or fields of study.

Although women's economic options vary widely in different cultures and in countries at different stages of economic develop-ment, women are increasingly drawn into market employment as the development process proceeds. On a global basis, 37 per cent of women over the age of 15 are in the labour force, comprising over one third of the labour force. Women's share in the labour force is highest in the developed countries: 43 per cent compared to 35 per cent in the developing countries. In the developing world there is considerable variation, as Table 7.1 shows. The high employment rates of women in East and Southeast Asia are linked to the region's high growth rates based on a development strategy of export-led industrialization and full utilization of human resources.

TABLE 7.1
Employment profile, cross-regional comparison: 1990–2 (%)

	Sub-Saharan Africa	Middle East and North Africa	South Asia	East and South-east Asia	Latin America and the Caribbean
Labour force	39	28	38	54	41
Women in labour force	37	19	28	42	34

Source: UNDP (1994) *Human Development Report 1994*, OUP, New York, Table 51, p. 210.

In developing countries, women's participation and contribution to the national product is insufficiently covered by national statis-tical systems due to the inadequate coverage of the informal sector and of women's unpaid family labour. (Men in similar situations, on the other hand, are usually designated self-employed in labour statistics.) The growing awareness of the importance of unpaid labour by women in developing countries has resulted in studies that attempt to quantify this economic contribution. These studies measure the activity either by the number of hours women spend at work, the economic value of this time, the volume of their production, or the value of what they produce.

Globally, most women are crowded into a handful of occupations with little potential for advancement. Table 7.2 shows a large percentage of women in the professional/technical, clerical/service, and sales labour force, and a small percentage in the manufacturing/transportation and the administration/management labour force. According to one cross-national study of 25 industrial countries, 'on the average, women are over-represented in professional, clerical, sales, and service occupations, and substantially under-represented in managerial and production jobs'.[3] But while women show an impressive entry into the banking, insurance and telecommunications industries, the jobs which have been listed as those likely to be increasingly in demand – computer analysts and programmers, software developers, systems analysts, and management analysts and consultants – are not those usually associated with women. Labour markets are thus likely to remain sex-segregated.

TABLE 7.2
Percentage of women in different occupations in the 1980s

	Professional/ technical	Clerical/ service	Sales	Manu- facturing/ transportation	Adminis- tration/ management
Developed regions	47	63	48	18	18
Latin America and the Caribbean	49	58	47	17	20
Africa	38	35	42	18	13
Asia and Pacific	37	38	29	17	10

Source: UN/DIESA, based on Women's Indicators and Statistics Data Base (WISTAT).
Note: The percentages show the unweighted averages of a number of countries in each region.

Global patterns of women's employment may be gleaned from data in the ILO's *Yearbook of Labour Statistics* for various years. Only a handful of countries report large percentages of women in the agricultural workforce: Malawi, Haiti, Indonesia, Pakistan, Sri Lanka, Thailand, and Turkey. Among European countries, only Greece has more women in agriculture than in any other sector. The manufacturing sector claims over 25 per cent of the female labour force only in the East Asian NICs, the former socialist countries, Tunisia, and Morocco. Throughout the world, the largest concentrations of women workers are in public and private services ('community, social, and personal services'), and especially in the areas of health, education, and social welfare. Women are paid less than men, especially in the manufacturing sector, where in countries like South Korea and Japan women workers' wages are only half of those of male workers. In other sectors, the gender gap is narrowing, but women still lack access to high-paying jobs and to managerial and supervisory positions. Moreover, women everywhere perform a balancing act between the market and the household, and public policy generally overlooks this gender difference.

The contribution of women to activities closely related to human development is known to be substantial. More than half of the first-level teachers in the world are women. In 1988, women made up 75 per cent of the first-level teaching staff in the developed countries and 77 per cent in Latin America. They made up 49 per cent of the first-level teaching staff in North Africa and 43 per cent in the Middle East and Asia. The percentage of women teachers at the second level is lower for all regions, since women are usually clustered in low-level jobs. But women teachers serve as motivators and role models and promote the increased participation of girls in school and other educational programmes.[4] As one expert notes, 'All the evidence from Third World countries shows a close link between women's education and social and economic development'.[5] Examining the literature and data, Blumberg concludes that 'there is now much evidence that women world wide make major contributions to the wealth of nations, and that the use and expansion of women's productive capacities is a necessary condition for social and economic progress'.[6]

Global economic restructuring and women workers

Macro-level phenomena such as technological change, structural adjustment programmes and liberalization measures, and the globalization of markets and production could have a significant impact – positive or negative – on women's work. Thus far, however, global economic and labour market developments in the 1980s, and continuing in the 1990s, threaten to undo the gains made by women in securing economic independence and in contributing to national development, while also imposing limitations on the capacity of governments, trade unions and women's organizations to improve women's employment opportunities and working and living conditions. The global spread of flexible labour practices and the supply-side structural adjustment economic strategy coincide with a decline in labour standards, employment insecurity, increased joblessness through industrial and other forms of restructuring, and a rise in atypical or precarious forms of employment that are casual, part-time, and temporary in nature, including home working. In some cases, technological advances have been unemployment-inducing. Where rationalization and the reduction of labour-intensive work are the primary goals, labour shedding tends to occur, particularly at the lower and more routine end of the skills spectrum where female industrial workers are generally found. Researchers have attributed much of the documented decline in women's employment in the textile industry in Argentina, Brazil and Italy in the 1980s to the introduction of digital automation and robotics. It has been suggested that the changes in equipment and processes necessitated by product innovation in response to increasing competition from developing countries has resulted in significant labour shedding in the European textile industry as a whole.[7]

The trend toward the rolling back of the State and the withering away of the redistributive, welfare state has major implications for women. Throughout the world women have sought employment in the public sector for its affirmative action policies, generous benefits, and implementation of labour codes. These have made the public sector – both public services and state-owned factories – a more woman-friendly employer than the private sector. In East Central Europe, the state sector has been shrinking fast in terms of output, income and employment. Not only have women lost jobs at a faster rate than men, but the loss of benefits such as free or cheap child care facilities and generous maternity leave affects women workers more directly and adversely. In China, new foreign-backed joint ventures producing clothing, toys and electronic goods hire women in large numbers, but these export-oriented factories have very exploitative labour practices. In Vietnam, women managers and workers alike express a preference for working in state-owned enterprises, where social protection and working conditions are more favourable than in the new and burgeoning private sector.[8] In the Middle East and North Africa, new export-oriented development strategies may increase the demand for female labour, but not necessarily in stable and salaried employment; home work or other forms of non-regular work are likely to expand instead, especially in Turkey, Tunisia, and Morocco. In Iran, although the female labour force is a small percentage of the total workforce, women in the public sector – whether professionals in the civil service or workers in state-owned enterprises – enjoy social security and benefits that elude women in the private sector.

Global economic restructuring seems to be expanding the numbers of home workers, who work for an employer but at home. A report from the Council of Europe suggested that there were about two million home workers in its 15 member countries. In Japan a survey found about one million home workers. In the Philippines around half a million home workers are believed to work in the garment industry. The garment industry also employs huge numbers of female home workers in Turkey, Tunisia, Morocco, and Egypt. In India the *bidi* (cigarette) industry alone employs over two million home workers, while a survey in Java in Indonesia found that 21 per cent of households were engaged in home-based work. Most home workers work in clothing, textiles, and other labour-intensive industries where the work can be fragmented and requires simple skills. In industrial countries such as France, the United Kingdom and the United States, home workers are more likely to be involved in services such as clerical work, laundry, or catering. In industrial countries there are also increasing numbers of tele-workers, persons working at home but in computer contact with their employers.

The relocation of clerical and data entry jobs to countries whose comparative advantage lies in a low-wage, well-educated workforce has resulted in telework offshore data processing and office administrative services, made possible by the growing tradability of those services over computer-communication lines. To date the main locations for such 'back-office' work have been in the Caribbean (with its proximity to the North American continent), India, mainland China, Singapore and the Philippines. In common with offshore manufacturing facilities, offshore services are often foreign-owned subsidiaries, many of which are physically located in Free Trade or EPZs to take advantage of the same incentives which include low-cost space, tax holidays, and the full repatriation of profits and dividends. A UN source notes that the jobs which 'are held almost exclusively by women are isolated from the organization, offer minimal opportunities for advancement, and little development of skills through formal or informal learning processes'.[9]

Home workers are mostly women, and their main problems are low pay, lack of social protection, and lack of coverage by labour legislation. According to the ILO, women make up at least 80 per cent of home workers globally, though the proportion can be much higher in countries such as the Netherlands, Greece, Ireland, and Italy. Home work may be attractive to women since it allows them to combine work with family care, but they may also be forced into home work because of their weaker position in the labour market. In the garment industry in Delhi, home workers on piece work have been found to earn half the minimum wage. In the Netherlands and Brazil home garment workers have been earning around one third as much as equivalent factory workers. Many home workers are isolated and thus vulnerable to exploitation, but they suffer further because the network of agents, contractors, and subcontractors takes a profit from their work. Home workers often work long hours and have to expose themselves and their families to risks from machinery and from flammable and other hazardous materials, but they often dare not complain either about wages or working conditions for fear of losing their jobs. Although trade unions traditionally have called for home working to be prohibited, more recently they have argued that existing legislation should be extended to home workers.[10]

Global economic restructuring has entailed increasing utilization of female labour in formal and non-regular employment. The growth of export-oriented industries and the trend towards flexibility in employment may be seen as a one-sided management strategy that short-changes large sections of the working population. If deskilling and downgrading of jobs is the dominant process of global economic restructuring, then supply-side policies that emphasize education and training will not change the growth in low-skill, low-wage jobs, though they may alleviate the plight of some workers at the very bottom. What the situation calls for, then, is nothing less than changing the course of economic restructuring. In the meantime, steps can be taken to eliminate exploitative work practices, institute the basic ILO conventions, and improve women's labour market positions, including their ability to combine productive and reproductive activities.

Industrial market economies

Since the 1970s, every country in the OECD has seen a rise in the proportion of women who enter the workforce. The disappearance of manufacturing jobs has affected mostly men. Meanwhile, service employment has grown. In particular, public services – in health care, education, administration and social work – have expanded, and here women have been the main beneficiaries. At the same time, women are more likely to work part-time. Between 1973 and 1990, the labour force participation rate for men fell from 88 to 83 per cent, while that for women increased from 48 to 60 per cent. For women this reflected an increasing desire to work and an increasing need to work, though neither aspiration was necessarily fulfilled since the unemployment rates for women are still typically higher than those for men. Another group with much higher-than-average levels of unemployment is young people. In Spain in 1991, while the overall unemployment rate was 16 per cent, that for people aged 16 to 19 was 31 per cent. Similarly, in Italy, the overall rate was 11 per cent but that for people aged 14 to 19 was 38 per cent. Rising unemployment and the expansion of part-time work (for women but also for men) may have put downward pressure on wages.[11]

Most OECD countries have seen an increase in long-term unemployment. The exception is the United States, where the average duration of unemployment is three months and the unemployment rate is lower than elsewhere. But this has been due to the creation of low-skill, low-wage service sector jobs. Indeed, much of the increase in female employment has been in these kinds of jobs, and in part-time and temporary employment. Elsewhere in OECD countries, the proportion of the workforce working part-time increased in the 1980s as full-time employment fell. There are now more than 50 million part-time workers in the industrialized market economies alone, and most of them are women.[12] In the OECD countries part-time women workers range from 65 per cent of the part-time labour force in Italy, Greece, and the United States to 90 per cent in Belgium and Germany. At the same time, and in a reflection of the feminization of labour trend, part-time work has increased for men as well, especially in New Zealand, the United Kingdom and the Netherlands. Whether for men or for women, part-time work is concentrated in service industries, especially the retail trade, hotels and catering, banking, and insurance. Part-time workers are on average paid lower hourly rates than full-time workers. They are unlikely to receive premium payments for overtime, and are generally excluded from other allowances such as holiday and sickness pay.[13] A 1991 survey by the European Union found that 37 per cent of part-time workers would prefer to work full-time.

For OECD countries, therefore, public policies are needed to protect part-time workers and home workers. Active labour market policies are also required to retrain and upgrade the skills of workers laid off from manufacturing and service sector jobs.

Eastern Europe and the former Soviet Union

Since the collapse of communism and the move towards marketization there have been substantial job losses and steep falls in GDP throughout the region. According to the Russian statistics institute Goskomstat, in 1993 there were 3 million unemployed persons in Russia, or an official unemployment rate of under 2 per cent, but Guy Standing of the ILO puts the real unemployment figure at 'a minimum of 10 per cent'.[14] In Eastern Europe, from the beginning of 1990 up to March 1992 the registered unemployed increased from 100,000 to 7.5 million at the beginning of 1994. Much of the unemployment burden is shouldered by young people and by women, and there is evidence of discrimination against ethnic minorities, suggesting a trend towards greater labour market segmentation. The rapid increase in the number of private sector jobs – whether through the privatization of state industries or the establishment of new businesses, especially shops and restaurants in Poland and Hungary – has not been sufficient to compensate for the loss of jobs in the state and cooperative sectors. At the same time, inflation has eroded real incomes as well as unemployment benefits in all countries of the region. Unemployment and inflation have led to an expansion of poverty at a time when the generous social policies of the past have been trimmed or eliminated. Because of the large percentages of single mothers and of female pensioners in some countries, the feminization of poverty could become a reality.

Everywhere, except Hungary and Slovenia, the unemployment rates are higher for women. (See Table 7.3 for gender-disaggregated unemployment rates.) In 1992, the unemployment rate in Bulgaria was 13.7 per cent for men, but 14.5 per cent for women; in Poland in 1992 it was 11.8 per cent for men and 14.9 per cent for women. There have been substantial lay-offs in sectors and occupations in which women predominate – in light industries, such as textiles and apparel, and in administrative jobs. Studies indicate that unemployed women find it difficult to get new jobs because employers prefer not to hire women in order to avoid the expense of maternity leave.[15]

Official statements and some studies assert that women have been more vulnerable to unemployment than men because of their lower level of vocational training (despite their higher level of general education). This may be true up to a point, and it does suggest the need for greater participation by women in retraining and skills-upgrading programmes. It must be acknowledged, however, that gender bias is largely responsible for this state of affairs. For example, statements of both government officials and employers tend to emphasize the traditional role of women within the home.[16] In Bulgaria and Poland there is evidence that men are increasingly taking jobs in formerly female-dominated service occupations that are now being upgraded and computerized. Where retraining is

TABLE 7.3
Unemployment rates by gender, selected Central and Eastern European countries, 1990–3

	1990	1991	1992	1993
Bulgaria				
Total %	1.7	11.1	14.1	16.4
Male %	–	–	13.7	–
Female %	–	–	14.5	–
Croatia				
Total %	8	14	15	–
Male %	6	11	12	–
Female %	11	16	18	–
Czechoslovakia				
Total %	1.0	6.9	5.1	5.1
Male %	0.9	5.9	4.7	–
Female %	1.0	7.3	5.4	–
Germany				
Total %	–	10.3	14.8	–
Male %	–	8.5	10.5	–
Female %	–	12.3	19.6	–
Hungary				
Total %	1.7	8.5	12.3	12.1
Male %	1.8	9.2	14.0	–
Female %	1.4	7.6	10.5	–
Poland				
Total %	3.5	9.7	13.3	15.7
Male %	3.2	7.9	11.8	–
Female %	3.8	11.4	14.9	–
Romania				
Total %	–	3.2	8.4	10.1
Male %	–	2.2	6.2	–
Female %	–	4.0	10.7	–
Slovenia				
Total %	4.7	8.2	11.5	15.6
Male %	4.5	8.5	12.1	–
Female %	4.8	7.9	10.8	–

Source: ILO *Yearbook of Labour Statistics 1993*, Table 9A; UN *World Economic and Social Survey 1994* (advance copy), Table VI.12.

being systematically provided, as in Hungary, research indicates a strong tendency towards gender segregation whereby men are moving into the technical and specialized areas while women gravitate towards data processing.[17] Maternity leave has become precarious and risky in the private sector. At a time when the cost of child care has increased and public services have deteriorated, the effects on the mobility of female labour are likely to be greater than those on male labour. Thus, in addition to active labour market policies and programmes that target women, every effort should be made to identify and redress gender discrimination in the economies in transition.

Latin America and the Caribbean

Two significant features that characterize the situation of women in employment in Latin America in the 1990s are the constantly growing numbers of women in the labour market, and their wider opportunities as regards access to formal education. The result is that, on average, women in the labour market have a higher level of education than do men. New employment opportunities with relatively good remuneration have appeared in the service sector, and especially in banking, insurance and telecommunications. In a number of countries in the region, industrial development, foreign investment and export manufacturing have contributed to significant increases in female industrial employment (for example, in Mexico, Brazil, Venezuela, Puerto Rico, Dominican Republic). On the other hand, the process of economic restructuring, entailing personnel cutbacks in the public sector and greater flexibility in the labour market, has resulted in higher rates of unemployment for women as well as a deterioration of working conditions. Meanwhile, social disparities have widened, and in a situation where women are assuming greater responsibilities for household management (20–30 per cent of all households are maintained by women), the phenomenon of the feminization of poverty is affecting millions of women and children.

Between 1980 and 1991 the average industrial wage fell by 17.5 per cent and the average minimum wage by 35 per cent; in Bolivia, Ecuador, Paraguay, Mexico and Peru, the wage falls were truly dramatic. Workers with better union organization and with the benefit of collective bargaining, such as those in construction and industry, saw their wages fall rather less (20 per cent). Unfortunately, women workers were not thus shielded, due to their lower levels of unionization in most countries. Perhaps the worst off were people in

the informal sector, who between 1980 and 1989 suffered an estimated 42 per cent drop in income.[18] But in the absence of a growth
of gainful employment, more and more people are drifting to the
informal sector, despite its precariousness. The number of informal
workers doubled during the decade, and these include domestic
staff, the self-employed, unpaid family workers, and those in micro-
enterprises. As a result, the informal sector's share of non-agricultural employment rose from 40 to 53 per cent. Even those still
employed by larger enterprises are now more likely to have precarious jobs, working on short-term contracts or sometimes working
at home, at wages far below those with stable jobs. An increasing
proportion of coffee, sugar cane, cotton, fruit, and vegetables for
export is produced by casual workers. According to a survey
conducted by PREALC, women account for the largest proportion of
home workers and temporary workers in agriculture.[19]

Caribbean countries generally are heavily dependent on the
export of primary commodities, on tourism, and on foreign investment in EPZs, where the majority of workers are female. Yet,
international competition is becoming ever fiercer in the traditional
primary industries, in light manufacturing and assembly operations,
and in tourism and data processing. Thus there exist high unemployment rates, especially among women and despite large-scale
emigration, particularly to North America. Urban decay and social
problems are also manifest. Many observers point to increases in
child malnutrition and vagrancy, as well as the emergence of
increasing numbers of street children, as evidence of deteriorating
social conditions. At the very least, this suggests an urgent need for
child care and youth programmes.

There has been much criticism, especially in the Women in
Development (WID) literature, of the social and gender effects of the
structural adjustment programmes, because of the burdens they
have placed on women's labour time and responsibility for household survival, because of the unemployment they have induced, and
because of the social disparities they have caused.[20] In 1990 some 46
per cent, or 192 million people, lived under the poverty line – 5 per
cent higher than at the beginning of the 1980s. About 22 per cent of
the Latin American population was considered 'extremely poor'.
Thus a major task is to reduce poverty and to increase equity. This
calls for greater investments in human resources, and especially in
women.

In many countries in the region, women's unemployment is
higher than men's, even though women make up a smaller proportion of the workforce, and the situation is most severe for younger

women. Unemployment rates of women are particularly high in Caribbean countries, especially Barbados, Jamaica, Panama, and Trinidad and Tobago. (For illustrations of differential male–female unemployment rates, see Figures 7.1 and 7.2.) In addition to active labour market policies, the feminization of unemployment, of poverty, and of low-wage work need to be addressed by public policies. The informal sector should not be regarded as a panacea. Measures should be taken to extend social protection to workers in the informal sector, in part-time work, and in home work. As one expert puts it: 'Expanding the employment opportunities of poor women is a key element of an effective social reform package that will reduce poverty and increase equity in the region.'[21]

Sub-Saharan Africa

Because of its peripheral status in the world economy, Africa has been most vulnerable to the global economic crisis. Growth stagnated in the 1970s and turned negative in the 1980s, and there have been steep declines in per capita GNP and in investment. The burden of foreign debt added to these problems and contributed to increasing poverty. Escaping from the downward spiral will mean offering much more productive work to Africa's people. This is a daunting challenge, for at least two reasons. First, the current population of 650 million is expected to grow at 3 per cent per year (compared with 1.8 per cent for the developing world as a whole). Second, a higher proportion of the population is joining the workforce; in particular, more women in the urban areas are looking for work outside the home to supplement their low family incomes.

The modern sector employs a small and declining proportion of workers – down from 10 per cent of the labour force in 1980 to 8 per cent in 1990. Indeed, wage employment in many countries is declining sharply – down 13 per cent in Niger between 1980 and 1985, and 5 per cent in Zambia between 1980 and 1988. As part of their economic adjustment packages most governments have sought to reduce expenditure on public sector employment. Women may have fared worse than men during many of these cutbacks. In Benin, while women represented only 6 per cent of those in parastatal and private formal employment, the proportion of women retrenched was as high as 21 per cent.[22] One specialist concludes that the small numbers of women working in the modern sector have been particularly affected by redundancy measures and have benefited least from the support measures, such as training and business enterprise programmes, adopted in many countries to mitigate their social effects.[23]

The indirect impact of male retrenchment and the substantial declines in real wages in the formal economy seem to have forced more women into the urban informal economy to augment family incomes. The fall in modern sector employment has been accompanied by a fall in wages, especially in the public sector, and a fall in the minimum wage. Economic pressures have led to a drop in school enrolment in some countries; in Nigeria it dropped from 89.3 per cent in 1982–3 to 61.6 per cent in 1987.[24] Concomitantly, there has been an expansion of the informal sector, which now employs 62.5 per cent of the urban labour force.[25] An increasing proportion of informal sector workers are women; between 1970 and 1985 their share of informal sector employment rose from 29 to around 35 per cent. Around 80 per cent of the women in the informal sector are traders. In recent years, however, the competition for informal sector jobs, particularly in trade, has meant that women are finding it less easy to enter the labour market. Many women are rural migrants who have travelled to cities as part of household survival strategies and return to their villages after accumulating some earnings.

Agriculture is by far the largest employment sector in Africa, offering a livelihood to between two thirds and three quarters of the population, most of whom are working for subsistence. Most people, particularly women, work extremely long hours within a gender division of labour that tends to allocate the most laborious, manual, and labour-intensive tasks to women. An International Fund for Agricultural Development (IFAD) report notes that 'new techniques have a bad habit of shifting economic control, employment, and profit from women to men', and cites the example of the Gambia, where introduction of a new technique turned the swamp rice cultivation from a women's activity into a men's activity.[26] Others single out the inadequacy of extension, credit and support systems which would enable women to access and make use of available innovations.[27]

The problems of Africa have been widely discussed and require concerted international action as well as changes in regional and domestic policies.[28] With respect to gender issues, it is important to increase women's access to means of production and to social and economic services. There need to be increases in women's literacy, school enrolments, educational attainment, and health care. And because of the high level of economic activity of African women and their increasing responsibility for households, credit schemes must be directed to women farmers and entrepreneurs.

The Middle East and North Africa (MENA)

Countries in the MENA region are suffering from a severe slow-down in economic growth, and in many countries there is now a recession. Some are implementing structural adjustment programmes with the assistance of the World Bank and the International Monetary Fund. The generally poor economic performance of the region has had a severe impact on employment. Many countries have been unable to provide work for the increased labour supply which has resulted from high population growth and the return of expatriate workers after the Gulf crisis. Although educational attainment has increased for both men and women, many studies suggest a mismatch between educational programmes and the requirements of new labour markets.[29]

Female labour force participation has generally been very low in this region, but in recent years there have been increases in professional fields in the service sector and in some kinds of industrial employment.[30] Significant undercounting of the female labour force continues; huge numbers of rural women are simply not counted in Iran, Jordan and Egypt, while in Turkey, Tunisia and Morocco, it is more the case that 'self-employed/own-account' women, women in unregistered workshops, and women who sew and knit at home as part of subcontracting arrangements are vastly under-enumerated. But even at the low official numbers, large percentages of the female labour force are unsalaried, and much of the private sector activity is informal. For example, Tunisia reported a total of 165,700 women in manufacturing in 1989, of whom 84,400 were salaried. Morocco, Tunisia and Turkey have experienced much success with their export-oriented strategy, especially in textiles and garments. In these countries, women constitute a large part of the unskilled labour force in the food and the garment and knitwear industries, and the share of female workers in factories producing for export markets is particularly high.[31] But we know that the expansion of Morocco's light manufacturing export industries, including textiles and garments, has not been accompanied by a growth of salaried employment. While industrial production, especially of export-oriented industries, grew faster than the rest of the economy, this has probably been accomplished through a growth of non-regular labour, including much female home work.

In the urban areas of MENA countries the female labour force is distributed across public services (where employment is salaried), formal employment in state-owned and some large private enterprises, and smaller private sector activities, where much of the employment is of a casual nature. Most educated Middle Eastern women prefer to work in public administration (their share is around 30 per cent), and the state-owned enterprises have also been favoured by job-seeking working-class women. A 1990 CAPMAS study in Egypt found that women reported more sexual harassment in the private sector than in the government sector.[32]

However, under current plans to cut back on the public sector wage bill and to promote export-oriented private sector activities, women's already fragile place in the urban labour market is being threatened, while working-class women can only expect unstable and temporary work without any benefits, or payment by piece-work, carried out at home. Unemployment rates, chronically high in some countries, could increase, especially if new entrants – which will include a growing supply of educated women, women maintaining households alone, or other women in economic need – cannot be accommodated in the modern sector. In many countries, the rate of unemployment is higher among women than among men; in Jordan, Egypt, Syria, Algeria, Iran and Turkey, educated women experience higher rates of unemployment than do educated men. In Iran, female unemployment is, at a whopping 25 per cent, far higher than the recorded male unemployment rate of 9 per cent.[33] In Egypt, the female and male unemployment rates are 28 and 6 per cent, respectively.[34] In Syria, though general unemployment in 1991 was 6.8 per cent, for women it was as high as 14 per cent. Israel's female and male unemployment rates in 1992 were 13.9 and 9.2 percent, respectively. Higher rates of female unemployment may be the result of gender discrimination, whereby at a time of slack in the labour market employers discriminate by preferring to hire males who are seen as the breadwinners of the household. As in other countries, women may also be seen as more expensive labour because of labour legislation requiring child care and maternity leave, especially in the public sector and in large private enterprises.

Clearly the supply of job-seeking women is increasing in MENA countries, whereas the demand for them is limited and inadequate to meet their employment and income needs. Will promotion of the private sector – including the expansion of tourism and denationalization of state-owned tourism-related enterprises – increase jobs for women? Current Tunisian economic policy is to promote tourism as a foreign exchange earner, but at present it is a heavily male-dominated sector. Women comprise a very small percentage (6 per cent) of workers in trade, restaurants and hotels.[35] (They are found in much larger numbers in other service sub-sectors, such as finance, insurance, real estate and business services, and of course in the education and health professions.) Tourism is one of Turkey's fastest growing industries. But although nearly two million people were involved in trade, restaurants and hotels in 1990, the female share of that workforce, at 86,000, was only about 5 per cent. It remains to be seen whether privatization will increase the demand for women employees, and whether the growing tourism industry will propel female-owned businesses.

In MENA countries, discrimination in labour markets should be identified and targeted. At the same time, education and training policies should target women's higher rates of illiteracy and lower educational attainment, in order that they become more competitive in the labour market. In particular, Morocco, Tunisia and Turkey should endeavour to make their female workers in the export-oriented industries more skilled and competitive.

South, East, and Southeast Asia

Asia is a heterogeneous region that includes countries with some of the world's most dynamic economies and industrious workforces, and countries with large populations of impoverished people. The region as a whole accounts for more than half (54 per cent in 1993) of the world's female labour force. In the 1970s and early 1980s, it was the growing supply of cheap and young female labour that was the cornerstone of successful export-oriented industrialization in East and Southeast Asia. Rapid outward-oriented industrialization, propelling these countries to NIC status, was therefore as much female-led as export-led. While generating unprecedented employment opportunities for women, industrial work exposed women to poor and often exploitative working conditions and occupational safety and health problems, and tended to be unstable.[36] (See Figure 7.3 for figures on women's employment as a proportion of general employment, in selected Asian countries.)

High levels of investment, both domestic and foreign (particularly from Taiwan, China and Japan), have fuelled the boom in exports and industrial output in what are now termed the second-generation NICs. In Thailand, foreign capital continues to flood in, attracted by low wage costs and by Thailand's expanding markets, both domestic and export. Unfortunately, economic growth and the expansion of female employment have not been accompanied by a diminution of the exploitation of factory workers and of sexual workers. At the same time, Thailand's secondary school enrolments are the lowest in the region. In Malaysia, the growth in non-agricultural employment has created jobs for women in export manufacturing and in private and public services. Along with educational attainment, increased labour force participation by women has helped to raise the age of first marriage and to lower fertility. In Indonesia, more and more women have entered the labour force, but according to one report, 'girl-child workers make up approximately 53 per cent of urban child workers'.[37] And there, as in some other countries, workers' rights are not observed and worker protests – including women workers who speak out – are dealt with severely.[38]

The labour force participation of women in South Asia, at about 28 per cent, is much lower than in East and Southeast Asia, at 42 per cent. In India, Pakistan and Bangladesh, cultural proscriptions, widespread illiteracy and early marriage limit female mobility. Pakistan's educational record has been a failure, especially where girls are concerned, and this is a cause of low female labour force participation. On the positive side, the growth in Bangladesh of the export garments industry and the activities of the Grameen Bank are important sources of income and employment for women. A 1989 labour force sample survey in Bangladesh found nearly 500,000 females involved in manufacturing (compared with 1.7 million men). In India, the Self-Employed Women's Association offers organization, legal recognition, and social protection for self-employed women. However, there has recently been an international outcry over the use of child labour in the South Asian countries.

Since the mid-1980s, the main influence on women's employment has been the impact of recession and structural adjustment. As in other regions, Asian women were more likely than men to be retrenched. They have been more vulnerable because of their concentration in the sectors most sensitive to international demand conditions and in direct production jobs which fluctuate closely with the actual level of enterprise operations, and because of the prevailing concept of women as secondary earners who are dispensable in tight employment situations. In Malaysia, more than half the total number retrenched in 1983–5 were from the two most 'feminized' industries (electronics and textiles), while in administrative services the largest employment cuts were among clerks, another feminized occupation.[39] In the NICs, female unemployment is low, and lower than men's. But in most Asian countries, female unemployment rates are high, especially in Sri Lanka and the Philippines, despite considerable labour out-migration. (For illustrations of differential male–female unemployment rates in selected countries of East and Southeast Asia, see Figure 7.4.) Pakistan's official unemployment rate in 1992 was 6.2 per cent, but the ILO estimates that combined open and disguised unemployment may now exceed 13 per cent. In an economic context of high male unemployment and a cultural context of patriarchal attitudes towards women, there is probably little encouragement of female employment. Although economic need is propelling more women into the labour market, the rise in female unemployment suggests a dramatic increase in the proportion of job-seeking women for whom opportunities are scarce. Given cultural constraints, Pakistani women are less mobile than are women from the Philippines and Sri Lanka.

In China and Vietnam, there have been rapid increases in unemployment, especially for women. In China, official policy stipulates that women be treated equally with men in employment, but in every sector women are in the lower-paying, less prestigious jobs. The 1988 'Women's Protection Law' provides a minimum of three months' maternity leave and additional child care benefits for women. However, as has occurred in East Central Europe, the expense of at least part of these provisions to private enterprises is widely believed to have increased discrimination against women workers. In Vietnam, there is evidence that the expansion of private sector jobs offering higher wages, especially in the tourism sector, may have led to increases in school drop-out rates among teenage girls – this is occurring in a context where a female factory worker typically has completed secondary school. With the contraction of the state sector, the promotion of the private sector, and the rise of unemployment, the household is re-emerging as a major unit of production. Persons employed in household production typically work long hours, and child labour is more likely to be deployed.[40] There are also reports of a resurgence of prostitution in Ho Chi Minh City (formerly Saigon), after a 20-year hiatus following liberation.

These developments in Asia suggest the need for several actions: promulgation of ILO conventions regarding workers' rights; ensuring that school enrolments remain high and that child labour does not expand; expanding productive employment for women and offering women incentives to leave the sex industry; and ensuring that active labour market policies include women workers in their programmes.

Towards greater investment in women

During the 1980s the rapid growth of female employment and women's entry into occupations previously dominated by men led one analyst to designate this trend 'the feminization of labour'.[41] Yet this has occurred in the context of economic liberalization, deregulation and privatization, leading to a more flexible workforce and the casualization of employment. The non-regular forms of employment, which are growing, are unstable and insecure, and often do not offer non-wage benefits to the women workers who are outside the coverage of standard labour legislation. The downscaling of the size of the public sector has also adversely affected women, not only because the government has been a major employer of women in many countries but also because wages and employment conditions are better on average in the public sector. At a time when some have called for an expansion of social protection in developing countries – including social policies that would enable women with family responsibilities to compete more equally with men – social security systems, the welfare state, and generous social benefits have come under attack in the developed world, including the former socialist countries.[42] At the same time, objections on the part of developed countries to the unfair comparative advantage of export-oriented developing countries – that is, the introduction of the social clause into international trade agreements directed at cheap female labour and sometimes child labour – could affect women's employment in those developing countries. And almost everywhere, women's unemployment rates are higher than men's, suggesting that while the supply of job-seeking women continues to expand, there remain serious barriers to women's ability to compete successfully in labour markets. Neither the current stage of global economic restructuring nor the reality of segmented labour markets is particularly conducive to enhanced employment opportunities and working conditions for women, especially in the developing world.

Yet it would be exceedingly short-sighted for policy makers to ignore the welfare and well-being of women, not only for reasons of equity and empowerment of women, but also for reasons of national development, which were discussed earlier in this chapter. Blumberg cogently describes the macro- and micro-level consequences of enhanced economic power for women, that is, employment and having income under their own control.[43] The link between employment and fertility has been widely discussed in the WID literature, and there is now consensus that women who enter into gainful employment marry later, begin childbearing later, and have fewer and healthier children than do women who remain outside the formal labour force. Women's productive activities have contributed significantly to the food supply, the large informal sector, service and farm labour forces, and to the export-manufacturing labour force. Indeed, in the developing countries there is a strong relationship between increases in female industrial employment, the growth of manufactured exports and national economic growth. The use and expansion of women's productive capacities, therefore, are necessary conditions for social and economic progress. In turn, women's contributions to social and economic development are enhanced by social policies and labour codes that acknowledge, value and facilitate their participation in both productive and reproductive activities. Recognition of these facts should spur governments and international organizations towards greater investment in the human resource development of women.

NOTES
1 UN (1991) *The World's Women: Trends and Statistics 1970–1990*, UN, New York.
2 The information and data are derived from ILO sources (e.g., *World Labour Report 1993; Yearbook of Labour Statistics 1993* and earlier years), and research findings and publications of the author. This chapter is part of the 1994–95 UNU/WIDER research project entitled 'Economic Restructuring, Women's Employment, and Social Policies in Industrializing and Transition Economies', of which the present author is the principal investigator. Eight collaborators from the transition economies are also preparing research papers within the project framework.
3 Charles, Maria (1992) 'Cross-national variation in occupational sex segregation', *American Sociological Review*, Vol. 57, No. 4, August, pp. 483–502. The quote appears on p. 490.
4 UN (1991) *World Economic Survey 1991*, UN, New York, pp. 190–1.
5 King, Elizabeth (1990) *Educating Girls and Women: Investing in Development*, The World Bank, Washington, DC, p. 6.
6 Blumberg, Rae Lesser (1989) *Making the Case for the Gender Variable: Women and the Wealth and Well-being of Nations*, Office of Women in Development, Agency for International Development, Washington DC, from the Executive Summary.
7 See, for example, Swasti Mitter (1993) 'Innovations in Work Organization at the Enterprise Level, Changes in Technology, and Women's Employment', BRIDGE Paper, Institute for Development Studies, Brighton.
8 Based on interviews by the author in Ho Chi Minh City and Hanoi, February 1994.
9 UN (1992) *World Investment Report: Transnational Corporations as Engines of Growth*, United Nations, New York, p. 186.
10 ILO, *World Labour Report 1993*, p. 27.
11 *Ibid.*, p. 19.
12 UN (1991) *World Economic Survey 1991*, UN/DIESA, New York, p. 190.
13 This does not hold true for Nordic countries, where part-time workers may be unionized and enjoy social protection. See the chapter by Nätti, in this volume.

14 ILO (1994) 'Russian "safety net" riddled with holes', *ILO Washington Focus*, Winter.
15 See V. M. Moghadam (ed.) (1993) *Democratic Reform and the Position of Women in Transitional Economies*, Clarendon Press, Oxford.
16 This has been well documented in the various chapters of *Democratic Reform, idem.*
17 A 1992 study for the ILO by Lado, Adamik and Toth, cited in 'Women workers in a changing global environment: framework for discussion', background paper prepared by the International Institute for Labour Studies (1994) for the International Forum on Equality for Women in the World of Work: Challenges for the Future, Geneva, 1-3 June, pp. 9–10.
18 ILO (1993) *World Labour Report 1993*, p. 24.
19 Cited in Petra Ulshoefer (1994) 'Comments on women's labour and employment in Latin America in the nineties', paper prepared for the International Forum on Equality for Women in the World of Work: Challenges for the Future, Geneva, 1–3 June, p. 2.
20 See, for example, relevant chapters in Lourdes Benería and Shelley Feldman (eds) (1992) *Unequal Burden: Economic Crises, Persistent Poverty, and Women's Work*, Westview Press, Boulder, CO.
21 Buvinic, Mayra (1993) 'Promoting employment among the urban poor in Latin America and the Caribbean: a gender analysis', prepared for the ILO, ICRW, Washington, DC, October, pp. 3–4.
22 ILO, *World Labour Report 1993*, p. 24.
23 Ouédraogo, Alice (1994) 'Women's employment in Africa: obstacles and challenges', paper prepared for the International Forum on Equality for Women in the World of Work: Challenges for the Future, Geneva, 1-3 June, p. 2.
24 UNICEF Situation Analysis, cited in Paulina K. Makinwa-Adebusoye (1994) 'Women migrants in Nigeria', *International Sociology*, Vol. 9, No. 2 June, p. 235.
25 ILO, *World Labour Report 1993*, p. 28.
26 IFAD, *Report on Rural Women Living in Poverty*, IFAD, Rome.
27 See Ingrid Palmer, *Gender and Population in the Adjustment of African Economies: Planning for Change*, ILO, Geneva.
28 See the chapter by Derseh Endale in Volume 2.
29 See Alan Richards and John Waterbury (1990) *A Political Economy of the Middle East*, Westview Press, Boulder, CO, Chapter 5; Sulayman Al-Qudsi, Ragui Assaad, and Radwan Shaban (1993) 'Labor Markets in the Arab Countries: A Survey', Economic Research Institute, Cairo.
30 For a detailed discussion, see V. M. Moghadam (1993) *Modernizing Women: Gender and Social Change in the Middle East*, Lynne Rienner Publishers, Boulder, CO, especially Chapter 2.
31 The information here is adapted from V. M. Moghadam (1994) 'Women in the textiles and garments industry in the Middle East and North Africa', paper prepared for the Conference on Women in the Global Economy: Making Connections, Institute for Research on Women, State University of New York, Albany, 22–24 April, and 'The political economy of female employment in the Arab region', in N. Khoury and V. M. Moghadam (eds) (1995) *Women's Economic Activities in the Arab World: Patterns, Determinants, Policies*, Zed Books, London.

32 Cited in *Al-Ahram Weekly*, 7 March 1991.
33 Moghadam, V. M. (1994) 'Mission Report: Islamic Republic of Iran, May 1994', UNU/WIDER, Helsinki, 26 May. The data on unemployment were obtained from the Statistical Centre, Tehran.
34 ILO (1994) *World Labour Report 1994*, p. 23.
35 They are also rarely found in the urban informal sector, according to a study by anthropologist Richard Lobban (1991) 'The urban informal sector in Tunis: a preliminary report', paper presented at the Annual Meeting of the Middle East Studies Association, Washington DC, November.
36 See the chapter by Tonguthai in this volume.
37 Mboi, Nafsiah (1993) 'Urban women in Indonesia: some issues of work and health', prepared for the Seminar on Women in Urban Areas, Santo Domingo, Dominican Republic, 22–25 November, p. 5.
38 In Indonesia, a 23-year-old worker named Marinsah, employed at a watch factory near Jakarta, was brutally tortured, raped, and murdered in late 1993 for leading a fight at her factory for a 15 cents a day wage increase. See 'The seamy underside of the Asian "miracle"', *World Press Review*, June 1994.
39 Lin Lean Lim (1994) 'Women at work in Asia and the Pacific: recent trends and future challenges', paper prepared for the International Forum on Equality for Women in the World of Work: Challenges for the Future, Geneva, 1–3 June, p. 2.
40 Moghadam, V. M. 'Market Reforms and Women's Economic Status: a Comparative Assessment of Eastern Europe and Russia, and Vietnam and China', Helsinki: UNU/WIDER, mimeo.
41 Standing, Guy (1989) 'Global feminization through flexible labour', *World Development*, Vol. 17, No. 7.
42 See Valentine M. Moghadam (1993) 'Social Protection and Women Workers in Asia', UNU/WIDER Working Paper No. 110, Helsinki.
43 Blumberg, Rae Lesser (1991) 'Income under female versus male control: hypotheses from a theory of gender stratification and data from the Third World', in Blumberg (ed.), *Gender, Family and Economy: The Triple Overlap*, Sage Publications, Newbury Park, CA.

FIGURE 7.1
Differential male–female unemployment figures, some countries in Latin America: 1983–92 (%)

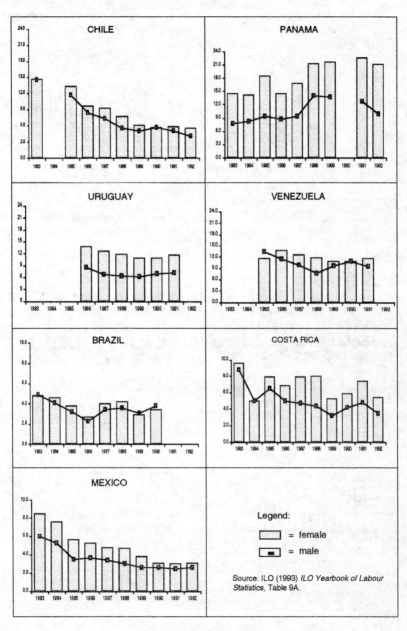

Source: ILO (1993) *ILO Yearbook of Labour Statistics*, Table 9A.

FIGURE 7.2
Differential male–female unemployment figures in the Caribbean:
1983–92 (%)

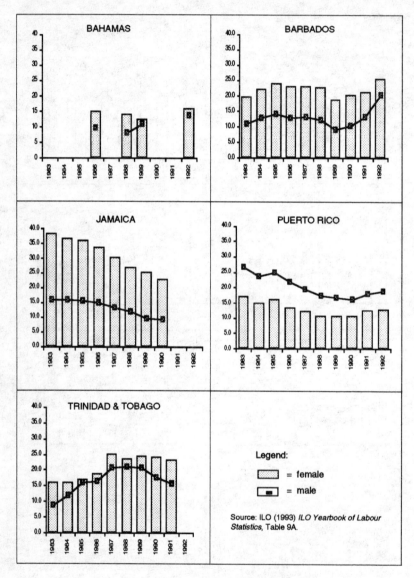

FIGURE 7.3
Number of women in total employment, some Asian countries
(in thousands)

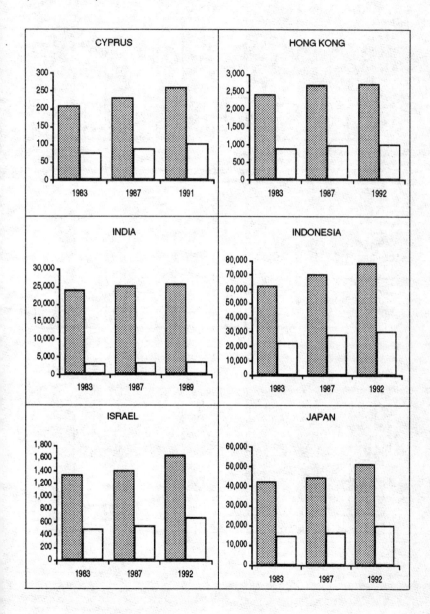

FIGURE 7.3 (cont)

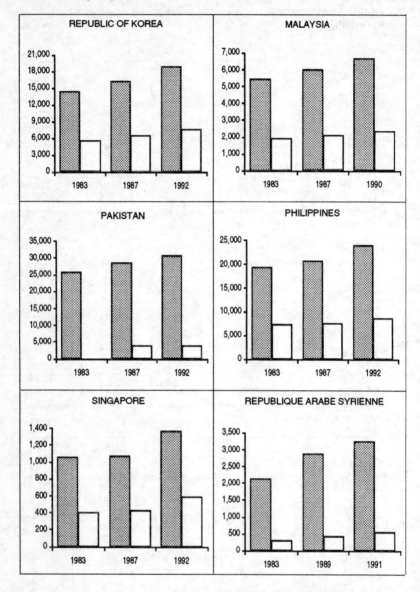

FIGURE 7.3 cont.

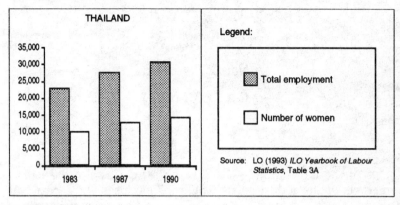

FIGURE 7.4
Differential male–female unemployment figures, some countries in East/
Southeast asia: 1983–92 (%)

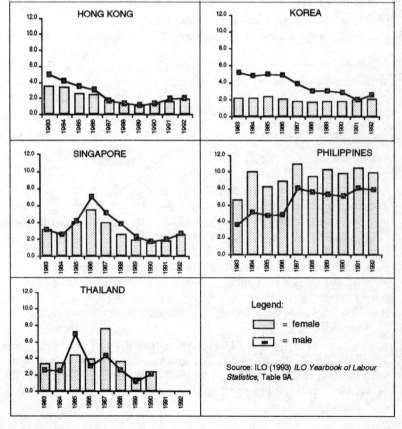

8

Flexible Work – A Risk or an Opportunity for Women?

A Nordic Perspective

– JOUKO NÄTTI –

One of the most striking changes in the structure of the labour markets of the industrialized countries has been the increase of women's employment, especially part-time employment. This chapter concentrates on women's employment and unemployment in the Nordic countries (Denmark, Finland, Norway and Sweden). In the first section the employment and participation rates in the Nordic and European Union countries and women's situation in the labour market are examined. In the second section, the recent high unemployment rates and the health effects of unemployment are discussed. The main aim of the article is to examine the consequences of part-time employment for women: are part-time jobs more precarious than full-time jobs, and are part-time jobs traps or perhaps rather bridges in the labour market?

Women's employment in the Nordic countries

EMPLOYMENT RATES IN THE NORDIC AND EU COUNTRIES
The employment rate is here defined as the share of the population in employment (employment/population). In the Nordic countries employment rates are very high (average 51 per cent in 1989) compared to European Union (EU) countries (average 41 per cent) (see Table 8.1). Furthermore, between 1973 and 1989 the increase in employment rates was more rapid in the Nordic countries (+ 4.4 percentage points) than in EU countries (+ 0.2 percentage points). In the United States and Japan, too, employment rates are higher compared to EU countries.

Changes in employment rates are affected by changes both in population and employment. The growth of population has been very similar in the Nordic and EU countries: the increase in population was about 5 per cent between 1973 and 1989 (see Table

TABLE 8.1
Employment rates in OECD countries: 1973, 1983 and 1989

Country	1973	1983	1989
Nordic countries	46.7	49.0	51.1
Denmark	47.5	46.7	50.9
Finland	46.2	49.0	49.6
Norway	41.6	46.3	47.6
Sweden	47.7	50.7	52.6
EU countries	40.4	38.7	40.6
Belgium	37.5	35.5	36.9
France	40.1	38.7	38.3
Germany	42.6	42.0	43.9
Greece	–	36.0	36.6
Ireland	34.4	31.7	30.6
Italy	35.3	36.2	36.7
Netherlands	–	34.5	40.8
Portugal	43.0	43.3	44.6
Spain	34.7	28.9	31.5
United Kingdom	44.0	41.3	46.2
United States	40.1	42.9	47.2
Japan	48.4	48.1	49.8

Source: OECD *Labour Force Statistics*, 1969–1989

TABLE 8.2
Employment and population changes in the Nordic and EU countries

Indicator	Denmark	Finland	Norway	Sweden	Nordic countries	EU countries
Total employment						
1973	2426	2194	1676	3879	10175	124887
1983	2420	2419	1945	4224	10998	124214
1989	2645	2494	2049	4466	11654	132480
Change 1973–89						
In thousands	+219	+300	+373	+587	+1479	+7593
Percentages	+9.0	+13.7	+22.2	+15.1	+14.5	+6.1
Components of growth						
Female employment	+212	+185	+307	+556	+1260	+9029
Service sector	+397	+466	+475	+819	+2500	+21094
Part-time jobs	+204	+25	+196	+343	+768	+9400[a]
Total population						
1973	5022	4666	3961	8137	21786	309426
1983	5114	4856	4128	8329	22427	320638
1989	5132	4964	4227	8493	22816	325981
Change 1973–89						
In thousands	+110	+298	+266	+356	+1030	+16555
Percentages	+2.2	+6.4	+6.7	+4.4	+4.7	+5.3

Source: OECD *Employment Outlook*,1993; OECD *Labour Force Statistics*, 1969–89.
a Estimate.

8.2). More variation can be found in employment: in the Nordic countries employment increased 15 per cent compared to 6 per cent in the EU countries in the period 1973–89. Both in the Nordic and EU countries the increase in employment was dominated by women's employment, the service sector and part-time jobs, which overlap each other. Thus, one of the main factors to be analysed in studying the employment rate is the role of women in the labour market and society.

THE INCREASE IN WOMEN'S PARTICIPATION IN THE LABOUR FORCE

On a global basis, 36 per cent of women over the age of 15 are in the labour force.[1] Especially in the Nordic countries, participation rates of women in the labour force are very high (the unweighted average was 75 per cent in 1992) compared to the global average or to the countries of Western Europe (average 54 per cent) (see Table 8.3). Furthermore, between 1973 and 1990 the increase in women's rates of participation was more rapid in the Nordic countries (+16 percentage points) than in Western Europe (+10 percentage points).

During the same period (1973–90) men's participation rates in the labour force decreased in all countries, though less in the Nordic than in the Western European countries. As a result, the gap between the participation rates of women and men declined to 8 per cent in the Nordic countries compared to 24 per cent in the Western European countries.

During the recession (1990–2) the participation rates of women in the labour force declined in all the Nordic countries except Denmark. Among men, the decrease was more rapid. The effects of recession and unemployment will be discussed later.

Accordingly, the share of women in the total labour force was almost half: in Sweden 48 per cent, in Finland 47 per cent, in Denmark 46 per cent and in Norway 44 per cent. In the EU countries, women accounted for 40 per cent of the total labour force in 1991. On a global basis, women comprise about one third of the labour force.[2]

As activity in the labour market has become the norm for most Nordic women, the role of full-time homemakers has become less common. This has enhanced women's economic authority and independence. In Finland especially, the full-time homemaker role of women has never been deeply rooted: from 1940 to the early 1960s only about one fourth of women aged 15 and over were full-time homemakers. In the other Nordic countries, the corresponding proportion of homemaker women was considerably higher. In the other Nordic countries, the participation of women in the labour force increased rapidly in the 1960s and 1970s, mainly on a part-time

TABLE 8.3
Women's and men's rates of participation in the labour force

Indicator	Denmark	Finland	Norway	Sweden	Nordic countries[a]	OECD countries
Women
1973	61.9	63.6	50.6	62.6	59.7	44.7
1983	74.2	72.7	65.5	76.6	72.3	49.8
1990	78.4	72.9	71.2	81.1	75.9	54.8
1992-	78.9	71.8	70.9	78.7	75.1	54.0
Change 1973–90	+16.5	+9.3	+20.6	+18.5	+16.2	+10.1
Change 1990–92	+0.5	-1.1	-0.3	-2.4	-0.8	-0.8
Men
1973	89.6	80.0	86.5	88.1	86.1	88.7
1983	87.6	82.0	87.2	85.9	85.7	82.3
1990	89.6	80.6	84.5	85.3	85.0	80.6
1992	88.5	78.5	83.0	82.7	83.2	78.3
Change 1973–90	0.0	+0.6	-2.0	-2.8	-1.1	-8.1
Change 1990–92	-1.1	-2.0	-0.5	-2.6	-1.8	-2.3

Source: OECD Employment Outlook, 1993
a Unweighted average

basis. In the late 1980s the proportion of women (age 25–54 years) engaged in full-time housework was about 17 per cent in Norway, 8 per cent in Norway, 7 per cent in Finland and 5 per cent in Sweden.[3]

The rapid increase in participation in the labour force among women is partly due to the high level of education of Nordic women and good overall post-war economic performance, but also due to active policies, such as the expansion of the welfare state.

The increased level of education has almost certainly intensified female labour market activity. In the Nordic countries the educational standard of women is higher and their schooling times are longer, on average, than in the OECD area.[4] For example, in Finland women are slightly ahead of men in the level of their all-round education, whereas men have more occupational training. On the other hand, there remain persistent sex differences in specialized fields, which partly have the effect of maintaining sex segregation in the labour market.

During the 1960s and 1970s the welfare state was expanded and the major social reforms were implemented, for example formal state education up to 16–18 years of age, national health care, and child-care services.[5] The expansion of the public service sector has offered jobs to women directly as well as indirectly, through the provision of social services which has encouraged the employment of women. The fast growth of moderately priced communal day-care facilities, in particular, has enabled women to hold paid jobs. In Finland, the number of day care places more than trebled between 1973 and 1986.

In all the Nordic countries, pre-school children (under 7 years old) are entitled to day care in an institution or in a family during the time their parents are at work or studying. Day care is mainly organized by local authorities. There are also care facilities for schoolchildren. In 1987, day care institutions and family day care covered 38–72 per cent of 3–4-year-old children and 58–77 per cent of 5–6-year-old children.[6]

Furthermore, in the Nordic countries every expectant or nursing mother is eligible for a maternity allowance. The payment period has been extended gradually, which has made it easier for women to remain in employment while being absent from work during maternity leave. Paid leave is longest in Sweden and next longest in Finland.

During the recession, maternity/parental leave in Finland has been shortened by two weeks and the level of compensation has been lowered from about 80 per cent to 66 per cent of former income. This reduction has been made as a reaction to the current economic situation in Finland which has also affected a range of other social benefits.[7]

In the Nordic countries, the father is entitled to share the last months of maternity/parental leave. For example, in Finland, the father also has a right to 6 to 12 days' paternity leave in connection with the child's birth. The number of fathers receiving paternity payments has steadily increased: in 1979, only 12 per cent of fathers used their right to paternity leave, whereas in 1991 this figure had risen to 45 per cent. Nonetheless, a minority of fathers take more than 6–12 days immediately following childbirth.[8]

The idea behind shared parental leave is partly that it makes it more difficult for employers to discriminate against young women on the basis of long maternity leave. It has also been argued that equal parenting is beneficial for the psychological development of both children and parents: children and parents have multiple role models. Research has shown that the physical health of employed, married women is usually better than that of non-employed, married women.[9]

WOMEN, CHILDREN AND WORK

The increase in women's participation in the labour force has been especially dramatic for women of childbearing and childrearing age. In the early 1970s, in the age group 25–34 years, less than half of European women were in the labour force, while in the late 1980s, the majority were participating: in the Nordic countries nine out of ten women, and in most Western European countries at least two out of three women.[10]

Accordingly, in the Nordic countries a greater proportion of mothers with children under three are employed (over 80 per cent) than of all women aged 15–64, while in most European Union (EU) countries, motherhood still shuts women out of the labour market.

In the Nordic countries, age-related female activity profiles have become increasingly continuous. In Sweden and Finland especially, they are currently very similar to those of men, both in profile and level. In most Western European countries, the age-related activity curve still shows a tendency for women to interrupt their paid work, even if this trend has become less marked in the 1980s.

In Finland, however, the new trend since the late 1980s is that, among women aged 25 to 34 years, the homemaker role has somewhat increased. In 1991, 13 per cent of the women in this age group were classified as homemakers. This is due to the generous home care allowances. The home care allowance is paid by the state for a child under the age of 3 immediately following parental leave. This allowance has been very popular: in 1990 it was paid to 75 per cent of the families (mostly women) entitled to it. On average, the home care allowance is used for a short period following the parental leave, usually until the child is 1.5 years old. Only 20 per cent of families (mostly women) used the home care benefits for the full 3 years. The home care role of women is temporary and relates to the social benefits provided by the state.[11]

Despite these social arrangements encouraging mothers to participate in paid work, the problem of combining work and family is well known to women in all the Nordic (and European) countries. A gendered pattern of time use is also common; women are responsible for housework, even when they work outside the home.[12] For many that means a double load, whereas men are free during the same period to invest in their careers.

In Finland, in particular, most employed women work full-time, that is, at least 35 hours per week. At the beginning of the 1990s only 16 per cent of employed Finnish women worked fewer than 35 hours per week. In the other Nordic countries, part-time work for women is much more common: 40–50 per cent of employed women work on a part-time basis. The weekly working hours of women are on average about two hours shorter than those of men.

In Finland, the presence of young children does not markedly influence the number of hours worked by mothers even if it tends to decrease their participation in the labour force temporarily. This is due to the home care allowance system. A vast majority of employed Finnish mothers of young children work longer hours than their counterparts in the other Nordic countries.

It can be argued that the longer the working hours in paid work, the less available women are for their family roles. Research, however, indicates that children of working mothers do not suffer physically or mentally. On the contrary, work is a positive factor for children and mothers alike. Nevertheless, studies show that a common concern among many employed mothers is a sense of 'not enough time' with their children and families.[13]

A preference among women for a shorter working week has come up in many studies, indicating that women, especially those with young children, would prefer shorter or more flexible work schedules. This arrangement would allow them more time to balance their job and child care responsibilities; it would also increase women's own control over their daily schedules.

In principle, part-time employment or an otherwise flexible arrangement for women may be appropriate in family situations where full-time employment would be stressful. However, part-time work for women is a controversial issue. On one hand, it can be seen as a compromise forced on women in a situation of rigid gender divisions characterized by a lack of family care services, a compromise made at the cost of low income, no social security, inconvenient working hours and a limited range of occupations. On the other hand, it gives women the benefits of an escape from home and possession of their own money, plus a chance to combine housework and paid work in a subjectively meaningful way, keeping women's total working hours to a reasonable number.[14]

SEX SEGREGATION AND THE WAGE GAP

In spite of the increasing feminization of the labour force and the normalization of women's employment, the labour market and occupations generally have remained sex-segregated.[15] In Finland in 1991, 44 per cent of all employed men and women worked in occupations where 90–100 per cent of the workers were of the same sex. Only about 10 per cent worked in occupations where the sex composition was more balanced. The sex segregation of the labour market is very similar in the other Nordic countries: sex segregation is greatest in Norway, followed by Sweden, and then by Finland and Denmark.

The high degree of sex segregation in the labour market in the Nordic countries is related to the rapid expansion of the service sector. There has been a great demand for labour in the traditional industries and occupations employing women, that is, in the clerical, the commercial, and the health care and social work sectors. Today, these sectors are almost exclusively dominated by women. Women have formed the core element of the welfare state. Partly because of the concentration of women in the public service sector, women have been less severely affected by unemployment than men who have mostly been employed in the private sector. However, women's jobs are now at risk.

For the past decade, the division of labour by sex has remained much the same, although some changes are taking place. Examples of transitional occupations are medicine and the legal profession.[16]

Besides sex segregation, another continuing problem for Nordic women is the wage gap between the sexes. Even though women have made great progress by entering new occupational domains and by making themselves indispensable in many fields, the wage gap between men and women is still markedly disadvantageous to women. In the Nordic countries, the gender gap in wages was smaller even the 1950s than in the OECD area on average. In the Nordic countries (excluding Finland) wage differentials also narrowed during the 1970s, although there was a slight increase during the late 1980s.[17]

The smallest wage differential in manufacturing among OECD countries in 1989 was in Sweden (11 per cent) and the greatest wage differential among the Nordic countries was in Finland (23 per cent), which coincides with the EU average.

During the recession, the gender gap in wages in Finland has tended to decrease due to the fact that extra benefits relating to working overtime and other special arrangements for men have been cut off. Now, there is an increasing gap, as regards quality of life, between the employed and unemployed.[18]

THE NORDIC WELFARE STATE – A MODEL IN TRANSITION

On average the share of social expenditure of GDP in the Nordic countries (24.3 per cent in the 1980s) is not much higher than in the EU countries (23.6 per cent). Still, the Nordic countries provide more universal social rights – but at the cost of higher taxation: the share of total taxation of GDP in the Nordic countries was 45.8 per cent (average in the 1980s) compared to 40 per cent in the EU countries.

The Nordic welfare state is highly institutionalized and the state has the role of a social engineer: it aims at redistribution. The commitment to full employment (at least before the recent recession) suggests that everybody – men and women – is directly related to employment. Nordic societies structure citizenship by means of labour market integration.[19] Thus, women's paid employment is no longer a choice in the Nordic countries; it now represents structural and cultural normality.

The Nordic social security system treats women as individuals. However, the state acknowledges that women and men are parents and carers in some phases of their lives. Social benefits related to parenthood are well developed. In principle these benefits are gender-neutral, in practice they are used mainly by women. Public services are therefore needed to help integrate mothers into employment.

The Nordic welfare states provide universal benefits at a moderate standard. The unique focus of the Nordic welfare model is on publicly maintained services. Welfare states of the EU type can be characterized as distribution states, whereas the Nordic type represents a service state.

Currently the Nordic welfare model is deeply challenged by European integration, economic problems, and political and ideological fluctuations, and the Nordic model is become increasingly unstable.

Unemployment and women

UNEMPLOYMENT RATES

In most European countries, women's employment is less secure than men's, and this is reflected in their higher unemployment rates. The paradoxical situation is that both employment and unemployment rates among women have increased, which also means that women understand themselves in relation to the labour market rather than by gender which is, by definition, outside it.[20]

In May 1993, the unemployment rate for women in the EU countries averaged over 12 per cent, whereas for men it was around 9 per cent. Between May 1985 and May 1993, the disparity in unemployment rates between women and men showed some signs of narrowing over the EU as a whole. Overall, there has been some tendency for the unemployment of women to rise over this period relative to that of men in the less developed parts of the EU, and to fall in the more developed parts.[21] However, in the Nordic countries, there is no noticeable gender difference in unemployment.

In Finland especially, unemployment increased rapidly during the early 1990s. In spite of the rapid increase in unemployment among women, the (official) unemployment rate is still lower for women (16 per cent in 1993) than for men (20 per cent). Accordingly, of all unemployed job seekers 41 per cent were women. However, if the figures for hidden unemployment (discouraged workers – persons who are without work and are available for it, but who are not actively seeking it) were included, the gap in unemployment rates between men and women would narrow, since the majority of the hidden unemployed are women (76 per cent in 1982, 56 per cent in 1991).

Paradoxically, the segregation of the labour market – at least to some degree – has been favourable rather than disastrous to Nordic women: segregation has been paralleled by the relative stability of women's employment. During economic slow-downs, because of the concentration of women in the public service sector, women have been less severely affected by unemployment than men, whose employment has mostly been in the private sector.

When the employment situation started to deteriorate rapidly in Finland in 1991, it hit first the traditional men's occupations in construction and manufacturing. Along with the continuing recession, unemployment has inevitably extended to the service sector both private and public, where the vast majority of employees are women. As a result, the number of unemployed women increased by 70 per cent from March 1992 to March 1994, while the increase during the same period was 31 per cent for men. The number of unemployed women increased most in the fields of health and social care, administrative and office work, sales and other services.

Increasing age seems to be a greater risk factor for unemployment among women than men. In the age group of 60 years and over, the unemployment rate among women (14 per cent) is higher than that among men (11 per cent). The lower unemployment rate of older men is partly explained by the fact that many men in this age group withdraw from the labour market via early retirement.

The current recession may mean gloomier future prospects for women than for men, for many reasons. The women's employment situation is deteriorating more rapidly than that of men. With continuing unemployment and the eventual termination of salary-based unemployment compensation, women whose husbands are working may end up totally without unemployment benefits. There is also some inequality in the daily allowances for the unemployed as a result of differentials in salary levels, women's salaries being lower. Furthermore, women's applications for unemployment allowances are more frequently turned down than those of men.[22]

HEALTH EFFECTS OF UNEMPLOYMENT

Research on job loss has brought out the negative impacts of unemployment on a broad scale, including economic problems and disruption of social contacts, as well as mental and physical disorders.[23] Family conflicts increase. The health consequences for both sexes are nearly equal according to the majority of studies. Some differences have, however, been demonstrated between men and women.

In Finland lengthy unemployment has led to an increase in mental health problems for both men and women, but the consequences have been more serious for men.[24] Other studies have indicated that job loss leads to an increase in suicide rates, stroke deaths, and the consumption of alcohol and drugs more frequently in men than in women. According to Kalimo and Vuori, it is possible that in the industrialized countries men have been more bound to work than women. For men, unemployment is worse than unsatisfactory work, while for women unsatisfactory work is worse than unemployment. In addition, women may be able to compensate for the lost work arena by being active in other social spheres more easily than men. For example, women with young children may see work as only one of several life projects more easily than men, and thus they may be able to adapt to unemployment better, especially if their economic situation is manageable.[25] However, differences other than those acquainted with gender primarily explain the health outcomes of unemployment. These moderating factors can be contextual or individual.

Important contextual factors moderating the effects of unemployment are the general economic situation of the society, the structure and scope of unemployment and other social security benefits, and the role of social networks. Thus the consequences of recession may proceed quite differently in different countries and at different periods.

The health consequences of unemployment depend to a great extent on the general economic situation of the society. During economic recession the resources available for people's health, together with the general service level of the society, deteriorate. Therefore, the lack of paid work is only one of many possible health risks, the effects of which may be accentuated by other simultaneous stresses.

The expected long duration of mass unemployment in Finland in the 1990s, along with the eventual dropping out of a large number of married women from among the recipients of unemployment benefits, may, according to Kalimo and Vuori, bring new problems in its wake, due not only to financial hardship, but also to the economic dependence of wives on their husbands.

The negative consequences of unemployment can be most effectively prevented by re-employment. When unemployment continues, functions that maintain activity – training and education, discussion groups, physical exercise and other purposeful hobbies – become of central importance.[26]

Flexible work – a risk or an opportunity for women?

The flexibility of labour markets, working time and employment contracts has been the great issue of industrial relations and labour protection since the 1980s. During the early 1990s, it has been suggested that part-time work, job sharing, early retirement and so on may be effective ways to combat rising unemployment in the OECD, including the Nordic countries. In international debates part-time work is widely condemned as a threat to full-time jobs, a precarious form of employment and a source of unequal treatment of women workers. It is also defended as a regular, well-protected way to reconcile the needs and preferences of workers with the operational requirements of organizations.[27] What are the Nordic experiences of part-time employment? Is part-time work a risk or an opportunity for women?

THE EXTENT OF PART-TIME WORK
The definitions of part-time work vary between countries, both regarding the underlying concepts and the methods of collecting data. In the Nordic countries, part-time employees are persons who (normally) work less than 35 hours a week (in Sweden), or less than 30 hours per week (in Finland) or who actually (during the survey week) worked less than 35 hours per week (in Norway).[28] In Denmark, part-time employees are persons who report that they work part-time (as in the EU labour-force survey). Because of the conceptual variation, valid conclusions as to the development of part-time work within the various countries can be drawn from national time series, but international comparisons of the character of part-time work should be made with caution.

The number of part-time workers in the industrialized market economies (15 OECD countries) grew from 37 million in 1978 to 48 million in 1987.[29] As a proportion of total employment, the share of

TABLE 8.4
Part-time employment as a proportion of total employment by gender: 1973, 1983 and 1992 (%)

Country	Total			Women			Men	
	1973	1983	1992	1973	1983	1992	1973	1992
France	5.1	9.7	12.7	11.2	20.0	24.5	1.4	3.6
Germany	7.7	12.6	14.1	20.0	30.0	30.7	1.0	2.2
Greece	–	6.5	4.8	–	12.1	8.4	–	2.8
Ireland	4.0	6.6	8.4	10.1	15.5	17.8	1.8	3.6
Italy	3.9	4.6	5.9	8.5	9.4	11.5	2.3	2.9
Luxembourg	5.5	6.3	6.9	13.9	17.0	16.5	1.0	1.3
Netherlands[a]	4.4	21.4	32.8	15.5	50.1	62.9	1.1	13.4
Portugal	–	–	7.2	–	–	11.0	–	4.2
Spain	–	–	5.9	–	–	13.7	–	2.0
United Kingdom	15.3	19.4	23.5	38.3	42.4	45.0	1.8	6.3
Australia	11.9	17.5	24.5	28.2	36.4	43.3	3.7	10.6
Austria	6.4	8.4	9.1	15.6	20.0	20.5	1.4	1.6
Canada	9.7	15.4	16.8	19.4	26.1	25.9	4.7	9.3
Japan	13.9	16.2	20.5	25.1	29.8	34.8	6.8	10.6
New Zealand	11.2	15.3	21.6	24.6	31.4	35.9	4.6	10.3
United States	15.6	18.4	17.5	26.8	28.1	25.4	8.6	10.8
Denmark	17.0	23.8	22.5	40.3	44.7	36.7	1.9	10.1
Sweden	18.0	24.8	24.3	38.8	45.9	41.3	3.7	8.4
Norway	23.5	29.0	26.9	47.6	54.4[c]	47.1	8.7	9.8
Finland	6.1[b]	8.3	7.9	10.2	12.5	10.4	2.3	5.5

Source: OECD,1993.   *a* Break in series 1985   *b* Data are for 1977   *c* Data from Norwegian Labour Force Survey

part-time employment grew from 13 per cent to 16 per cent. To the extent that this growth reflects voluntary behaviour by workers it has important implications for economic welfare, because it allows an increased number of workers to be employed at any given level of aggregate demand.[30]

In most Nordic countries, the proportion of part-time work of all female employment is considerable (37–47 per cent), except in Finland (11 per cent). Among the EU countries, only Britain and the Netherlands have a high level of part-time employment.[31] Among other OECD countries, Australia, New Zealand and Japan have a high proportion of female part-time employment.

During the 1960s and 1970s, the number and proportion of female part-time employees grew in all the Nordic countries. Since the early 1980s, however, the proportion of female part-timers has declined (see Table 8.4). In the EU countries, as a whole, the proportion of female part-time employment to all female employment increased from 28 per cent in 1983 to over 30 per cent in 1989.

In the Nordic countries, male part-time employment, compared with that of women, has grown steadily. In 1992, the proportion of male part-time employment was 6–10 per cent. In the EU countries, the proportion of part-time work to total male employment increased from 2 per cent in 1983 to 4 per cent in 1989.[32]

Another important difference between the Nordic and the EU countries is the number of hours usually worked per week (contractual working hours) in part-time work. In most EU countries, the proportion of a small number of working hours (1–20 hours per week) in part-time employment is much higher (57–67 per cent) than in the Nordic countries, and it increased between 1975 and 1985.[33] The higher percentage of the small number of working hours may imply that the proportion of marginal or casual part-time work is expanding.[34] In the Nordic countries, the proportion of a small number of working hours (less than 20 hours per week) of part-time employment as a whole was (1991) highest in Norway[35] (50 per cent) and Finland (46 per cent), and lowest in Sweden (only 17 per cent). Similar differences are evident also in actual working hours (hours worked in the reference week per employed person at work): the number of part-timers' weekly hours was smallest in Finland (17.8) and largest in Sweden (24.7).[36] Especially in Sweden, working a little less than 35 hours a week is increasingly regarded as normal practice.[37] The number of working hours is important in many ways. A small number of hours usually means a lower income and dependence on additional allowances or on a main earner in the household. In addition, access to social benefits and the social security system is generally best for part-timers working more than 20 hours a week and worst for those working less than 16 hours.[38]

Exclusion from protection by labour law is another major factor, explaining the increase in precarious, i.e. marginal, jobs.[39] Concerning provisions in labour legislation (dismissal protection, leave entitlements, right to pro-rated pay, etc.) there are definite restrictions on the degree of protection offered to part-time employees in the labour legislation of some EU countries (the Netherlands, UK). But even in other EU countries part-time workers are often treated in discriminatory fashion, especially with regard to fringe benefits regulated under collective agreements.[40]

Thus, the degree of protection of part-time workers through either legislation or collective bargaining does not seem to be closely associated with its extent.[41] While the Nordic countries, especially, have extensive protection and very high proportions of part-time employees, other countries (the UK or the Netherlands, for example) with high proportions of part-time workers offer much less protection. At the same time, some countries with relatively advanced protection (Southern European countries, for example) have small proportions of part-time employees.

In the Nordic context Finland seems to be an exception: the comparative proportion of female part-time work is distinctly smaller, and the characteristics of Finnish part-time work differ from those of the other Nordic countries, too. The different development in Finland – compared with the other Nordic countries – may, at least partly, be a result of earlier developments in female employment. The female rate of participation in the labour force in Finland was formerly much higher than in the other Nordic or Western European countries: in 1950, it was 60 per cent in Finland, 50 per cent in Denmark, 37 per cent in Norway and 35 per cent in Sweden. In 1992, the female participation rate was at almost the same high level in all the Nordic countries (from 71 per cent in Norway to 79 per cent in Sweden). In the other Nordic countries, the considerable increase in female economic activity was the result of increased part-time work, but in Finland the tradition of full-time work has dominated the female labour market.[42] In the other Nordic countries, an additional source of part-time work was the fact that women working full-time reduced the number of their working hours. This was the case especially in Sweden where rising marginal tax rates, the introduction of the partial pension, and increased opportunities for parents with pre-school children to work fewer hours may have caused women to reduce the number of working hours.[43]

The willingness to work on a part-time basis depends also on economic conditions. In Finland, the level of wages and standard of living were formerly lower than in the other Nordic countries. There are also important differences in housing policy: the proportion of rented flats is significantly lower in Finland than in the other Nordic countries. Accordingly, the high cost of acquiring a house or an owner-occupied flat usually means full-time working. All these factors have restricted the possibilities of employees to choose part-time work in Finland. Thus, the proportion of full-time workers wishing to work shorter weeks has been lower in Finland than in the other Nordic countries. In addition, the concentration of part-time jobs in only a few occupations has restricted realization of the willingness of full-timers to work shorter weeks.

The decrease in female part-time work in the Nordic countries since 1982 may imply that the dynamics of part-time work are changing in these countries. The positive effects of increased female employment are outweighed by the negative effects of the decreasing proportion of part-time work. Sundström argues that the main reason for declining part-time work in Sweden has been tax reforms from 1983 onwards, whereby marginal tax rates for full-time workers were reduced stepwise, while those of part-time workers were raised.[44] In the Danish debate, increased restrictions in unemployment benefits for part-timers played their part. In addition to these changes, there may be other factors. One explanation for the decrease in part-time work among the middle age groups may be the rising level of education, which entails willingness to work full-time.[45] On the demand side, an important change is the break in the expansion of the public sector. From the 1960s to the early 1980s, employment grew much faster in the public than in the private sector.[46] In the late 1980s, the public sector's share of total employment declined in Sweden, was stable in Denmark, and grew slower than earlier in Norway and Finland. In the Nordic countries (except in Finland) the public sector (health and social services, education) has employed more than half of all female part-timers.

PART-TIME EMPLOYEES AND JOBS
Part-time work is heavily gendered, which indicates its connections with the wider differences between the sexes in family, labour market and society.[47] The vast majority of part-time employees are women (in 1991, 83 per cent in Sweden, but only 66 per cent in Finland). However, of all part-time employees, the proportion of women has declined during the last decade.[48] The trend has been the same in the EU countries.

Part-time work is more common among married than unmarried

women (except in Finland). Accordingly, most female part-time employees are married, although their proportion of all female part-time employees has declined. In 1991, the number was highest in Norway (77 per cent) and lowest in Finland (57 per cent). Considering all female part-time employment in the EU countries, the comparative proportion of married women has also declined, from 82 per cent in 1983 to 77 per cent in 1989.[49] This may indicate that the link between family status (marriage) and part-time work is loosening. However, most female part-timers still live in households where there is another (usually full-time) earner.

In addition to gender, part-time work varies with age. The proportion of part-timers is largest among employees under 20 years or over 60 years of age. The differences between the various age groups are more conspicuous among men than women. For women, but not for men, part-time work is usual also in the middle age groups.

Part-time work has expanded most rapidly among the youngest age groups, and to a lesser extent among older workers – women and men alike. The rapid growth in part-time work among young people is usually explained by the fact that most of them combine studying and work, because of the inadequacy of financial aid for studies.[50] Many studies also indicate that the youngest age groups are more affected by consumer culture. However, most Nordic female part-time employees are 25–59 years old (68–80 per cent in 1991), but the proportion of teenage (15–19 years) part-timers (18 per cent) is also considerable, except in Sweden (6 per cent) and Norway (7 per cent). Thus, Swedish and Norwegian part-timers are still typically middle-aged, married women, while in the other Nordic countries the proportion of younger part-timers is growing.

The age distribution of male part-timers is quite different: many male part-timers are either teenagers (45 per cent in Denmark) or over 60 years old, especially in Norway (18 per cent) and Sweden (24 per cent). This is partly due to the extensive part-time retirement scheme in these countries, especially in Sweden. In Finland, by contrast, the proportion of older male part-timers is only 10 per cent. In addition, shorter working weeks are more common for male than for female part-timers. Thus for men, part-time work is a temporary way of entering and leaving the labour market. For women, part-time employment is a more stable way of participating in the labour market. In other words, women and men work on a part-time basis at different times in the life cycle.

Most female part-timers work in services and retail trade. In Finland, agriculture and financing are also notable areas of employment for part-timers. Similarly, in most EU countries part-time work is concentrated in services and trade, while in less industrialized countries it is more usual in agriculture.[51] The proportion of part-time work is smallest in (male-dominated) manufacturing, construction and transport.

Part-time work is often seen in part as a way by employers to achieve numerical flexibility.[52] Numerical flexibility means the ability of enterprises to adjust the number of workers or working hours to changes in the level of demand for them. Indeed, part-time work is usual in industries where the demand for products and services typically varies in the short term (e.g. retail trade). In most of the Nordic countries, however, part-time work is typical in the public sector as well (health and social services, education). In the public sector, the classification of part-time workers as a numerically flexible workforce is more problematic. Thus, part-time work is common both in skilled and less skilled occupations. In Finland, however, part-time work has been concentrated in the private sector and less skilled occupations. This factor has implications for the nature of part-time jobs, as will be seen later.

ARE PART-TIME JOBS PRECARIOUS?

In the debate on atypical employment it is often assumed that these forms of employment are more precarious than standard employment relationships. According to Rodgers, the concept of precariousness involves instability, lack of protection, insecurity and social or economic vulnerability, and it is a combination of these factors that characterizes precarious jobs.[53] Thus, there are several dimensions to precariousness, and the boundaries of the concept are to some extent arbitrary. Because of limited data, we can use only a few indicators. In this study, part-time jobs are classified as precarious if they are characterized by low union density (which is usually associated with the control of work and protection), discontinuity, and unstable work history.

The concentration of part-time workers in small establishments may be one reason for the lower unionization rate among part-time wage and salary earners as compared with full-timers (Table 8.5).[54] The difference in unionization between female part-time and full-time workers is smallest in Sweden (80 per cent vs 86 per cent) and greatest in Finland (44 per cent vs 78 per cent). In Norway, the gap between female part-timers and full-timers narrowed considerably from 1978 to 1985.[55] The development was similar in Sweden and Finland, though less distinct and less restricted to women. Compared to most EU countries, however, the union density of part-timers is high in the Nordic countries.

Another indicator of the integration of the part-time workers into the labour market is job continuity, which is here defined (in a narrow sense) as the overlap between part-time and temporary work. In Finland especially, female part-timers have temporary jobs more often than full-timers (34 per cent vs 16 per cent), although half of the part-timers said that they did not want a permanent job.[56] However, the overlap between part-time and temporary work increased during the 1980s. This may indicate the casualization of Finnish part-time work. The phenomenon was evident earlier in Norway, too, but during the 1980s the gap between female part-timers and full-timers narrowed (in contrast to Finland), which may reflect the normalization of part-time work.[57] Also in Sweden, the gap between part-timers and full-timers is narrow.[58]

Differences between Finland and the other Nordic countries are

TABLE 8.5
Unionization rate, proportion of temporary jobs and working time preferences in part-time and full-time work (female wage and salary earners, percentages)

Country and year		Unionization rate		Proportion of temporary jobs		Involuntary	
		Part-time	Full-time	Part-time	Full-time	Part-time[a]	Full-time[b]
Denmark	1982	76	89	–	–	–	–
Finland	1981	–	–	23	10	32	21
	1986	37	78	24	13	26	20
	1989	44	78	32	13	21	19
	1990	44	75	34	16	–	–
Norway	1978	31	54	31	12	13	29
	1985	55	61	14	13	22	24
Sweden	1978	69	–	–	–	–	–
	1984	–	–	–	–	22	26
	1987	80	86	17	16	–	–

Notes: a Proportion of part-timers wanting a longer working week.
                 b Proportion of full-timers wanting a shorter working week.
Denmark: part-time = 1–29 hours per week. *Source: Arbejdstidundersogelsen 1982*, p. 72 (both sexes).
Finland: Part-time = 1–29 hours per week. *Source* for 1990: *Survey of Working Conditions.*
                 Source for 1981, 1986, 1989: *Annual Labour Force Survey* (temporary = *määräaikainen*; fixed-term).
Norway: Part-time = 1–34 hours pre week. *Source:* Ellingsaeter (1979), pp. 61, 73, 88; Ellingsaeter (1989), p. 72, 76 (temporary = *inte fast anmstatt*).
Sweden: Part-time = 1–34 hours per week. *Source* for 1978: Pettersson 1981, p. 201. *Source* for 1984: DELFA. *Source* for 1987: Deltidsarbete 1988, pp. 25, 18 (temporary = *tidsbegränsad*).

obvious also in the work history of part-timers. Nordic female part-timers are usually older than full-timers (as in most EU countries as well),[59] but not in Finland. Moreover, in Finland job tenure is clearly shorter in female part-time work than in full-time work (5.2 vs 8.5 years),[60] and the gap remains even when age is controlled for; in Sweden the difference is minor (6.4 vs 6.7 years).[61] This may reveal the more temporary character of female part-time work in Finland as compared with the other Nordic countries. In addition, Finnish female part-timers were more often unemployed (26 per cent vs 19 per cent) than full-timers during the last five years.[62] This was not the case in Sweden[63] or Germany.[64] However, in 1990 the unemployment gap between Finnish part-timers and full-timers disappeared among women (but not among men), at least partly because of a decline in female unemployment.[65]

BRIDGES OR TRAPS?
Part-time employment seems to be a heterogeneous phenomenon.[66] We can assume that some individuals may be forced to accept part-time work in the absence of alternatives (involuntary part-time work), while some individuals may, in fact, prefer part-time work (voluntary part-time work). In this study part-time work is classified as a bridge or a trap depending on (1) whether the taking up of part-time work has been voluntary or involuntary, and (2) whether part-time work is associated with frequent job moves. Part-time work is interpreted as a trap when it is involuntary and when there are few opportunities of getting a full-time job.

During the last three decades, in most of the Nordic countries (with the exception of Finland) part-time work has been an important alternative to full-time work for women. For men, part-time work has tended to be a short-time way of entering or leaving the labour market. At the individual level, a crucial criterion is the motivation for part-time work. In the Nordic countries, most part-timers work voluntarily on a part-time basis, preferring this form of employment. Having a young child[67] is the commonest reason for Swedish women (29 per cent) to work part-time,[68] while in Finland studying (26 per cent) and child care (25 per cent) were the main categories reported.[69] In Sweden the commonest reason among men is health or age (29 per cent), but in Finland studying (37 per cent).

Despite the provision of state-supported day care possibilities, the decision to work on a part-time basis is often caused by family obligations. As is well known, women take care of most household duties. According to a Finnish survey of working conditions, 38 per cent of female part-timers (and 16 per cent of full-timers) said that during their working history they had chosen part-time work for family reasons. Only 7 per cent of male part-timers (and 2 per cent of full-timers) gave the same answer. Therefore, to what extent women's choices of working hours are voluntary or not is a complex question.

Involuntary part-time work usually means part-time work for labour market reasons. The dominant form of involuntary part-time work relates to the inability to find a full-time job, while economic reasons such as short-time working account for a minority of cases. This explains why involuntary part-time employment is closely linked to the business cycle.[70] Moreover, comparison of data on involuntary part-time employment in different countries requires considerable care.

Involuntary part-time work, defined as part-time work for labour market reasons, varies with unemployment. In the late 1980s, the proportion of female part-timers for labour market reasons was 16 per cent in Sweden (female unemployment rate 2 per cent)[71] and Finland (female unemployment rate 4 per cent).[72] Ten years earlier (1977) – in connection with a higher unemployment rate in Finland (8 per cent) – the proportion of involuntary part-time work was higher (23 per cent).

The connection between involuntary part-time work and unemployment can also be examined at a regional and individual level. Involuntary part-time work varies with the regional un-employment rate. Accordingly, involuntary part-timers had been unemployed more often than other part-timers during the previous 12 months (37 per cent vs 8 per cent).[73]

Another means of estimating the proportion of involuntary part-time work is to find out what kind of working time part-timers prefer. In Finland, the proportion of those part-timers who would like to shift to full-time work used to be considerable (32 per cent of female part-timers in 1982). In the late 1980s, however, the proportion of involuntary part-time work to total part-time work declined – in a context of diminishing unemployment. As regards Norwegian and Swedish part-timers, the proportion used to be lower, but in the 1980s there was a rapid increase in involuntary part-time work. In addition, the proportion of full-time workers wishing to work shorter weeks was formerly higher in Sweden and Norway than in Finland, but, again, the gap narrowed in the 1980s. Further, involuntary part-time work seems more common for men than women – as in most Western European countries.[74]

To what extent part-time work can be regarded as a trap or a bridge depends also on the mobility between part-time and full-time work. Mobility in this respect is considerable, especially among part-timers: before their present jobs, 34 per cent of the Finnish female part-timers had been in full-time jobs and 19 per cent in part-time jobs; 22 per cent had been studying, 18 per cent had taken care of the household, 6 per cent had been self-employed and only 2 per cent had been unemployed.[75] As regards female full-timers, 6 per cent of them had been in part-time jobs, while most had either been in full-time jobs (58 per cent) or studying (19 per cent). The results may indicate that changes from full-time to part-time work are easier than changes in the opposite direction. Similar findings have also been made in Germany.[76] However, when using panel data the picture is more heterogeneous. According to the results of Santamäki-Vuori and Sauramo,[77] the position of part-time employees was distinctly more changeable than that of full-time employees during a follow-up period of 15 months (1987–8): part-timers were more likely to change jobs (40 per cent of part-timers, 18 per cent of full-timers), to leave the labour force (20 per cent vs 6 per cent) and to become unemployed (8 per cent vs 4 per cent). However, the fact that in most cases the job changes of part-time employees involved a transfer to full-time jobs suggests that the opportunities for changing working hours may not be quite so limited.[78] Even among those willing to change their working hours, the wishes appeared to be more likely to be fulfilled among part-timers than full-timers.[79] Furthermore, in Sweden the proportion of women who switched from part-time to full-time work rose in the 1980s.[80]

Thus, most female part-timers have preferred part-time work, and the proportion of involuntary part-time work has been quite small. In Finland, the proportion of involuntary part-time work used to be higher than in the other Nordic countries. Yet the mobility between Finnish part-time and full-time work is considerable, especially among part-timers, and correspondingly the opportunities for changing working hours are not so limited. Therefore, for most part-time workers, part-time jobs seem to be bridges rather than traps.

Policy implications

The overall growth of part-time work in industrialized countries is not a uniform process. There are big differences in the extent and increase of part-time employment among countries. As compared to most Western European countries, part-time employment is considerable among Nordic women. Part-time work accounts for over 40 per cent of all employed women in most Nordic countries (but in Finland only one in nine), whereas in the EU countries the average share is less than 30 per cent. Thus, in a quantitative sense, the classification of part-time work as a form of atypical employment may be misleading.

The situation of part-timers in the labour market seems to vary in the Nordic countries. On the one hand, the gaps between part-time and full-time work (unionization rate, continuity of jobs) have narrowed in Sweden and Norway, which may reflect the normalization of part-time work in these countries. Thus, Goldthorpe's assumption that the growth of part-time work has led to a considerable expansion of the secondary labour force would not seem to apply to most Nordic countries.[81] Part-time work, therefore, does not inevitably lead to the marginalization of women in the labour market. Crucial factors for the normalization of part-time work seem to be relatively long hours, job security and full social security benefits. On the other hand, the situation of part-timers in the Finnish labour market seems still to be more precarious than that of full-timers. Therefore, the classification of part-time work as a form of atypical employment fits Finland better than the other Nordic countries. However, there is also considerable mobility between part-time and full-time work, especially among part-timers, and part-time work is usually done voluntarily.

Thus, part-time employment covers a broad spectrum of employment forms, ranging from marginal forms of labour market participation to forms of employment which hardly differ from regular full-time employment. According to Nordic experience, part-time work could provide great opportunities to those who seek to balance work with family, education or other priorities. In many European countries, such opportunities exist only for those who do not need to support themselves solely on part-time earnings.[82] In addition, part-time work often implies low pay and lack of social benefits. To improve the situation, efforts should be made by governments, trade unions and employers to integrate part-time employees into legally guaranteed schemes and into collective agreements. Within the EU, efforts (directive proposals) are being made to harmonize the guaranteed minimum standards for part-time workers. Still, there is fear in some quarters that improved protection of part-time workers may increase rigidities and harm competitiveness. However, the contribution of less-than-proportional pay and benefits for part-time workers to lower costs is very small and is concentrated in service occupations which mainly concern domestic consumption.[83] If conditions of part-time employees are improved on an international scale, the implication for competitiveness would be negligible. Without a serious upgrading of the status of part-time work, real possibilities for better jobs for women are likely to be long delayed.

NOTES

1 See chapter by Moghadam in this volume.
2 *Ibid.*
3 Allen, T. (1992) 'The Nordic model of gender equality', TTT discussion papers, No. 116, Helsinki.
4 *Ibid.*
5 *Ibid.*
6 See *Social Security in the Nordic Countries 1990*, p. 98; and OECD (1990) *Employment Outlook*, p 140.
7 Säntti, R. (1993) 'Parents and child care leave', in K. Kauppinen-Toropainen (ed.), *OECD Panel Group on Women, Work and Health, National Report: Finland*, The Ministry of Social Affairs and Health, Helsinki.
8 Kauppinen-Toropainen, K. (1993) 'Introduction', in K. Kauppinen-Toropainen (ed.).
9 *Ibid.*
10 Rantalaiho, L. and R. Julkunen (1994) 'Women in Western Europe: socioeconomic restructuring and crisis in gender contracts', *Journal of Women's History*, Vol. 5, No. 3, pp. 11–29.
11 Säntti (1993).
12 Rantalaiho and Julkunen (1994).
13 Kauppinen-Toropainen (1993).
14 Rantalaiho and Julkunen (1994) pp. 21–2.
15 *Ibid.*, p. 19.
16 Kauppinen-Toropainen (1993) p. 4.
17 OECD (1991) *Employment Outlook*, Paris.
18 Kandolin, I. (1993) 'Women's labour force participation and sex segregation in working life', in K. Kauppinen-Toropainen (ed.).
19 Esping-Andersen, G. (1990) *The Three Worlds of Welfare Capitalism*, Polity Press, Cambridge; and Rantalaiho and Julkunen (1994).
20 Rantalaiho and Julkunen (1994) p. 20.
21 'Employment in Europe 1993', Commission of the European Communities, Brussels.
22 Kalimo, R. and J. Vuori (1993) 'Unemployment and health: women's resources and coping', in K. Kauppinen-Toropainen (ed.).
23 *Ibid.*
24 Lahelma, E. (1989) 'Unemployment, re-employment and mental well-being. A panel survey of industrial jobseekers in Finland', *Scandinavian Journal of Social Medicine*, Supplement 43.
25 Kalimo and Vuori (1993) p. 184.
26 *Ibid.*, p. 185.

27 ILO (1989) *Conditions of Work Digest*, Vol. 8, No. 1: Part-time work, p. 3.
28 In 1989, the definition of part-time work was changed in the Norwegian labour force survey. Part-time employees are persons who work 1–36 hours a week (settled/average working hours), with the exception of persons with 30–6 working hours who classify themselves as full-time workers (*Arbeidmarkedstatistikk* 1989, p. 73). Because of a break in the time-series, the older definition of part-time work is mainly used in this study.
29 ILO (1989) pp. 32–3.
30 Ehrenberg, R. G., P. Rosenberg and J. Li (1988) 'Part-time employment in the United States', in R. A. Hart (ed.), *Employment, Unemployment and Labor Utilization*, Hyman, London.
31 See Rubery, J. (1989) 'Precarious forms of work in the United Kingdom', in G. Rodgers and J. Rodgers (eds); Konle-Seidl, R. and U. Walwei (1991) 'Potential for flexibility in EC countries', *Labour* No. 5, pp. 175–93; and Drew, E. (1992) 'The part-time option? Women and part-time work in the European Community', *Women's Studies International Forum*, Vol. 15, pp. 607–14.
32 Eurostat (1991) 'Employment and Unemployment' (Eurostat 3C).
33 Marshall, A. (1989) 'The sequel of unemployment: the changing role of part-time and temporary work in Western Europe', in G. Rodgers and J. Rodgers (eds), p. 19.
34 Büchtemann, C. and S. Quack (1989) ' "Bridges" or "traps"? Non-standard employment in the Federal Republic of Germany', in G. Rodgers and J. Rodgers (eds), p. 115.
35 The high proportion of short part-time employment (less than 20 hours per week) in Norway may partly be a result of using *actual* working hours as a reference point. According to Ellingsaeter's results (1989, p. 69), the proportion of those part-timers who usually work 1–14 hours per week declined from 34 per cent in 1978 to 21 per cent in 1985, whereas the proportion of those working 15–24 hours per week increased from 41 per cent to 56 per cent during the same period.
36 OECD (1990) *Employment Outlook*, Paris, pp. 26–7.
37 Maier, F. (1991) 'Part-time work, social security protection and labour law: an international comparison', *Policy and Politics*, Vol. 19, No. 1, pp. 1–11.
38 See ILO (1989); and Delsen, L. (1991) 'Atypical employment relations and government policy in Europe', *Labour*, Vol. 5, pp. 123–49.
39 Maier (1991).
40 Konle-Seidl and Walwei (1991) p. 186.
41 ILO (1989) p. 28.
42 Pfau-Effinger, B. (1993) 'Modernisation, culture and part-time employment: the example of Finland and West Germany', *Work, Employment and Society*, Vol. 7, pp. 451–64.
43 Sundström, M. (1987) *A Study in the Growth of Part-time Work in Sweden*, Arbetslivscentrum, Stockholm.
44 *Ibid.*
45 Blank, R. (1989) 'The role of part-time work in women's labor market choices over time', *American Economic Review*, Vol. 79, pp. 295–9.
46 OECD (1989) *Employment Outlook*, Paris, p. 167.

47 Beechey, V. and T. Perkins (1987) *A Matter of Hours. Women, Part-time Work and the Labour Market*, Polity Press, Cambridge.
48 OECD (1991) *Employment Outlook*, Paris, p. 46.
49 Eurostat (1991).
50 In Finland, about half the students in higher education have jobs during the term. University studies usually take 5–8 years and the grant system does not cover all living costs. In addition, every fifth high-school student and every third vocational school student was working during the school term. Among all those students who were working while studying, 39 per cent had part-time jobs. Correspondingly, most (70 per cent) young (15–24 years old) part-timers were working on a part-time basis because of their studies (LFS 1989).
51 de Neubourg, C. (1985) 'Part-time work: an international quantitative comparison', *International Labour Review*, Vol. 124, pp. 559–76; and OECD (1983) pp. 50–1.
52 Atkinson, J. (1987) 'Flexibility or fragmentation', *Labour and Society*, Vol. 12, pp. 87–105; Pollert, A. (1988) 'The "flexible firm": fixation or fact?', *Work, Employment and Society*, Vol. 2, pp. 281–316; Hakim, C. (1990) '"Core and periphery" in employers' workforce strategies: evidence from the 1987 ELUS survey', *Work, Employment and Society*, Vol. 4, pp. 157–88; Walby, S. (1990) *Theorizing Patriarchy*, Blackwell, Oxford; and Penn, R. (1992) 'Flexibility in Britain during the 1980s', in N. Gilbert, R. Burrows, and A. Pollert (eds), *Fordism and Flexibility*, MacMillan, Basingstoke.
53 Rodgers, G. (1989) 'Precarious work in Western Europe: the state of debate', in G. Rodgers and J. Rodgers (eds).
54 Ellingsaeter, A. L. (1979) *Deltidsundersoegelsen*, Statistisk Sentralbyrå, Rapporter 79, p. 4, Oslo; and OECD (1985) p. 91 .
55 Ellingsaeter, A. L. (1989) Normalisering av deltidsarbeidet, Statistisk Sentralbyrå, Sociale og økonomiske studier 71, Oslo.
56 SWC (1990) *Survey on Working Conditions Data*, Statistics, Helsinki, Finland.
57 Ellingsaeter (1989) p. 71.
58 *Deltidsarbete* (1988) Statistiska Centralbyrån, IAM 1988:2, Stockholm.
59 Neubourg (1985) pp. 564–5.
60 SWC (1990) *Survey on Working Conditions Data*, Statistics, Helsinki, Finland.
61 Pettersson, M. (1981) *Deltidsarbete i Sverige*, Arbetslivscentrum, Stockholm.
62 SWC (1984) *Survey on Working Conditions Data*, Statistics, Helsinki, Finland.
63 Pettersson (1981) p. 135.
64 Büchtemann and Quack (1989) pp. 125–6.
65 SWC (1990) *Survey on Working Conditions Data*, Statistics, Helsinki, Finland.
66 Tilly, C. (1992) 'Dualism in part-time employment', *Industrial Relations*, Vol. 31, pp. 330–47.
67 The lack of (state-supported) child care, by contrast, is nowadays a very uncommon reason for working on a part-time basis (only 1 per cent of female part-timers reported this reason in 1987 in Finland and in

166   WOMEN IN THE LABOUR MARKETS

Sweden). In all Nordic countries, pre-school children (under 7 years old) are entitled to day care in an institution or in a family for the time their parents are working or studying. The extent of state-supported child care is largest in Denmark and smallest in Norway. The differences in child care, however, do not explain the differences in part-time work between the Nordic countries.

68 Deltidsarbete (1988) and LFS (1987)
69 LFS (1987) *Labour Force Survey*, Statistics, Helsinki, Finland.
70 OECD (1993) *Employment Outlook*, Paris, p. 14.
71 See Deltidsarbete (1988).
72 LFS (1987) *Labour Force Survey*, Statistics, Helsinki, Finland.
73 LFS (1991) *Labour Force Survey*, Statistics, Helsinki, Finland.
74 Marshall (1989) pp. 20–1; and OECD (1990) p. 182.
75 SWC (1990) *Survey on Working Conditions Data*, Statistics, Helsinki, Finland.
76 Büchtemann and Quack (1989) p. 127.
77 Santamäki-Vuori, T. and P. Sauramo (1990) *Atypical Forms of Employment and Labour Market Dynamics in Finland*, Labour Institute for Economic Research (TTT), Discussion Papers 101, Helsinki.
78 *Ibid.*, pp. 33–4.
79 *Ibid.*
80 Sundström, M. (1991) 'Part-time work in Sweden: trends and equality effects', *Journal of Economic Issues*, Vol. 25, pp. 167–78.
81 Goldthorpe, J. (1985) 'The end of convergence: corporatist and dualistic tendencies in modern Western societies', in B. Roberts, R. Finnegan and D. Gallie (eds), *New Approaches to Economic Life*, Manchester University Press, Manchester.
82 Maier (1991).
83 ILO (1989).

9

Asian Women in Manufacturing: New Challenges, Old Problems

– PAWADEE TONGUTHAI –

Several Asian countries recorded very high economic growth in the second half of the 1980s, with some such as the East Asian Newly Industrializing Countries (NICs) and Thailand attaining double-digit rates.[1] The main driving forces behind their achievements were inflows of foreign investment and exports of manufacturing products. Recent world events may have slowed down the impressive performance, but it is still widely expected that some of the Southeast Asian countries will soon be accorded the newly industrializing status, as Japan was in the 1960s, and the Republic of Korea, Taiwan, the Republic of China, Hong Kong and Singapore were in the 1970s.

The economic performance of countries that have chosen the path of export-led industrialization is greatly influenced by world trade and investment conditions. The globalization of manufacturing production and changes in technological and demand conditions are forcing producers to make several adjustments in order to remain competitive in the world market. As producers change the capital–technology–labour mix, shifting towards the first two productive factors, many low-skilled tasks will inevitably become redundant.

Export-oriented firms have attempted to reduce the fixed part of labour cost by substituting temporary or part-time workers for full-time wage employees. One alternative is subcontracting to home-based workers or small informal enterprises. Women workers, particularly those who are married with young children, or in the older age groups, predominate in both types of production arrangements.

Women are currently the disadvantaged group in the manufacturing sector and are ill-equipped to face the new challenges as they have low levels of education and skills. A wide range of education, training, and retraining programmes are urgently needed to facilitate their skills acquisition and their integration into the next stage of industrialization.

This chapter highlights the impact on women workers in economies that rely on low-wage labour as a springboard for industrial development. Such strategy has, no doubt, attracted a large amount of investment from both local and foreign sources and in a short time helped increased national incomes several times. But, for the millions of women who have played an integral role in supporting that success, what have they got in return for their efforts? With the economies undergoing rapid transformation, are women workers able to keep up the pace and move to the next stage of development along with the rest of the economy?

Industrialization in Asia and the role of women

More than half (56 per cent) of the 828 million women officially estimated to be in the labour force world wide in 1990 were in Asia, with over 35 per cent in East Asia.[2] A significant difference in the labour force participation rates between men and women still exists in most countries, with the latter being much lower. In Malaysia, for example, although female labour force participation rose significantly to 48 per cent in 1992, it still lagged far behind the 86 per cent for men. The highest degree of disparity was found in the countries of South Asia, with the exception of Sri Lanka which has had an outstanding record of equal access to education for both boys and girls. Women's participation rates remain below 10 per cent in Bangladesh and Pakistan, while they exceed 50 per cent in many countries of East and Southeast Asia which also show narrowing disparity between rates for men and women, such as China, Mongolia, Vietnam and Thailand.[3]

The expansion of female economic activity is attributed to the rapid expansion of educational facilities as well as increased access to them by women. Education has also led to changes in the attitudes of women as they become aware of other available options in their lives, apart from marriage and childbearing. The success of family planning programmes and the resulting smaller number of children as well as the availability of labour-saving home appliances has also substantially reduced women's domestic burden.

Women's employment, however, is still characterized by an M-shaped or a bi-modal pattern. There are high participation rates among younger age groups who enter the labour force immediately after leaving school, generally earlier than men due to the shorter period of education. With a high incidence of dropping-out after marriage and the birth of their first child, the participation rates decline noticeably, then high participation rates appear again as middle-aged women re-enter the labour market.[4] This pattern reflects a widespread social perception in Asia about the primacy of women's domestic role. Such discontinuity in women's labour market experience is likely to affect adversely women's earnings and career advancement, making them more likely to be concentrated in the lower occupational categories. Once a woman drops out of the labour market for marriage and child bearing, it is very difficult to return to full-time employment. Women usually obtain re-employment only in less secure, more irregular jobs.

In more industrially advanced countries, the bottom of the 'M' has been lifted recently as more women continue working after marriage and childbirth. This could be, as in the case of Japan, a result of women's struggle for their rights and better social conditions, particularly the availability of child care centres.[5]

The role of women in the economy of Asian countries changes according to the transformation of the economic structure, from agriculture to manufacturing and then to services. The obvious pattern is that of the decline in the participation of both sexes in agricultural activities, with that of women being at a slower rate. Demand from the manufacturing sector in the initial stages of industrialization is mainly for assembly-line production workers. As the agricultural sector is usually undergoing its own transformation with increasing mechanization, those low-skilled positions are easily filled by the surplus labour released from agricultural activities.

Although the original emphasis and direction of industrialization efforts in Asian countries varied, the same path was ultimately chosen, that is, export-oriented manufacturing, making the most of the low-skilled inexpensive workforce these countries all have in abundance. Such a strategy has dramatically changed women's role, status and opportunities.

Factories established during the initial period of industrialization were those producing goods that used almost entirely female labour, such as textile products and electrical equipment. Textile and garment making are activities widely believed to be women's specialities as they are the tasks women have always been responsible for in their traditional household duties. Production of electrical equipment and parts is supposed to require patience, careful attention to detail and nimble fingers – qualities commonly thought to be found in women more than in men.

A large number of women left their rural villages to find jobs in the cities in countries where women's economic activities outside their homes received social acceptance and there were no restrictions against young women migrating alone. They were drawn by the promise of a much more exciting and brighter future than working on farms. Particularly striking were the cases of Thailand and the Philippines where the number of young women in the age group 11–19 years who migrated to the capital cities was twice as large as that of the men.[6]

In Malaysia, the implementation of the New Economic Policy in the 1970s and ethnic employment quotas encouraged the participation of Malays, who were located largely in the rural areas, in the new economic sector. The emphasis on export-oriented industries created employment opportunities for women, resulting in a massive entry of women into the manufacturing sector. Young Malay women migrated from rural areas to factories in the Free Trade Zones.[7]

New economic opportunities opened up for Indonesian women with the government's commitment to reduce the country's dependence on oil export and diversify to manufacturing. The Indonesian government played another important role by setting a higher marriage age through the marriage law. The expansion of educational programmes also enabled women to find jobs at better pay than previously.

Although employment opportunities for women were plentiful, most of the women workers were concentrated in the unskilled category, while being noticeably underrepresented among the categories of supervisors and technicians. Furthermore, opportunities for women in the formal sector were limited and they were overwhelmingly found in the group of workers who were paid on a daily, piece-rate basis.[8] Compared with men in the same age and educational group, women were paid far less. Their employment was characterized by very low wages, long work hours, and low occupational safety and health standards.

Through the new employment opportunities, women were able to earn cash, most of them for the first time in their lives. Their status was elevated from unpaid family workers toiling all day long in the fields to that of the family breadwinners. Their earnings were used to buy dresses, jewellery, presents for their friends and families, or to send their younger brothers and sisters to schools, and to build new houses for their ageing parents – the last option being the greatest sign of gratitude that a good Asian daughter could ever show. In Thailand, it has almost become a competition among parents to see whose daughters can send most money home. Needless to say, this puts a great pressure on women to work very hard to fulfil their parents' expectation. Strangely enough, parents seem to expect this show of gratitude from daughters, but not from sons. A daughter who leaves home for work in the cities and never sends money home is considered to have committed a great sin, and can hardly hope to receive a warm welcome home.

These Asian economies still have more than 50 per cent of their populations in agriculture. Until recently, therefore, young women still felt attached to the farms and did not consider factory life to be their future. They chose factory work only because there was little or no other option in the villages that could give them nearly as much return. That attitude explains why they have tolerated bad working conditions, poor wages, and the lack of promotion. They have also been reluctant to invest in training and to join labour unions.

Even when they would like to become union members, the right is sometimes denied them, as in the case of several Export Processing Zones (EPZs) in the NICs and Southeast Asian countries. When governments try to outdo one another in offering attractive packages to foreign investors, workers' welfare is often sacrificed as labour codes, along with employment conditions, are relaxed or ignored.

The Malaysian government still frowns upon labour activities and the government-controlled press tends to report unfavourably about labour leaders. The continuing success of the economy has also quelled any comments about the restriction on unionization. In such a tight labour market, minimum wage legislation is not found to be necessary, as industry determines its own basic wage or minimum guarantee for all workers.

The changing technological and economic environment

IN THE MANUFACTURING SECTOR

The global trading system has been undergoing great changes as a result of advances in information-intensive technology and telecommunication, as well as the creation of regional trading blocks. When the East Asian NICs were facing restrictions on their import quotas and rising labour costs at home, one sure route of escape was to move their production facilities to the Southeast Asian countries. The move is now under way to the rest of Asia. China, Vietnam, Laos PDR, Bangladesh, Sri Lanka and even Mongolia are entering the picture in the competition in the labour-intensive and low-skilled industries.

Ever since producers in the developing countries of Asia have used the advantage of low-cost labour to produce and export light manufacturing goods, they have been gaining an increasing share of the world market. To counteract the disadvantages in wages and labour shortage, producers in Western countries have therefore been

under increasing pressure to improve their productivity by introducing new technologies and innovative management practices.
Those adjustments have been going on continually. Today it can be
said that, for many manufacturing products, the comparative
advantage no longer depends on having a large pool of low-cost
labour. Advanced technology and increased productivity can almost
perfectly compensate for the shortage of labour and high wages.

In highly capital-intensive industry, such as textiles, technological
innovations have penetrated all phases of production, making the
industry highly automated, leading to greater machine speeds and
improved product designs. The impact on employment has been to
reduce the proportion of unskilled labourers while increasing that of
technical and skilled personnel.[9]

For garment production, however, the degree of automation is
much lower than in textiles. There is still plenty of room for products
aimed at the middle and the low end of the market which can be
produced by using cheap labour. Major changes are found in
organizational arrangements, with closer cooperation between
buyers and suppliers in terms of designs and reduction in the time
lag between the placing of orders and the delivery of products. The
consequence is shorter runs and pressure for more flexibility in production. Competition relies as much on marketing as on reducing
production costs.

One strategy chosen by manufacturing firms to achieve flexibility
and to cut down on production costs has been to minimize the fixed-
cost portion of labour by reducing the number of permanent workers,
especially the low-skilled group. Firms prefer to employ multi-
skilled workers as permanent workers, with their greater flexibility
for information-intensive work. Tasks that require a large proportion of low-skilled labour are put out, or subcontracted, to smaller
firms or to home-based workers.

Two systems of employment, therefore, emerge as a consequence
of such an arrangement.[10] Workers in the same firm can be divided
into two groups. The first group, the core workers, receive high
wages, job security, good working conditions, and opportunities for
skills development and promotion. The second group, the peripheral workers, are either subcontractors or workers who are only
hired by the firms temporarily. They are poorly paid and have to
work long hours, but have little security and are not entitled to
protection from the labour law.

Firms that do not rely on subcontractors to increase output prefer
to use existing workers to do overtime work rather than recruit new
ones. The latter option necessitates increasing production capacity,

which most firms are reluctant to do unless they are certain that the increase could be sustained for a reasonably long period of time.

Even within the factory setting, several measures have been devised by employers to extract as much work as possible from the workers, such as setting extremely high target outputs and offering a reward, such as a gold necklace. A tremendous strain is put on the workers' physical and mental health. Those who hope to win the prize don't take even a ten-minute lunch break so they can rush back to the machines and work towards that impossibly high target output. The use of stimulants is common and even encouraged by employers.

Challenges and problems for women workers

The export orientation of industrialization which relies on low-cost labour has drawn unskilled young women into the manufacturing process with little preparation and hardly any further development of skills. The qualities which have made these women attractive as workers to both local and foreign investors are their innate abilities as women, in particular their dexterity and obedience. The nature of the tasks they have been assigned to perform requires little training.

For the new production and trading environments, however, the need for labour-intensive work has been significantly reduced, shifted towards cognitive skills in technology and in the management of organizations. Given that women have been employed mainly in unskilled and semi-skilled tasks, this change in skills requirements implies a decline in demand for their labour. In order to keep up with the fast-changing international market and technology, these women require skills upgrading and intensive training and retraining – an investment which very few of them can afford.

The world of work for Asian women is changing very fast. Their lives are being increasingly threatened by the introduction of new technologies and changes in world market conditions – both factors which are beyond their control. All the Asian economies, regardless of the size of their labour pools, currently seem to be obsessed with the drive towards new technology, hoping that it will be the passport to the status of an NIC.

Malaysia has set its sights on an even more ambitious goal. It intends to by-pass the newly industrializing stage and jump right on to the next stage, setting the national goal to be a fully industrialized nation by the year 2020. Indonesia is moving towards highly capital-intensive and prestigious industry, such as the aircraft industry, while downgrading the importance of labour-intensive industry such as footwear or garments which has been the major source of employment for women.

Under the new forms of work organization such as subcontracting, workers are paid less than their counterparts in the formal sector because of the piece-rate basis. In addition, these women have no channel to air their problems or to seek ways to improve their pay and working conditions. The nature of their employment and the smaller size of the production unit make it difficult to organize and this leads to a lack of security. In countries such as the Philippines where labour unions have a history of being very strong and aggressive, subcontracting can be used as a way to hide the firm's effort to reduce the bargaining power of labour.

Industrialization in Southeast Asia will soon no longer be simply a low-wage affair. Technologically advanced industries requiring just a small number of highly skilled workers have been established while the traditional industries offering 'women's jobs', such as textiles and electronics, have been laying off workers. The numbers began with a few hundred, but may soon reach into tens of thousands per year.

Few women are in a position to deal with the problems currently confronting them. Their daily work, which may be up to 12–14 hours a day, leaves them no time to make plans for the future. Women with a relatively good education may be able to afford the time and may possess the means to adjust their skills and knowledge, but the low-skilled workers with only primary or lower secondary school education have almost no chance to develop their skills and become equal partners in the next stage of development.

The average level of education for women workers is low, and technical knowledge practically non-existent. Among Thai manufacturing workers, 80 per cent have at the most six years of education. Even if by some miracle an all-out attempt to increase the rate of continuation from primary to secondary school is completely successful, Thailand will still have more than 70 per cent of its manufacturing workforce with just six years of education by the year 2000.[11]

Although the new technologies and changing market conditions may also affect other industries where men are concentrated, the greatest and most immediate threat is in industries that have been depending on low-wage women workers. When the day comes that these labour-intensive industries reach the end of their cycle, can new jobs be found for the women workers?

Faced with budget constraints, Asian governments are very slow

in considering skill development schemes, preferring to let each
factory arrange its own training programme. The only countries in
which such programmes have worked are the ones that have already
left the labour-intensive stage behind and entered the technology-
intensive stage of labour shortage with a corresponding need for
highly skilled human resources. In the labour surplus countries,
skills development programmes face a lot of difficulty getting off the
ground.

Experiences of Japan and the East Asian NICs

Many of the problems currently facing Asian women working in the
manufacturing sector are similar to what women workers
experienced several decades or even a hundred years ago. What we
now observe in the Southeast Asian countries and what will soon
emerge in China, Laos PDR, Vietnam, Bangladesh and Sri Lanka has
been experienced before by Japan in the 1970s and by the Asia NICs
in the 1980s. The problems are simply being repeated, with the
addition of new challenges from the changing world situations.

The 'economic miracle' of the East Asian countries had been
based on export-oriented industrialization and foreign investment.
Their high growth rates were made possible by light industries such
as textile and garments, an abundant and inexpensive supply of
female labour, and a controlled labour force. Under dictatorial
political regimes, union activity did not have much chance to
flourish. Low unionization was further caused by the location of
many industries in the EPZ where they are accorded the status of
essential industries and their workers were thus not allowed to
strike.

In Japan, since industrialization began around the end of the
1800s, workers in the textile industry had been young, unmarried
women who migrated from rural areas to work temporarily in the
cities. The employment contracts were essentially between factory
owners and the women's parents or brothers. Working conditions
were extremely bad, and the standard working hours were twelve
hours per day or more. Dormitories and food were unsanitary,
factories were dusty and diseases were widespread. Most of the
women who quitted their jobs did so by running away.[12]

Gradually, the situation for women workers in terms of wages
and working conditions improved, due mainly to sustained
economic growth and the increased demand for labour. Migration
also declined as the crowded situation in the cities, together with the

problems of water and air pollution, had forced the government to find alternatives for these women in their own rural communities. Rural industrialization policies provided firms with incentives that were favourable enough to decentralize the location of their factories. The garment industry was among the first to move into rural areas, employing mostly married women in factories that were set up in all kinds of places such as abandoned schools and old bowling alleys in order to minimize capital investment.[13] Then others followed, including high-tech companies such as those which produce semi-conductors. The shortage of labour was another major factor behind the relocation. These local factories provided employment opportunities for farmers' wives looking to supplement their families' declining incomes because of the cutback in rice production induced by government policy.

Women with high school education preferred clerical, sales or service jobs to the monotonous jobs on the assembly line, so the firms had to shift their recruiting to middle-aged or older housewives as a source of part-time labour. However, although women may have been brought into the labour market when labour shortage occurred, they were also the first to be released when business conditions were down. Their role was essentially that of an adjustment valve, bearing the main burden of business fluctuation.[14]

Technological change also affected women's employment in Japan, particularly between the end of 1960s and 1970s when mechanization and automation were introduced on a large scale. Mechanization occurred rather gradually in old industries, such as textiles, but much more rapidly in electronics and food industries. Initially, the introduction of factory automation and other labour-saving devices expanded women's opportunities as certain tasks were deskilled and became monotonous. Firms were thus able to put women in positions formerly occupied by men, taking advantage of women's cheaper wages.[15]

The negative impact on Japanese women was not apparent, even though factory automation in Japan proceeded around three times faster than in Europe and the United States. The reason was that many women routinely quit their jobs after marriage and childbirth. Firms could therefore reduce the number of workers significantly when they also stopped hiring new workers at the same time.

In addition, Japanese firms have subtle ways to encourage women to retire early, either by putting psychological pressure on them or assigning them very difficult work. Furthermore, a majority of women did not mind working part-time or being full-time housewives, depending on their husbands' incomes. Therefore, although there have been many dismissals, they have not been regarded as unemployment problems. Even among widows, middle-aged women or those whose husbands were unemployed, the number was not large enough to draw public attention.

However, part-time employment has resulted in insecure positions and poor working conditions, while hours worked are comparable to full-time employment. The only difference between part-time and full-time employment is the former's irregular, insecure status. Once a Japanese woman leaves a job after getting married or giving birth, it is extremely difficult for her to return to full-time employment.

During the industrialization process in Korea, the labour-intensive, assembly type industries have been the fundamental force enabling the country to achieve rapid economic growth in a very short time. The primary source of labour supply to Seoul's manufacturing sector has been underemployed family agricultural workers, unemployed people or economically inactive workers from other areas. They have been paid low wages – as little as 60 per cent or less of wages paid to men.[16]

As the labour pool of unskilled workers in the rural areas was exhausted, labour force participation by young females in the age groups 15–19 and 20–24 declined. Facing serious labour shortage, firms drew in married women who chose the hourly or flexible employment system. Child-care facilities were introduced in order to entice this group of workers. The high-wage firms, however, preferred male workers. The customary practice has been that males are hired through regular job opening advertisement and females are hired through personal connections with those already employed.[17]

Early retirement programmes that apply only to women are typical. Married women are discouraged from entering or continuing to work in both clerical and production jobs. Employment contracts used by private firms often specify that women will retire when they marry.[18]

An overwhelming proportion of female workers are in low-wage industries, such as textiles, garments and fabricated metal. Their employment is much less stable than that of male workers. Female employment structure may be characterized as involving low wages and job insecurity.

There is also an increasing tendency in Korea to employ women as temporary and daily-paid workers. They do not enjoy the right to collective bargaining and are not entitled to other benefits enjoyed by permanent employees and are, therefore, more vulnerable to exploitation.

Conclusions

The situation for Asian women in the manufacturing industries described in this chapter has been going on for several decades and is getting worse. Southeast Asian governments are now directing their focus towards automation and advanced technology. Sophisticated, technology-intensive factories spring up all over the region. Globalization of production and marketing is putting Asian countries in direct competition with each other, each one clamouring for a larger share in the world market. In the process, women are being retrenched, and wages of women who remain in employment are being driven down.

Planners seem to be more preoccupied with the shortage of engineers, technicians and middle management, while the countless low-level workers who are not in a position to invest in upgrading or retraining are given lower priority.

The seriousness of the problem has remained largely hidden up to now because of the farming sector. The existence of support from this sector has been acting as a buffer or a relief valve for the economy when industrial activities are down. Women workers know they can always return home where food and shelter, at least, will be available. But how long can the economy and society of these countries remain flexible, absorbing the labour released from the factories?

Many of the countries in Asia are reaching a major turning point. To ensure that the turning point brings less tension and leads to a peaceful coexistence of various groups in society, priority must be given to the social consequences of industrialization, and greater attention must be paid to the more equal sharing of economic benefits.

In Japan and the NICs, the importance of the manufacturing sector as an employer of female labour is declining. The shift to capital- and technology-intensive manufacturing has led to the relocation of the labour-intensive portion of manufacturing activities – normally those with a high content of female labour – to other countries. Thus, although demand for women workers is declining in Southeast Asia, it will increase in other countries of the region which are trying to follow the same path of export-led industrialization.[19]

As the process of structural adjustment accelerates, the emphasis is increasingly on technological changes, greater labour flexibility, and a growing trend towards a reduction in formal sector employment and a rise in casual labour. It is essential that social safety nets be created for workers who will lose employment.

The transitional economies face problems similar to those of countries undergoing structural adjustment programmes. Adopting the market economy system has brought challenges to be overcome, requiring knowledge and economic efficiency. There is an emphasis on producing for export, drawing young rural women into export-oriented employment. At the same time, the collapse of the socialist system has led to the breakdown of the system of welfare support. Workers displaced by the introduction of new technologies have no recourse or social safety net. The most vulnerable group is older women whose skill and basic education are too low to be of much help in adapting to the new and advanced technologies.

The challenges ahead in manufacturing affect these countries and their women workers in differing degrees. In Japan and the NICs, which have been experiencing the situation of labour shortage, the issue for the female labour force is thus not so much employment creation as improving the conditions and types of employment already available to women.

In Southeast Asian countries, the manufacturing sector is grow-ing very fast and export earnings are crucial to their economic growth. As manufacturing activities and the role of women are still concentrated in the textile, garment and electronics industries, the challenges lie in helping women workers cope with the gradual shift to technology and knowledge-intensive production. At the same time, with the increase in the casualization of labour, the urgent tasks of increasing productivity and upgrading conditions of female labour in the informal sector must be addressed.

Agriculture, which has been the traditional source of employment for women, still absorbs more than 50 per cent of total employment. The rate of growth, however, has slowed down considerably. Furthermore, the establishment of new agricultural institutions means women are having more difficulty in gaining access to credit. New agricultural technology which is invariably labour-saving reduces demand for women's labour and pushes women to look for jobs in activities outside the farms.

East Asia's success is commonly attributed to the well-educated population and easily trained labour force.[20] In the East Asian NICs, great emphasis has always been placed on education. During the period of technological changes in labour-intensive industries, women manufacturing workers did not have much difficulty making a transition to service work because most of them already had at least a high school education. Such a background made it easier for them to be trained for the new jobs.

The problems currently facing women workers in some of Asia's fastest growing sub-regions, Southeast Asia in particular, may linger much longer, however, and could have a potentially more serious effect. Education is the major barrier that stands between the almost-NICs like Thailand and Malaysia and the East Asian success cases.

Human capital formation, with emphasis on a secondary level of education and on increasing women's access to technical and non-traditional training, must be given high priority. The expansion of women's employment in the subcontracting and home-based sector requires the urgent upgrading of technology and improvement of working conditions for workers in the informal sector.

Finally, the process of development planning must take into account women's concerns. Higher representation of women in positions of economic and political power may enhance these efforts.

NOTES
1 Asian Development Bank (1993) *Asian Development Outlook*, Oxford University Press.
2 International Labour Office (1993) *World Labour Report 1993*, International Labour Organization, Geneva.
3 United Nations Industrial Development Organization (UNIDO) (1994) 'Participation of women in manufacturing: patterns, determinants and future trends regional analysis, ESCAP region', a draft report.
4 Economic and Social Commission for Asia and the Pacific (ESCAP) (1994) 'Review and appraisal of implementation of the Nairobi forward-looking strategies for the advancement of women; regional priority issues and proposals for action: women in economic development', paper for the Second Asian and Pacific Ministerial Conference on Women in Development, Jakarta.
5 Hiroki, Michiko (1993) 'Restructuring and employment of women', paper for the East Asian Women Workers Activists Meeting, Tokyo.
6 'Promoting employment, occupational mobility and skill formation for women in manufacturing: trends and evidence from selected countries of Asia and the Pacific Region', paper for UNIDO/ESCAP Validation Workshop on Participation of Women in Manufacturing: Regional Analysis of Patterns, Determinants and Future Trends in Asia and the Pacific, Bangkok.
7 Ariffin, Jamilah (1992) *Women and Development in Malaysia*, Pelanduk Publications, Malaysia.
8 Lin Lean Lim (1992) *Employment Situation and Training Needs of Women Workers in Garment and Food/Tobacco Processing in Surabaya/Sidoarjo, Indonesia*, a report submitted to UNDP/ILO as part of project preparation for the Industrial Skills Development Project.
9 UNIDO (1993) *Changing Techno-Economic Environment in the Textile and Clothing Industry: Implications for the Role of Women in Asian Developing Countries*, Vienna.

10 Van Liemt, Gijsbert (ed.) (1992) *Industry on the Move*, International Labour Office, Geneva.
11 Sussangkarn, Chalongphob (1991) 'Education, labour markets and economic development: policy simulations', Research Report Nos 1–2, Thailand Development Research Institute Year-end Conference, Bangkok.
12 Hazama, Hiroshi (1976) 'Changes in lifestyle of industrial workers' in Hugh Patrick (ed.) *Japanese Industrialization and its Social Consequences*, University of California Press, Berkeley, Los Angeles, London; Tsurumi, E. Patricia (1991) *Women in the Thread Mills of Meiji Japan*, Princeton University Press, New Jersey; and Hiroki (1993).
13 Shiozawa, Miyoko and Michiko Hiroki (1988) *Discrimination Against Women Workers in Japan*, Asian Women Workers' Center, Tokyo, Japan.
14 *Ibid.*
15 See chapter by Yashiro (1994) in this volume.
16 ESCAP (1994).
17 *Ibid.*
18 Cho, Hyoung (1987) 'Women's labour force participation and their status in the economy: Republic of Korea and Hong Kong' in *Women's Economic Participation in Asia and the Pacific*, ESCAP, Bangkok.
19 UNIDO (1994).
20 World Bank (1993) *The East Asian Miracle: Economic Growth and Public Policy*, Oxford University Press, New York.

– PART III –

Internationalization and Global Responses

10

The 'New' International Competition: Effects on Employment

– MICHEL FOUQUIN, AGNÈS CHEVALLIER –

– JEAN PISANI-FERRY –

In 1993, the United States had a heated debate on the ratification of NAFTA, the German government expressed concern about the future of *Standort Deutschland* – that is, about the country's ability to remain attractive for manufacturing investment[1] – and, in France, a well-publicized parliamentary report warned that *délocalisations* are a threat to employment and called for a strengthening of EU protection against imports from cheap labour countries.[2] During the UNU/WIDER conference many Scandinavian participants posed similar questions. Each country clearly had specific concerns: US citizens were worried about Mexico 'sucking' away North American jobs (Ross Perot's *dixit*) and thereby bringing stagnant US wages down further; the Germans were suffering from an overvalued real exchange rate and were wondering who would invest in the former German Democratic Republic (GDR) when wages in the Czech republic were ten times lower; French politicians were, for obvious reasons, anxious about the rise in mass unemployment; and Scandinavian participants were worried about the possibility of maintaining their social welfare schemes in the face of new competition and their entry into the European Union. Yet these debates had a common feature – the potential competition from emerging manufacturing exporters. In all these countries, as well as in many others, a widespread view is held that a dramatic change in international trade and investment is under way, and that industrialized countries are losing ground at an accelerated pace. Another view held by the IMF and the OECD is that unemployment problems are only a consequence of imperfect domestic labour markets, more flexibility in these markets being the solution.

Is the fear of international competition warranted – or is it mainly a side-effect of the recession and an attempt to find scapegoats instead of addressing domestically rooted problems? This issue has been discussed by many economists over the last few years, especially in the US, where the main focus of the discussion has been whether trade with low-wage countries has caused an increase in the wage gap over the last two decades.[3]

In this chapter, we first analyse the impact of trade on labour markets. Second, we concentrate on trade and aim at determining whether there is an observable acceleration in the emergence of new competitors to the established industrial powers, and whether there are indications that the trend is likely to accelerate further in the near future. We base ourselves on very rough and unsophisticated analysis of standard indicators: trade shares and patterns, foreign direct investment (FDI) and labour costs. As all these indicators are by definition backward-looking, a more forward-looking perspective is also adopted through a short survey of the current policies of developing economies and the economies in transition. Finally, we briefly discuss whether there is evidence that this competition is 'unfair'.

Wage gap and international trade[4]

To answer the first question we mostly use studies made by US economists of the US economy. The fact is that there is, in the US as well as in some European countries (in particular in Great Britain), an increasing inequality between wage earners.

First, the average net hourly wage of non-manual workers increased at the rate of 1.77 per cent per year at constant prices during 1959 and 1973, then it decreased at the rate of 0.73 per cent per year between 1974 and 1993. The same change in trend is seen for the average cost (i.e. social benefits included) which rose by 3 per cent per year before 1973 and at only 0.66 per cent since.

Second, the decline in purchasing power of the average wage is not a homogeneous trend; there is simultaneously an increase in inequality among different categories of workers. Beginning in the early 1970s inequality has since increased dramatically. Between 1970 and 1989, the average salary of the 10 per cent best-paid workers among active males was 1.8 times higher than it used to be when compared to the 10 per cent lowest-paid people: inequality of primary income has increased by 80 per cent.

If we go into more detail we find that for men between 25 and 34 years old, salaried men with the highest skills have increased their income between 1975 and 1990 by 25 per cent compared to the non-qualified people. Inequality has increased the most for young people as old workers benefit from acquired advantages. Trade unions tend to make concessions at the expense of the new workers, protecting more the interests of the old workers (who are union members).

There are different explanations. First, there is the labour supply: the relative supply rise of one category should, everything being equal, lower its relative compensation, but if we look at the facts we see that the relative supply of high- and middle-skilled workers has increased very rapidly in the US, which is going against the expected effect. There is no specific explanation for this movement.[5] The decline of labour union membership and the rise of the number of immigrants (20 per cent of the category of people without diplomas) are not important enough to explain such a discriminatory change.

Many economists believe that technical progress is the main source of change in relative wages. To be invented, introduced and used, technical progress needs high-skilled workers. Technical progress in general can replace low-skilled workers but it cannot replace high-skilled workers. So there is a clear bias in favour of high-skilled workers and against low-skilled workers. In fact employment has decreased mostly in low-skilled labour-intensive activities. The share in employment of manufacturing industries, with low and medium technological content, has been declining from 26 per cent in 1968 to 14 per cent in 1993. On balance, sectors with a high-skilled labour content (such as financial or business services, insurance, high-tech industries) have increased their share. If we look at the comparative advantage of the US, we can also see that low-skilled activities are subject to the strongest increase of imports coming from developing countries, while high-skilled activities are, in general, sectors in which the US has a strong and increasing comparative advantage.

In fact the US economy became an economy open to international trade. Measured by the share of international trade (export plus import) in GDP, the ratio was stable at 6–8 per cent up to the 1970s, then it grew rapidly towards 22 per cent in 1991. As a consequence, the competitive pressure of international trade must have increased dramatically in the US. We might also mention the fact that in the manufacturing sector the increase has been much more dramatic.

The link between international trade and the rise in wage inequality in the US became an object of political controversy during the last presidential election. What is more, the neo-classical theory of international trade clearly predicts such an outcome. If we follow the Stolper Samuelson classical demonstration we know that for a country like the US, which has a relatively abundant supply of qualified workers, trade openness will drive the country to become more specialized in high-skilled labour-intensive goods, and this will lower relatively the production of low-skilled labour-intensive goods. This evolution introduces a decline in the demand for low-skilled labour and a rise in demand for high-skilled workers. In the case of full employment the adjustment is made through wage changes – that is, through an increase in the wage gap. A secondary effect is that, under the hypothesis of full employment, there is an increase in the relative use of low-skilled workers in both industries. Several statistical tests have been tried to find a correlation between the wage gap and trade openness during the 1980s. In the US manufacturing industries, the employment elasticity to the price of imports is around 0.3: a decline of 10 per cent in import prices would reduce employment by 3 per cent. In the 1970s the change in wages was satisfactorily explained through the relative variation in supply and demand for labour, but this was no longer the case in the 1980s. A 1 per cent decrease in the trade balance would depreciate low-skilled workers' wages by 3 per cent[6] and appreciate high-skilled workers' wages by 1 to 2 per cent.[7]

Other economists deny the existence of such a direct link between international trade and the wage gap.[8] First they mention the fact that the decline in wages has not increased the demand for low-skilled labour, but this argument does not take into account the fact that simultaneously there has been a strong increase in the supply of high-skilled workers.

The same study shows that the relative price of high-tech goods has not increased (in fact in the computers and VLSI industry it has decreased dramatically). This is not in conformity with the standard theory and, in fact, the theory does not account for strong technical progress.

Another study shows that an increase in trade in high-tech goods with the rest of the world increased the wages of high-skilled workers; on the other hand, an increase in the import ratio in basic goods decreased the salary of low-skilled workers in this sector.[9] This study supports the idea of trade having a strong impact on wage inequality. Nevertheless it is still difficult to measure the employment impact of trade, because goods exported by developing countries are no longer produced in the North, and countries of the South cannot often produce the same goods as are made in the North. Products are not truly substitutable.

In that respect, accounting for the employment content of trade gives interesting results.[10] For the North, trade with the South has no significant effect on high-skilled employment but a strong impact on low-skilled employment with a loss of 6 per cent, which translates into 3 per cent of total employment. This could explain a third of the rise in structural unemployment. For the South the effect would be positive and increase employment by 3 per cent. On the whole the welfare effect is positive for both regions.

It is clear that international trade has had an important impact on wage inequality in the US. Even the strong increase in the supply of qualified workers has not been strong enough to balance that effect. It seems also that this phenomenon is becoming evident in most OECD countries, and that in some of these countries it has met with strong resistance because of fears that it may be responsible for an increase in structural unemployment.

The chapter in Volume II by Derseh Endale emphasizes the problems in Africa. The chapter shows clear-cut evidence that there is a general rise in unemployment in Africa and that there is a dramatic increase in highly qualified people. Although one may suspect a bias in the census which overestimates underemployment for highly qualified people because they live in urban areas and have easier access to bureaucrats than illiterate rural workers, there is nevertheless an increase in the waste of human resources and inadequate development of people in Africa. On the other hand, the chapter by Valentine Moghadam shows that export-led industrialization has led to increased employment for men and especially women. M. Fouquin (1990) has shown that there has been a much greater increase in real wages in East Asia than in the Western developed countries, and that the gap in wages has been diminishing rapidly. There is also strong evidence that the increase in wages was faster in East Asia for highly qualified people than for blue collar workers. The conclusion may be that development reduces international inequality between growing nations but increases inequality between citizens.

The new competition in perspective

At first sight, trade with less developed countries (LDCs) and/or relocation of production facilities there is a poor candidate for explaining unemployment problems in the North. For France (the picture is roughly similar in big European countries) imports from non-OECD countries account for less than 12 per cent of total imports and outward direct investment is less than 7 per cent.

This picture is obviously misleading. Bilateral trade data fail to take into account competition in third markets. FDI data cover a limited amount of the total investment made in LDCs (in fact, we know that employment by French affiliates amounts to 23 per cent of total manufacturing employment in France). The reason is that these data ignore the fact that relocation of production facilities does not necessarily imply a direct investment abroad by the same country. Furthermore, relocation is a very narrow concept whose relevance is disputable. What is important is that emerging countries have access to Northern technology, that they build up production facilities, that they produce goods designed for the developed countries' markets, and that finally the goods are exported. Therefore the first indicator of the emergence of new competitors is trade.

Figure 10.1 presents the share of developing countries (including NICs) in world exports of manufactured goods. There is clearly an upward trend, though no clear evidence of a recent acceleration.

FIGURE 10.1
Developing countries' share of world manufacturing exports

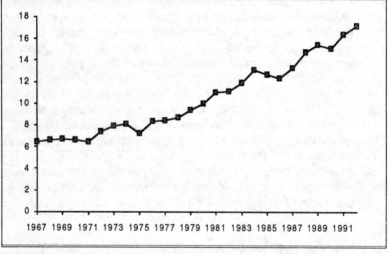

Source: CEPII–CHELEM

Figure 10.1 indicates that the share of developing countries in world exports of manufactured goods has gained about 10 percentage points over the last two decades. How dramatic is this gain? In order to put it in a historical perspective, Table 10.1 provides elements on the changes in market shares over the last century. Two interesting references are: the rise of Germany and the US at the end of the nineteenth century; and that of Japan after the Second World War. In both cases, changes in market shares were of a similar order of magnitude (10 percentage points), though spread out over a longer period of time (four decades rather than two).

TABLE 10.1
Export market shares: 1870–1987 (%)

	1870	1913	1950	1973	1987
France	16.8	10.3	8.7	9.4	8.9
Germany	13.1	19.1	5.7	17.4	17.7
United Kingdom	30.1	19.9	18.0	7.6	7.9
USA	12.5	18.5	29.2	18.4	15.3
Japan	0.5	2.5	2.3	9.5	13.9
Others	27.0	29.7	36.1	37.6	36.2
Industrialized countries	100	100	100	100	100

Source: Maddison, A. (1991) *Dynamic Forces in Capitalist Development,* Oxford.

Acceleration is also apparent when one looks at the performance of individual exporters (Figure 10.2). Starting in the mid-1950s when exports had recovered from the consequences of the war, it took 15 years for Japan to multiply its export volume by a factor of ten. The corresponding achievement was reduced to 12 years for Korea and Taiwan. If present trends continue, it should be some 10 years for China. This suggests the existence of some kind of learning curve for emerging countries, but not all countries are able to achieve comparable performances: Figure 10.2 also shows that Mexico and the Mediterranean countries are on a different path. In fact, an important issue (to which we shall return below) is whether the experience of successful emergent countries can be repeated.

Until recently, FDI data did not indicate any accelerated drive towards relocation. On the contrary, most of the growth in FDI in the 1980s (from US$50 billion a year in the early 1980s to US$200 billion a year in the late 1980s) arose from increases in FDI among industrialized countries (and to a large extent among European countries). According to CEPII calculations, the share of developing countries in the stock of inward FDI actually decreased from 25 per cent in 1980 to 17 per cent in 1990 (de Laubier 1993).

Recent changes unambiguously indicate a resumption of the growth of inward FDI in developing countries, which is part of a more general trend towards an increase in private financial flows to developing countries. According to the IMF, FDI in LDCs increased from US$10.7 billion in 1988 to US$28 billion in 1991 and to US$47.3 billion in 1993.[11] Even a flow of that size, however, represents only about 1 per cent of domestic investment in industrialized countries, and 2–3 per cent of domestic investment in LDCs. Furthermore, FDI by Western firms in low-wage Asian countries is a small fraction of this total.[12] This can hardly be considered a dramatic move.

A different picture emerges, however, when one adopts the point of view of dynamic recipient economies. China is a good case. According to Lemoine et al.,[13] inward FDI represented 8–10 per cent of total Chinese gross capital formation in 1992, and 25–30 per cent of investment in machinery and equipment.[14] These proportions are higher for coastal regions like Guandong, where FDI amounts to 30 per cent of total investment. FDI can therefore be considered instrumental in the accelerated development of China's coastal regions. Another example is Mexico, where FDI represents some 10 per cent of total domestic investment.

A number of observations can be made in order to reconcile these two pictures:

1   FDI is concentrated in a small number of countries (and frequently in a small number of regions within countries) where it makes a significant contribution to capital formation and growth;

2   In the case of China and some other Asian countries, FDI comes from Hong Kong rather than from industrialized countries; in fact, Hong Kong accounted for 70 per cent of Chinese inward FDI in 1992;

3   Last but not least, FDI does not capture the web of inter-enterprise relations that links firms from the South and the North through a number of interrelated agreements.

LABOUR COSTS

Labour cost differences are extremely wide between developed industrialized economies and developing economies or economies in transition. Typical figures give an order of magnitude of 1:5 between NICs and industrialized countries. They reach 1:10 for second-tier NICs and 1:20 to 1:40 for large underdeveloped economies like China and India.

As illustrated by Figure 10.2, the width of this gap is without precedent. In the nineteenth century or at the beginning of the twentieth century, wage differentials did not exceed 1:5. For example, wages in Italy were one fifth of wages in the US and half those of the UK.[15] Moreover, although they were emerging economies, wages in the US and Canada were significantly higher than those in Western Europe. This was because these countries were rich in natural resources, but poor in labour.[16]

FIGURE 10.2
Labour cost at current exchange rate (United States = 100)

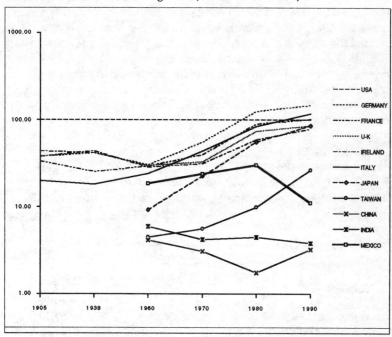

Source: J. G. Williamson (1992) NBER/DAE WP No. 36 (February)

The obvious explanation for these differences is that productivity levels are also very far apart. Available comparisons (which are rather rough) show that differences in productivity levels in manufacturing are of the same order of magnitude as differences in labour costs. According to recent research carried out using the 'industry of origin' approach,[17] productivity is 4 per cent of the US level in China,[18] 6 per cent in India, 20 per cent in Korea.[19] Corresponding figures for labour costs were 3 per cent, 6 per cent and 26 per cent in 1990.[20]

However, productivity in new, marginal production facilities is normally much higher than average productivity in emerging economies. Assuming that world-class technology is made available through FDI or licensing agreements, there are not many reasons why productivity, in the modern export-oriented sectors, should be much lower than in industrial countries. Evidence of such dualism can be found in productivity data at the industry level. According to

Ruoen and Szirmai, already in 1985 productivity in the Chinese rubber and plastic footwear industry was 45 per cent as high as in the US, while it was only 0.5 per cent as high for chemical fertilizers (similar observations were also made for the Korean case). This is consistent with the observation that the marginal productivity of capital is much higher in the South than in the North. In sectors where investment in modern capital goods and management has taken place, the result has been a dramatic improvement in labour productivity. Such a situation obviously gives a very significant unit cost advantage to the exporting sector.

INDUSTRY ISSUES
Trade between developed and developing countries is generally expected to be of the inter-industry rather than intra-industry type. This is because comparative advantage, rather than economies of

TABLE 10.2
Ten top market shares in North–South trade: 1992

A Southern shares in northern imports, top ten (%)	
Clothing	53.53
Knitwear	49.60
Leather	49.56
Consumer electronics	44.33
Carpets	36.45
Electronic components	32.69
Clock making	29.86
Toys, sports equipment and miscellaneous	29.63
Articles in wood	27.32
Computer equipment	23.58
Memo: All manufacturing	15.34
B Northern shares in southern imports, top ten (%)	
Aeronautics	98.29
Precision instruments	93.89
Construction equipment	92.65
Engines	91.52
Arms	91.06
Vehicle components	89.92
Pharmaceuticals	88.82
Specialized machines	88.20
Commercial vehicles	87.95
Machine tools	87.32
Memo: All manufacturing	74.66

Source: CEPII-CHELEM data bank.

scale, is the main source of gains from trade. It is well known that intra-industry flows dominate North-North trade, while inter-industry flows dominate North–South trade.

While both types of trade yield welfare gains, inter-industry trade imposes a higher structural adjustment burden upon the economy. This is because this burden is essentially concentrated in certain industries, regions, and categories of employees (the low-skilled categories), instead of being more uniformly distributed.

Table 10.2 illustrates this point. It lists the top ten or ten major categories of manufacturing industries in both North–South and South–North trade (including intra-EU and other intra-regional trade). In each case, industries are ranked according to the share of the exporting region in the other region's total imports.

Development policies and outward-oriented growth

Until the 1980s, the number of countries actually pursuing export-oriented policies was limited to the so-called Asian Tigers (Korea, Taiwan, Singapore and Hong Kong, whose combined population is less than one tenth that of the OECD). The view that a dramatic change in world trade is under way is partly based on the important increase in the number of countries involved in international supply of manufactured goods. Together with the demise of the Eastern bloc, the spread of outward-oriented policies across the developing world during the 1980s is responsible for this increase.

THE SPREAD OF OUTWARD-ORIENTED POLICIES
In the first years of the 1980s, ideological and economic conditions were mustered to spread trade liberalization and outward-oriented growth policies across the developing world.

During the 1970s, theoretical studies and empirical investigations started to question the validity of the protectionist view which had dominated development economics and development policies for years. Serious drawbacks of these policies were pointed out. They had excessively encouraged industrialization at the cost of reducing the incentives for expanding agriculture and exports. High protection in the import-competing sectors had produced high negative effective protection in the export sectors, mainly through currency overvaluation. The results were a worsening of income distribution, the reduction of savings, increases in the rate of unemployment, and very low rates of capacity utilization.[21] Opening up to competition – both external and internal – seemed to be the way to raise economic efficiency. The dramatic contrast between the success of the four Asian NICs and the failure of the inward-looking economies of Latin America gave strong support to this argument. Export promotion strategies started to be strongly advocated as a superior development strategy.

Of course, during the 1970s, most developing countries had registered rather high growth performances compared to their historical records, but in the inward-oriented economies, this growth was mainly financed by rising indebtedness, sometimes at unsustainable levels.

The debt crisis in 1982 played a major role in reshaping policy views regarding development strategies. Export gains appeared to be the safest way to finance imports. In the short term, the financial assistance from Bretton Woods institutions was the only way out of financial crisis. The adoption by indebted countries of structural adjustment programmes designed with these institutions became the condition required by creditors for debt restructuring and financial assistance. The fact that most of the developing countries were faced with major debt burdens led to a rapid spread of adjustment programmes over the developing world. Trade liberalization has been a central part of these adjustment packages. Forty-two countries have received loans from the World Bank during the 1980s with the express purpose of reforming their trade regimes.[22]

TRADE LIBERALIZATION AND DEVALUATION

The objectives of trade liberalization were to reduce the anti-export bias and to improve allocation efficiency by liberalizing the import regime. The aim was to transform international trade into 'the engine of growth'.

At the same time, it is worth noting that the definition of trade liberalization is far from unanimous. Opinions among economists range between reducing the degree of anti-export bias and implementing free trade. For some, a policy of export orientation is consistent with a moderate degree of protection. Moreover, many authors point out that the four most successful East Asian exporters – although definitely outward-oriented – have pursued protectionist strategies simultaneously in some of their industries.

However, in recent years, many developing countries have liberalized their tariff regimes by simplifying tariff structures, reducing rates and eliminating quantitative restrictions. More than 20 of them have become GATT members during the past ten years.

Apart from the elimination of anti-export bias through trade liberalization, currency devaluation has been a powerful means of export promotion. The devaluations, as long as they raise import prices, have simultaneously helped to ensure that tariff liberalization remains consistent with balance of payments goals. Many countries adopted a floating exchange rate system in the course of the 1980s. The result was a significant depreciation of their currencies against the dollar and the other major currencies

The success of these outward-oriented policies is illustrated by the data provided by the IMF in 1993.[23] The acceleration of export growth and the diversification of exports, towards non-traditional and manufactured goods, were rather impressive in some cases.

PROSPECTS

Is 'trade optimism' definitively about to overcome 'trade pessimism'? Three arguments support the optimistic view.

First, a positive association between exports and economic growth is found in many empirical investigations (such as the survey made by the World Bank in 1992). This correlation does not prove causality, but it does give some weight to those who advocate export-oriented policies. Second, export performance is lasting. It seems to be subject to strong hysteresis. 'Once a decisive increase in export is achieved, the process tends to be self-perpetuating even when the originally advantageous circumstances reverse somewhat.' In Korea or Turkey, for example, exports were not affected by the appreciation of the currency.[24] Third, the supply response to an increase in the price of an exportable is large, and often very quick.

Furthermore, the trade opening of Eastern Europe and the former Soviet Union will contribute to an increase in the supply of manufactured goods. However, some important questions have not yet received clear-cut answers. Some refer to the export supply. For those countries which succeeded in export promotion, a critical question is whether the rapid growth and diversification of exports can be sustained. The hysteresis previously mentioned was observed in relatively short periods. Comparisons made between adjusting countries and non-adjusting countries show that the former tend to do better in export and economic growth, but worse in investment.[25] This means an increase in efficiency of investment, but raises concern about future export capacity and competitiveness. Other questions emerge about those countries which have not yet succeeded in manufacturing export. Would they react to the opening of their economies in the same way as their predecessors did – or is this kind of positive reaction only typical of semi-industrialized countries? Is export promotion feasible in countries where import substitution industrialization has failed totally? Negative answers would mean that the number of competing nations in the next decade will not exceed by much the present number.

Finally, questions arise about the demand side. As supply from the emerging countries increases, it is not clear whether competition among this group of countries will develop (through price competition and the search for privileged access to the Western markets) or whether the range of goods supplied by low-cost producers will expand. There are also questions about the developed countries' behaviour. During the 1980s, 20 out of 24 industrial countries increased their protection against manufactured or processed products from LDCs. This growing protection and the recession in the industrialized countries raise the recurrent adding-up problem: export-oriented policies have proved successful when implemented by a small number of small countries – can they also succeed if undertaken by a large number of large countries?

Unfair competition?

The competition from emerging countries has frequently been considered 'unfair'. In this section, we discuss on what grounds it could be regarded as such.

Discussions of unfair competition are frequently confused and inconclusive. There are several reasons for this. First, it is an extremely difficult issue analytically, because it touches on different fields of research and analysis which are the subject of separate theories: trade economics, international monetary economics (because of the exchange rate), and the theory of justice. Second, there is no generally accepted definition of fairness in international trade. Third, there is no generally accepted definition of what appropriate social standards are. Fourth, differences in social norms are no obstacle to trade, either at the theoretical or at the practical level. We will therefore limit ourselves to a few remarks.

However wide they are, differences in labour wage and non-wage costs, the degree of social protection, or the extent of regulation in the workplace *per se* are not sufficient reasons for regarding the emerging economies' competition as unfair. Legitimate motives for concern may arise, however, on purely economic grounds.[26] This happens if there is evidence that a country is behaving in a beggar-thy-neighbour fashion. In that respect, two cases deserve closer examination.

An obvious possibility is exchange rate policy. Maintaining an undervalued real exchange rate, that is, keeping the value of labour at international prices below the level consistent with productivity, can help attract foreign capital and gain market shares at the expense of neighbouring countries.[27]

There has been discussion among French economists on this particular issue, under the heading 'monetary dumping'.[28] The empirical evidence is mixed, since the appropriate level of an exchange rate is extremely difficult to assess. Purchasing Power Parity is the only available norm at hand; however, it is empirically rather rough and theoretically biased.[29] Some estimates indicate, for example, that the Chinese yuan and the baht of Thailand are significantly undervalued, but there is no clear consensus in that respect.

In the case of a deliberate undervaluation of the exchange rate, the appropriate response should be to ask the IMF to tighten its surveillance role *vis-à-vis* the country. Exchange rate policies are subject to multilateral surveillance (Article 4 of the IMF statutes), and the Fund is entrusted with this role. However, the main concern of multilateral organizations in the recent decades has been to assist and advise individual countries in their stabilization and growth policies. This suggests the possibility of a country-by-country bias, in which the global effects of the individual countries' exchange rate policies have been overlooked.

Readjusting some exchange rates will not really change the nature of the problem. As discussed above, emerging economies are characterized by wide differences in productivity among industries and enterprises. The standard example is the existence of a large, low-productivity agricultural sector, but the same reasoning can be applied to countries in transition. There, a traditional and inefficient state sector, whose 'value added' is very low and can even be negative at international prices in some industries, coexists with a new, modern one. Similar observations can be made in the case of countries who have recently dismantled trade protection. In such cases of pronounced dualism, should the exchange rate be set at a level consistent with unit labour costs in the traditional or in the efficient sector? The appropriate response should probably be for these countries to rely more on another instrument, namely tariffs, in order to protect the traditional sector, rather than to ensure that the traditional sector remains viable through an undervaluation of the exchange rate,[30] but this would conflict with liberalization objectives, at least on political economy grounds. The sad truth is that there is probably no satisfactory solution to the problem.

A different case is that of a deliberate lowering of social standards by a government in an attempt to attract foreign capital. It should be emphasized that governments do not necessarily face incentives to take such action. Social standards can be perfectly justified on purely economic grounds, as they correct market failures and help in achieving efficiency. For example, prohibiting child labour or regulating working time can help raise economic efficiency through creating favourable conditions for the accumulation of human capital. Governments should therefore implement this type of regulation on pure economic efficiency grounds.[31] However, governments can adopt sub-optimal standards in an attempt to attract capital and to gain more from this capital inflow than they lose from the inadequate character of the regulation. This is what could be considered social dumping, and as generally in the case of coordination problems, the appropriate response should probably be found in a multilateral framework through a mix of rules and explicit coordination.

Conclusions

This chapter began by asking whether competition from the emerging countries will increase and accelerate. The short answer is that it will. For decades, international economists have been wondering why capital did not flow to the developing world, where the marginal productivity of investment (MPI) was much higher than in the North. In addition to human capital (which was not a sufficient factor), the standard answers were political risk and externality effects.[32] Political risk has been, in part, removed through wide-ranging reforms supported by the governments of the North and by international organizations. As human and physical capital have begun to accumulate, externalities now contribute to an acceleration of growth and in the catching-up process.

The rise of this new competition is obviously a major challenge to the developed economies, especially to the European ones. The problem it raises is neither a problem of trade imbalances (because emerging economies, with the exception of Taiwan, exhibit no tendency to systematic trade surplus), nor a problem for growth (the aggregate effect of this new competition might well be positive for economic growth in the North),[33] but it is obviously a problem for unskilled labour in the North. As mentioned earlier, there is an intense debate about the impact of that kind of trade on wage inequality and/or employment. For us it is clear that the impact is important whether it is a direct impact or an indirect one (increased competition increases the pressure to rationalize production in the short run). As the pressure will increase in the future it is of paramount importance in developed countries to adapt human capital accumulation to these trends. Another major problem comes from the location of new competition and new partnership. Japan, which is very close to Asian NICs, has many opportunities to make profit from Asian development; on the other hand, Europe is facing the difficulties (and sharing the cost) of the transition process in Eastern Europe, not to speak of Africa and the Middle East. A more intensive cooperation of developed countries is urgently needed.

NOTES
1 BMWI (1993) *Zur Zukunftversicherung des Standortes Deustchland*, September.
2 Arthuis, J. (1993) *Rapport sur l'incidence Èconomique et fiscal des délocalisations*. Sénat, June.
3 Cortès, O. and S. Jean (1994) *Commerce international et marché du travail: critique des mÈthodes d'analyse sur le cas des Etats-Unis*, mimeo, CEPII, May.
4 This section is translated from O. Cortes and S. Jean (1994) in *La Lettre du CEPII*, March.
5 Bound, J. and G. Johnson (1992) 'Changes in the structure of wages in the 1980s: an evaluation of alternative explanations', *The American Economic Review*; Borjas G., R. Freeman and L. Katz, 'On the labour effects of immigration and trade', NBER Working Paper, No. 3761.
6 Revanga, A. (1992) 'Exporting jobs: the impact of import competition on employment and wages in US manufacturing', *The Quarterly Journal of Economics*, No. 107 (February).
7 Murphy, K. M. and F. Welch (1992) 'The structure of wages', *The Quarterly Journal of Economics*, No. 107 (February).
8 Lawrence R. and M. J. Slaughter (1993) 'Trade and US wages: great sucking or small hiccup?', Brookings Papers on Economic Activity: Microeconomics.
9 Oliveira-Martins, J. (1993) 'Market structure, international trade and relative wages', OECD Working Paper No. 134.
10 Wood, A. (1992) 'The factor content of North–South trade in manufactures reconsidered', Weltwirtschaftliches Archiv.
11 *World Economic Outlook*, April 1994.
12 Laubier, D. de (1994) 'Les implantations dans le Sud-Est asiatique: des craintes excessives?', *Economie internationale*, No. 57 (premier trimestre).
13 Lemoine, F., M. Dramé, and A. de Saint-Vaulry (1994) 'Hong Kong – Chine: un dragon à deux têtes', *Economie internationale*, No. 57 (premier trimestre).
14 Proportions vary according to the exchange rate used for calculations.
15 Based on data provided in Williamson (1992) NBER, Working Paper No. 36.
16 In O'Rourke, K. and J. G. Williamson (1992) 'Were Hecksche-Ohlin

right', NBER, Working Paper No. 37 (June). Williamson argues that this is precisely the context in which the factor price equalization theorem was put forward.

17 Ark, B. van (1993) 'The ICOP approach – its implications and applicability', in A. Szirmai, B. van Ark and D. Pilat (eds) *Explaining Economic Growth*, Elsevier.

18 Ruoen, R. and A. Szirmai (1993) *China's Manufacturing Performance: An Industry of Origin Comparison [preliminary]*, mimeo, August.

19 Figures refer to the second half of the 1980s.

20 Source: CEPII data base on labour costs, based on US Bureau of Labour statistics data and other sources.

21 Edwards, S. (1993) 'Openness, trade liberalisation, and growth in developing countries', *Journal of Economic Literature*, Vol. 31: 1358–93 (September).

22 Rodrick, D. (1992) 'The limits of trade policy reform in developing countries', *Journal of Economic Perspectives*, Vol. 6, No. 1 (Winter) pp. 87–105.

23 IMF (1993) BIS Economic Papers No. 39 (November).

24 Rodrick, D. (1993) *Trade and Industrial Policy Reform in Developing Countries: A Review of Recent Theory and Evidence*, NBER Working Paper No. 4417.

25 *Ibid*.

26 We leave aside the ethical and humanitarian dimensions of the issue. In these cases, the primary motive for international intervention does not arise from economic considerations, and the rational motive for using economic sanctions (trade sanctions, for example) is essentially a matter of efficiency. Economists would generally warn against the use of economic sanctions, because of the risk of overlap (or contradiction) between general humanitarian objectives and narrowly defined economic interests. When feasible, an explicit conditionality in the operation of international organizations would be preferable. But this is, in any event, a separate debate.

27 To the extent that the issue is the average level of wages with respect to the rest of the world, it can be assimilated to a real exchange-rate problem.

28 Lafay, G., and J. M. Siroën (1994) *Maîtriser le libre-échange*, Economica; and Pisani-Ferry, J. (1993) *Délocalisation et compétition du Sud*, Report for the French Planning Agency.

29 A well-known bias is the so-called 'Balassa effect', which states that as productivity differences between developed and developing economies are smaller for the non-tradables sector than for the tradables sector, the equilibrium exchange rate of a developing country (that is, the PPP exchange rate for tradables) is lower than the PPP exchange rate.

30 This was suggested a few years ago by McKinnon in the context of economies in transition.

31 This argument was put forward in the CEPR 1993 report on Monitoring European Integration.

32 Lucas, R. (1990) 'Why doesn't capital flow from rich to poor countries?', *American Economic Review* (May). Using a standard Cobb-Douglas production function, Lucas computed that on the basis of relative GDP

per capita, MPI in India should be 60 times higher than in the US! This evaluation is scaled down to 5 if human capital endowments are taken into account. The rest can be accounted for by political risk or the external effects of human capital accumulation.

33 Mathieu and Sterdyniak (1994) consider that the net effect of the emergence of Asian competitors has been to lower French GDP by 1.3 percentage points. However, the counterpart of this loss is likely to be a net gain for Japan. The overall effect of the emerging countries' competition should be distinguished from its distribution among industrial economies.

11

Globalization and the Restructuring
of the European Labour Market:
The Role of Migration

– H.W. OVERBEEK –

Since the mid-1970s there has been a rapid increase in the numbers of international refugees and (illegal) migrants. Western Europe has been one of the major regions of destination for these population movements. Many observers have spoken of a crisis, and three factors seem to warrant such a characterization: the rapid growth in the numbers of international migrants between the mid-1970s and the late 1980s; the presumed loss of control by governments of trans-border movements; and the rise of right-wing extremism in Western Europe mobilizing anti-immigrant sentiments.

Other aspects of the immigration issue have received less attention in the public debate. Nevertheless, as the following pages will illustrate, the issue of immigration is closely related to the process of the restructuring of the labour market taking place under the impact of intensifying global competition. We will attempt to highlight the interconnections between the processes of globalization, labour market restructuring, and the building of a joint European immigration policy.

First, this chapter will briefly discuss alternative explanations for this increased migration before it discusses the process of globalization, the changing structure of the welfare state and, in particular, the labour market in Europe as well as the role of immigrants in these processes, and finally the way in which these changes are reflected in the emerging new European immigration regime.

Explaining the international migration and refugee crisis

Explanations of international migration, and particularly of the refugee crisis of the 1990s, involve a variety of factors. One type of explanation considers the present refugee crisis in terms of such unique events as the collapse of 'really existing socialism' (leading to

East–West migration) or the effects of civil war, famines, or natural disasters in many Third World states (leading to increased migration from South to North). A second type of explanation accords primary importance to long-term factors such as the demographic and development gap between the North and the South. This approach is also known as the root causes approach. Finally, a third type of explanation points at the restructuring of the world political and economic order taking place since the 1970s as the main reason for the rapid increase in South–North migration since the 1980s.

This chapter departs from the viewpoint that a comprehensive explanation of contemporary migration movements should in fact consist of a combination of these three perspectives. The historical process is layered, and a recognition of this important insight allows a better understanding of the interconnections between different processes. Concretely, the current migration and refugee crisis is to be understood as the composite outcome of various historical processes with a rhythm and a dynamic of their own.

THE SHORT-TERM REALITY OF THE CRISIS
The European and North American member states of the Inter-Governmental Consultations on Asylum, Refugee and Migration Policies[1] recorded almost 200,000 asylum applications in 1985 (up from 92,400 in 1983), and 644,900 in 1991, with another 71,000 applications recorded in Australia (16,000) and in Central and Southern Europe (55,000).[2] These numbers have led to reactions little short of panic in West European government circles.

One of the first reactions has been to call for assistance to refugees to be given in their region of origin. This call, uncritically repeated by politicians of most persuasions, ignores completely the fact that refugees overwhelmingly remain within their region of origin. By 1992, the world counted 17 million officially registered refugees and asylum seekers. Of those 17 million, 13.2 million (78 per cent) were located in the Third World, a further 2 million refugees from the former Yugoslavia were located in European countries (the bulk in Croatia, Serbia, Slovenia, Hungary, Austria – that is, in their own region), and some 1.8 million (just over 10 per cent) in Western Europe and North America.[3] In addition, some 4 million people in the Third World are considered to be in refugee-like situations, and an estimated 23 million people are internally displaced. In Western Europe, with a *per capita* GNP of between US$15,000 and US$30,000, asylum seekers make up 0.3 per cent of the population; in Malawi, with its *per capita* income of US$180, the figure stands at 10 per cent.[4]

The regions producing the largest numbers of refugees in the 1980s were Afghanistan (3 million Afghans fled to Iran, 3 million to Pakistan), the Horn of Africa (more than 2 million refugees in and from Sudan, Ethiopia, Somalia, Kenya), Southern Africa (over 1.5 million Mozambicans and 0.5 million Angolans), Yugoslavia (2 million), and Central America and the Caribbean (1.2 million).[5] Very recent hotbeds of refugee-producing conflicts have been the Caucasian region of the former Soviet Union, Myanmar (Burma), Haiti, and (yet again) Burundi and Rwanda. Behind each of these statistics lies a unique tale of human drama, of political upheaval, of dictatorship and exploitation, of ethnic or religious strife, and of superpower politics. It is only by taking the particulars of the situation in specified countries or regions into account, such as the precise trajectory of the drama in Yugoslavia, the clan wars in Somalia, or the political games played with the Haitian refugees in the Caribbean waters, that one can understand each case in its full complexity.

Simultaneously, however, the length of the list of crises and cases suggests that, in their totality, they cannot be understood only in terms of their own specificities. An explanation in more structural terms is called for.

ROOT CAUSES

The opposite approach to the question of the determination of migrant and refugee flows is the search for root causes. In approaches of this type, three fundamental processes stand out: demographic pressure, poverty, and ecological deterioration. It must be emphasized here that the three factors are not independent but interrelated. Poverty leads to erosion of land and loss of forests, population pressure is not an absolute variable, but is related to economic and ecological carrying capacity. In fact, we have here the determinants of what in many cases is a fatal triangle, the short-term outcome of which can be only marginally affected by human intervention.

When looked at from this perspective, migration can be explained in terms of the interaction of push and pull factors originating from ecological, demographic and socio-economic disparities. The demographic transition model predicts that countries in the second and third stages of modernization (with a rapidly declining death rate and a continued high birth rate) will display high mass-emigration potentials. Countries in the fourth stage of modernization, with stagnant populations, will become immigration countries. If the recent population explosion in the Third World is extrapolated into the future and combined with data about the structural poverty of the region in question, it can then be concluded that migration pressures will continue to rise, unless something drastic is undertaken.

And indeed, the most authoritative projections of world population are alarming, especially in the case of the differential growth rates of the countries of the European Union on one hand, and the African continent on the other. Over the period 1980–91, GNP *per capita* grew by an average of 2.3 per cent annually in the countries of the Organization for Economic Cooperation and Development (OECD); the average annual change in *per capita* GNP was negative both in sub-Saharan Africa (minus 1.2 per cent) and in the Middle East and North Africa (minus 2.4 per cent).[6] The projected population growth for these regions in the years 1991–2000 is 0.5 per cent per year for the OECD, against 2.9 per cent for the Middle East and North Africa, and 3 per cent for sub-Saharan Africa. By 2020, the population of the EU will be back at the 1990 level, while the population of the African continent will have more than doubled.

Demographic pressure and poverty are closely linked. Two reports prepared in the 1980s under the authority of the former UN High Commissioner for Refugees, Sadruddin Aga Khan, identified underdevelopment as the root cause of South–North migration and refugee movements. Aga Khan noted that

unless you really address the problem of development, you are never going to be able to circumscribe movements of people, whether they are refugees for economic, political or ecological reasons.[7]

Whatever the validity of these explanations for longer-term patterns of migration and population movement, they do not suffice if we want to understand the rapid increase in the numbers of migrants and refugees since the late 1970s. The facts contradict the hypothesis that extreme poverty produces migration and refugees: generally speaking, the poorest people do not migrate across borders, and where they do (Haiti, for example) they are, in fact, the last social stratum to join the migration.[8] Additional conditions (of a political nature) have to apply for poverty to lead to migration. In his analysis of labour migration from underdeveloped to developed countries, Alejandro Portes came to the same conclusion:

labor migration does not occur through external comparisons of economic advantage between countries and regions but requires the penetration of economic and political institutions of the centers into peripheral and outlying areas.[9]

There is every reason to assume that the same holds true for spontaneous movements of asylum seekers to Europe and the USA. The trek of Central American and Caribbean asylum seekers to the USA has everything to do with the historical role of the USA and of American capital in the region, just as the massive flow of asylum seekers from Central and Eastern Europe to Germany cannot be explained only by the factors of proximity and constitutional leniency, but must also be understood in the context of Germany's historical ties with the regions in question. Germany's role in the unfolding drama in Yugoslavia is a case in point. The role of the state (both in sending and in receiving countries) is thus of paramount importance. That states are not always successful in regulating migration flows does not change the fundamental fact that 'it is precisely the control which states exercise over borders that defines international migration as a distinctive social process'.[10]

It is states which have often initiated and usually regulated flows of migrant labour, and it is states which have determined who will be recognized as refugees and will have a place to take refuge in.

In order to be able to analyse the structural context in which the role of states in circumscribing migration has developed in the past two decades, we need to introduce a medium-term perspective.

GLOBAL RESTRUCTURING

The state does not exist in isolation, is not an independent variable, but is inserted in a complex structure: it is shaped by social forces (national and transnational), and by the manner of its insertion into the world order. The relationships between these three levels are not unilinear but reciprocal, each 'containing, as well as bearing the impact of, the others'.[11]

In this chapter, the focus will be on the way in which changes taking place since the 1970s, both in the sphere of social forces (becoming more and more transnational) and in the world order, differentially affect the state in different parts of the world, and particularly the state in its role as regulator of migration and refugee movements.

First, the transformation of the world economy since the early 1970s has resulted in the emergence of global finance, global production, and an increasingly global labour market. Against the backdrop of this globalizing tendency, new growth regions in the world economy attract large flows of labour, while other regions are marginalized and become exporters of labour. The end of the Cold War and the collapse of Soviet power have transformed the world order in the political and military-strategic spheres as well.

A second dimension of the process of global restructuring is the collapse of stable social structures in large parts of the Third World, and more recently in the former socialist countries of Eastern Europe. In many of these countries, civil society was weakly developed, and it was the state which provided a measure of social cohesion and political stability. The breakdown of the state in these cases (whether as a result of the imposition of structural adjustment and liberalization, the withdrawal of military and financial aid after the end of the Cold War, or the collapse of really existing socialism) releases and intensifies social, religious, ethnic, and nationality tensions to the point where a rapidly growing number of people have to flee for fear of violence and war.

Thirdly, the concomitant restructuring of the social relations of production on a global scale takes place in several dimensions. Technological changes lead to a recomposition of the working class, involving a new segmentation of the labour market along lines of gender, ethnicity, and age. The welfare state is redefined, trimmed, hollowed out, and all of these processes have an impact on the size, direction, and nature of migration movements.[12]

The impact of global restructuring on the core

In the developed industrial countries, global restructuring also implies the restructuring of the social relations of production: the replacement of the Fordist organization of mass production with the concomitant entrenched power of organized labour and the safety net of the Keynesian welfare state by the new structures of post-Fordist flexible accumulation and the run-down of mass production, the traditional stronghold of the (white, male) organized working class.[13] The structures of tripartism and state corporatism are replaced by enterprise corporatism, just-in-time delivery systems and sub-contracting. This process is accompanied by the expansion of the service sector employing non-established workers (women, ethnic minorities, migrants). According to Cox, these processes amount to the establishment of a core–periphery structure within the advanced capitalist economies, with increased mobility of labour matching the liberalization of trade and finance.

The core of the labour market is composed of highly skilled, highly paid labour. The restructuring of production and the rise of such new global sectors as transnational advertising have created a highly internationalized labour market with a great deal of cross-border migration of professional transients.

On the periphery of the increasingly bifurcated labour market we

find the 'use of a more precariously employed labour force segmented by ethnicity, gender, nationality, or religion'.[14]

According to a recent survey of the Dutch labour market, this
bifurcation has occurred and the legal labour market for immigrants
exists mainly in two segments: the upper range of the labour market,
including the segment of expatriate workers being employed by
their own overseas company; and the segment of 'temporary,
artistic, or low paid work of a more secondary or irregular nature'.[15]

Below this lowest rung of the legal labour market we find the
subterranean segment of illegal labour. From the point of view of the
eventual position on the labour market it makes little difference
whether we look at illegal economic migrants or at refused asylum
seekers who have gone underground; they all have to survive in the
seams of the official economy.[16] Throughout the OECD countries,
this development is reflected particularly in the peripheralization of
labour in the global cities. One element has been the re-emergence of
domestic labour: a rapidly growing demand for domestic workers is
filled by large numbers of Third World women, replaced in Western
Europe in recent years by East European women. Looking at another
sector, Ross and Trachte have analysed the reappearance of
sweatshop production in the New York garment industry, and
conclude that

> There exists within New York, the global city, a substantial growing
> segment of the labor force whose conditions of production resemble
> those of the labor force in the Third World.... Sweatshops in New York
> are the logical consequence of the globalization of production in the
> garment industry and the consequent competition for jobs between
> segments of the global reserve of labor.[17]

In many European metropolises, too, sweatshop production
utilizing illegal immigrant labour has become significant. Thus in
Amsterdam there are, by the estimate of the Public Prosecutor,
around 500 illegal sweatshops in the garment industry alone, mostly
employing illegal Turkish immigrant workers.[18] And the phenomenon is not restricted to the garment industry. Spain recently
concluded an agreement with Morocco which regulated the
recruitment of temporary workers. In Spain migrant workers are
primarily employed in construction: the World Exhibition in Seville
and the Olympic Games in Barcelona were made possible through
their efforts.[19] In Italy, it is estimated that the informal sector
accounts for 20 per cent of GDP.[20] In California, it is estimated that
half of the state's million agricultural workers are illegal Mexican
immigrants, with the proportion rising rapidly.[21] And in France,

Immigrant labour ... is part of a clandestine workforce which keeps the wheels going round. The construction industry, including the Channel Tunnel, relies on it; the fashion industry would collapse without it; domestic service would evaporate.[22]

This global restructuring also implies the end of national welfare states. The logic of inter-state competition imposes further and further flexibilization and weakens the position of labour. The imperative of flexible accumulation erodes the protective shield of the state in the core. Under the impact of competitiveness, the Keynesian welfare state is gradually trimmed down, more quickly where resistance is weak (as in the USA or Britain), more slowly where resistance is tougher (Germany, Scandinavia), but unmistakably in the same direction. Bob Jessop has given this process the label 'hollowing out'. The Keynesian welfare state is hollowed out, eroded from within, and in the process transformed into a Schumpeterian workfare state (SWS).

Its distinctive economic and social objectives can be summarized in abstract terms as: to promote product, process, organizational, and market innovation and enhance the structural competitiveness of open economies mainly through supply-side intervention; and to subordinate social policy to the demands of labour market flexibility and structural competitiveness.[23] A growing supply of irregular, non-unionized, low-paid labour is essential for the SWS, and undocumented immigration is quite functional from this perspective.

The employment of foreign labour has become a condition for the continued existence of many small and medium-sized firms, and thus there is a substantial interest in continued (illegal) immigration.[24] Several authors argue (it would take us too far to pursue the point in more detail here) that immigration has a positive long-term economic effect (in terms of job creation, income generation, and reproduction of the labour force).

This effect is not restricted to the economic effect of legal immigration. The official labour market and the illegal or informal labour market are not separated by a watertight screen; they are connected and operate as communicating vessels. It is even possible to argue that policies devised to diminish illegal immigration, in effect strengthen the development of a segmented labour market and hence the demand for illegal migrant workers.

On the other hand, there are political forces which successfully use the economic and social crisis in order to mobilize xenophobia and racism in order to create a climate of social and political unrest. The governments in Western Europe are under increasing pressure from different sides, and attempt to maintain a balance between the compelling logic of interstate competition and the rising pressure upon them from the right. These contradictions are also reflected in the emerging European immigration regime.

Towards a European immigration and refugee regime

To some extent, it may be said that the Triadic regions have developed differential ways and means of dealing with the pressures generated by the globalization process. Japan has aimed at externalizing the effects as much as possible by exporting the production processes instead of importing labour. But the nature of certain industries (e.g. construction) limits the applicability of such a strategy. On the other hand, Western Europe as a whole might be said to have internalized the segmentation of its labour market, but there, too, there are important differences between the major European countries determined by their different histories and the different ways social compromises have become institutionalized over time. In North America there are yet other mixes to be observed. It is, however, not too audacious to remark that there are clear tendencies towards convergence of developments and policies between the core regions. Since the mid-1980s there is an intensification of cooperation in this field among the OECD member states and the member states of the Council of Europe. These contacts are for the time being limited to the level of intergovernmental consultation.

The member states of the EU have gone further and have gradually developed elements of a joint policy in the sphere of migration and asylum. This intensification is usually explained by the perceived need for a common policy after the abolition of internal border controls with the Single Market Act signed in 1986.[25] In the emerging common policy a number of elements can be discerned, each reflecting aspects of the developments which we have sketched briefly in the earlier sections.

The first concern of the European states has been to develop a system for dealing with those asylum seekers who succeed in reaching the territory of the EU and call on the established procedures for dealing with asylum requests. The main instruments of this system are the Schengen Agreement, the Dublin Convention, and the introduction of the concept of safe countries. The Schengen Treaty of 1985 (devised primarily to coordinate the policing of international crime and terrorism after the abolition of border controls) and the Schengen Execution Agreement of 1990 (ratified but still not in operation), concluded between first five and now nine EU members

(Britain, Ireland and Denmark are not part of Schengenland), purports to determine the responsibility for examining asylum requests within Schengenland. The Dublin Convention Determining the State Responsible for Examining Applications for Asylum Lodged in One of the Member States of the European Communities (drafted by the Ad Hoc Group on Immigration) does the same, but in this case for all 12 members of the EU. Both Schengen and Dublin are clear on one point: asylum requests will not be heard by more than one of the contracting parties. Both treaties, however, fail to guarantee that a refugee's request will be materially examined by at least one of the contracting states:

> Every Contracting Party retains the right, on the basis of its own laws and in conformity with its international commitments, to refuse entry to an applicant for asylum or to remove him to a Third State (Schengen Agreement, Article 29(2)).

The two arrangements in effect restrict severely the access of asylum seekers to a fair hearing of their case, and in this sense contradict the 1951 Geneva Refugee Convention. The Geneva Convention was further eroded by the introduction of the notion of safe countries by the ministerial conference held in London in December 1992, making it possible to send back without a hearing of their case those asylum claimants coming from countries deemed to be safe. The preservation of national autonomy in the determination of the criteria to be applied leads to a spiral of 'downward harmonization' resembling a self-propelling series of competitive currency devaluations. Moves by one state to restrict access to its asylum procedures or directly to its labour markets lead to similar responses by neighbouring states (as with the Dutch responses to the change in the German Constitution of 1993).

It is remarkable that the 'common' policies designed to restrict the access for asylum seekers and to limit their rights are essentially constituted outside the framework of the EU: European policy in this field is not supranational but inter-governmental. This is true not only for the Schengen Agreement, but for the Dublin Convention as well. Those EU institutions that should, at the supranational level, guarantee the rule of law – the European Court of Justice and the European Parliament – are thus effectively excluded from having any dealing with the formation and implementation of asylum policy.

In a similar vein, the position of migrants legally residing in the European Union has also been under attack, particularly with respect to their rights to family reunification and their right to form new families by marrying spouses from the country of origin.[26] Although these rights are guaranteed by international treaties, too, they have been subject to a process of continuous erosion by the EU states. In May 1993, the European Council meeting in Copenhagen called for punitive measures (including extradition) against legal immigrants employing illegal ones, marking the first time in the debate over illegal immigration that the position of legally resident immigrants has been questioned.[27]

European policies, however, are not limited to those immigrants and asylum seekers who succeed in reaching Union territory. A second pillar supporting the emerging structure is formed by the policies aimed at lowering the number of actual arrivals.

For asylum seekers arriving through the air, these policies focus on carrier sanctions, tougher visa requirements, and on-the-spot screening. The Dutch government, to give one example, in November 1993 concluded a successful three-month experiment of stationing immigration officers at Nairobi Airport to screen potential Somali refugees and to send these, when caught, to the UNHCR camps in Northern Kenya.

Asylum seekers travelling from or through states sharing borders with the EU are increasingly faced with a *cordon sanitaire* erected along the outer limits of the European Union. To the south, Morocco and Spain concluded a bilateral agreement in 1992 by which Morocco undertakes to take back all persons illegally entering Spain through Morocco.[28] North Africa has been looked upon with some anxiety by the European Commission in the past. In its 1990 Report on Immigration Policies, the Commission expressed its concern over demographic developments in the Maghreb (Commission 1990). In a report prepared for the Trilateral Commission, Doris Meissner takes a different view. She sees the Sahara as 'the real development rift to Europe's South' and, drawing a parallel with NAFTA, calls for an EU–Maghreb Association which would create a zone 'which will to some extent absorb migration pressures from more distant areas'.[29] This seems in line with the policy the Maghreb states are attempting to establish, beginning with the formation of the Union du Maghreb Arabe in 1989.

To the east, the Central European states of the Visegrad Group (Poland, Czech Republic, Slovakia, Hungary) have also agreed with the Schengen states to take back asylum seekers and illegal migrants. Similar arrangements exist bilaterally between Germany and Romania and between Germany and Bulgaria.[30] In exchange, the Western states assist technically and financially to cope with the consequences of this policy: Romania was offered DM30 million and

Bulgaria accepted an offer of DM28 million in 1992.[31] In 1993/4, Germany promised Poland DM120 million in order to improve its border controls. The result of this policy is rapidly becoming visible. More and more immigrants (from the region itself as well as from Asia and Africa) establish themselves in Central Europe and the Balkans.[32] And with improved surveillance capacity on the borders between Central Europe and the former Soviet Union, problems accumulate there. By August 1993, more than 20,000 asylum seekers from Somalia, Afghanistan and Iraq were stranded in Moscow alone. This is in addition to the more than 2 million refugees in Russia from former Soviet republics such as Georgia, Azerbaijan, and Tadjikstan. Although Russia signed the Geneva Treaty last year, the representative of the UNHCR considers it irresponsible to consider Russia as a safe country fit to receive so many refugees.[33]

And yet, it would be a mistake to think that Western Europe's borders are being closed completely. There are, to begin with, still certain categories of refugees who can successfully claim asylum (refugees from the former Yugoslavia, for example). In any case, it has never been the intention of the EU countries to block all immigration. As has been argued earlier, there is in the European economies a structural demand for cheap and irregular labour. Only part of this demand can be supplied by domestic labour, which must be complemented by immigrant labour. It is therefore no wonder that a strong pro-immigration lobby exists, openly in the United States and more indirectly in the European Union. Employers and would-be employees in many small and medium-sized firms (in construction, horticulture and the garment industry, for example) share an interest in evading immigration controls, but transnational firms, too, have recently given a cautious first signal that they would consider increased temporary immigration as a useful tool to further flexibilize the European labour market.[34]

It would seem that Germany has taken the lead in experimenting with ways to profit from the opening of the East. Since 1989 it has concluded agreements with Hungary, Poland and Czechoslovakia (now the Czech Republic) to regulate seasonal migrant labour. Recruitment for longer periods is limited to a maximum of 70,000 per year, but the possibility of obtaining a work permit for three months has been used by 120,000 Easterners in the first ten months of 1991 alone.[35] It must also be remembered that the agreement of 1991 between the Schengen countries and Poland has abolished the visa requirement for Poles for visits of up to three months. This has made it a lot easier for Polish migrant workers to work, temporarily or for longer periods, in the West.

Conclusion

We have argued in this chapter that the rapid rise in the numbers of refugees in the recent past was a process of world-wide dimensions, to be explained by the conjuncture of long-term demographic and developmental factors, short-term unique events, and such structural phenomena as the reorganization of the world economy since the 1970s and the collapse of the Cold War order. In all cases, the effects of these developments on the role and position of the state are of central importance.

In the Third World globalization erodes the capacity of the state to guarantee social cohesion. Liberalization and structural adjustment lead to a de-articulation of the state and of the existing social structures. Existing latent conflicts are triggered by this development, which explains an important part of the increased flow of migrants and refugees during the past two decades.

The official response in the EU/OECD area has been somewhat ambiguous. Governments are caught up in a web of contradictory interests and tendencies. On one side, the logic of global economic restructuring (liberalization, flexibilization) dictates acceptance of relatively high levels of immigration. On the other, the entrenched interests connected with the welfare state (pushed forward by the rise of the extreme right) attempt to maintain nationally or regionally compartmentalized labour markets such as that of the Nordic Union or the emerging European and North American arrangements. Given existing differentials between different regions of the global system (in terms of income or more generally of socio-economic and political conditions) this is an impossible task in the long run.

The solution to the contradictions arising out of the clash of these forces cannot be an even further expansion of the market at the expense of social control. Advocates of untrammelled liberalism should recall Karl Polanyi's conclusion that *laissez-faire* is not the natural order of things: 'free markets could never have come into being merely by allowing things to take their course ... *laissez-faire* itself was enforced by the state'.[36] Historical development is like the movement of a pendulum, swinging between the poles of economic liberalism and social protection. The economic liberalism of the nineteenth century made way for corporatism and welfare state capitalism. In their turn, since the 1970s, corporatism has been pushed back by the rise of neo-liberalism. Now, on the threshold of the twenty-first century, we are confronted by the consequences of this swing of the pendulum: many of today's problems of global unemployment and mass migration arise out of too little, not too much regulation and protection. It is time for the pendulum to swing the other way. There is scope and need for public intervention and protection. In the age of globalization, it is essential that this intervention should take a multilateral form. And notwithstanding its many shortcomings, what better forum than the United Nations system?

NOTES
1 The Inter-Governmental Consultations on Asylum, Refugee and Migration Policies in Europe, North America and Australia (Geneva); the members are Australia, Austria, Belgium, Canada, Denmark, Finland, France, Germany, Italy, the Netherlands, Norway, Spain, Sweden, Switzerland, the United Kingdom and the United States.
2 United Nations Population Fund (UNFPA) (1993) *The State of World Populations 1993*, United Nations, New York.
3 *El País*, 18 April 1993.
4 Collinson, S. (1993) *Europe and International Migration*, RIIA/Pinter, London.
5 UNFPA (1993) p. 32; *El Pais*, 18 April 1993.
6 World Bank (1993) *World Development Report 1993*, World Bank, Washington.
7 Zolberg, A. R. (1989) 'The next waves: migration theory for a changing world', *International Migration Review*, Vol. 23, No. 3, pp. 403–30.
8 Cf. Zolberg (1989) p. 260.
9 Portes, A. (1978) 'Migration and underdevelopment', *Politics & Society*, Vol. 8, No. 1, pp. 1–48.
10 Zolberg (1989).
11 Cox, R. W. (1986) 'Social forces, states and world orders: beyond international relations theory', in R. O. Keohane (ed.), *Neorealism and its Critics*, Columbia University Press, New York, pp. 204–54.
12 Jessop, B. (1992) 'Changing forms and functions of the state in an era of globalization and regionalization', paper presented to EAPE Conference, Paris, 4–7 November.
13 Cf. Cox, R. W. (1987) *Production, Power, and World Order. Social Forces in the Making of History*, Columbia University Press, New York.
14 Cox, R. W. (1992) 'Global perestroika', pp. 26–43 in Ralph Miliband and Leo Panitch (eds), *Socialist Register*, Merlin Press, London.
15 Muus, Ph. J. (1992) 'Nederland: iInternationale migratie, arbeidsmarkt en sociale zekerheid', pp. 5–41 in *Migratie, Arbeidsmarkt en Sociale Zekerheid*, Sociaal-Economische Raad, Den Haag.
16 The distinction is difficult to make in any case: the line between the two is drawn on the basis of changing legal interpretation and, worse, on the basis of political expediency, only partially reflecting the individual backgrounds of the persons involved; see Collinson (1993): pp. 25–6, and Widgren (1989) p. 602.
17 Ross, R., and K. Trachte (1983) 'Global cities and global classes: the

peripheralization of labor in New York City', *Review*, Vol. 6, No. 3, pp. 393–431.
18 *NRC Handelsblad*, 8 October 1993.
19 Lemoine, M. (1992) 'Les naufragès de la migration vers le Nord', *Le Monde Diplomatique*, December, pp. 22–3.
20 Collinson, S. (1993) p. 124.
21 *The Economist*, 27 March 1993.
22 *Financial Times*, 2 February 1990.
23 Jessop, B. (1992) p. 2.
24 Brochmann, G. (1993) ' "Fortress Europe" – a European immigration regime in the making?', in SamPol 1993, pp. 117–32; and also Collinson, S. (1993) pp. 14–15.
25 Cf. Brochmann, G. (1991) "Fortress Europe" and the moral debt burden: immigration from the "South" to the European Economic Community', *Cooperation and Conflict*, No. 26, pp. 185–95.
26 *Ibid.*, pp. 188–9.
27 *NRC Handelsblad*, 1 June 1993
28 Lemoine, M. (1992).
29 Meissner, D., *et al.* (1993) *International Migration Challenges in a New Era. Policy Perspectives and Priorities for Europe, Japan, North America and the International Community*, The Triangle Papers No. 44, The Trilateral Commission, New York/Paris/Tokyo.
30 King, M. (1993) 'The dynamics of inclusion and exclusion of refugees between Eastern, Central and Western Europe', paper presented to ECPR Joint Sessions Workshops, Leiden, April.
31 *Ibid.*
32 *Migration News Sheet*, July 1994, p. 1.
33 *NRC Handelsblad*, 13 August 1993.
34 Cf. Monod, Jérôme (1991) *Reshaping Europe, A Report from the European Round Table of Industrialists*, ERT, Brussels.
35 Bieling, H.-J. (1993) *Nationalstaat und Migration im 'Postfordismus' – Gewerkschaften vor der Zerreiszprobe*, Forschungsgruppe Europäische Gemeinschaften (FEG), Studie Nr. 2, Philipps-Universität Marburg.
36 Polanyi, K. (1944, 1957) *The Great Transformation. The Political and Economic Origins of Our Time*, Beacon Press, Boston.

12

The Internationalization
of the Labour Market

– MEINE PIETER VAN DIJK –

The internationalization of the labour market is an ongoing process. Jobs are moving South rapidly because of the price of labour in the South, but also because of improved communication and the liberalization of different economies. This has made capital and labour even more mobile than before.

A continuous process of the spatial relocation of industries and services is taking place, as well as ongoing industrial restructuring and economic adjustment processes at the macro-, meso- (sectoral) and micro-levels.[1] This implies that more flexibility of labour is required. Skill availability and development, geographical mobility and job mobility are three forms of labour flexibility. It is argued in this chapter that this flexibility facilitates labour adjustment to the ongoing economic restructuring. Differences in the labour adjustment processes in Japan, the United States and Europe are highlighted. Recent proposals on how to increase productive employment are discussed to see whether possibilities exist for a social safety net.

The question of how to achieve an optimal international division of labour is an old one, but requires some reconsideration. In this chapter we look at a number of policies which could be useful to achieve such a distribution of employment.

The new international division of labour

The present international division of labour is the result of a largely spontaneous or autonomous process. The 1980s inflicted a historical shock on the world economy. The long-run performance of the industrial sector in a large number of African and Latin American countries has been interrupted. The debt crisis of 1982 and the subsequent world-wide economic recession have resulted in a deep contraction of productive employment in those countries. At the same time, industrial employment increased significantly in Southeast Asia. Employment grew in the US at an average of 2.1 per cent over the period 1982–90, while in the EU employment rose by just 0.9 per cent per year. An estimated 100 out of 850 million inhabitants in rural China, for example, are actually moving to the south and the cities to seek low-wage industrial employment.

The new international division of labour can only be understood by giving due weight to the following factors:

1   The private sector has created most of the jobs;

2   The industrial sector has taken a leading role (strongly related to other sectors of the economy like the tertiary and primary sectors);

3   The new industries have been financed by local and very often by international capital which was brought into the country;

4   Financial markets have played an important role. They transfer capital from savers to borrowers, agglomerate capital, monitor its use, select projects, enforce contracts, transfer, share and pool risks, and record transactions;[2]

5   The choice of the location of industries in the world and within countries has not been determined only by endowments or simple factors such as wage levels. It has not been decided by governments, but by private entrepreneurs. Economic activities tend to cluster in cities, industrial districts or other attractive locations.

A new theory of the international division of labour, based on market-driven choices, would have enormous consequences for parts of the world such as:

1   Marginalization of other countries which do not participate in the race, such as a number of African countries whose share in world trade is actually declining;

2   Increasing inequality at the international, but also at the national level; in developed countries this could lead to a dualistic society with important groups being left out;

3   Continuing economic warfare with Europe, the United States and East Asia as the major actors;

4   Decreasing wages in those countries which have to compete, particularly for unskilled and low-skilled labour, which tends to become abundant, either through migration or the reduced need for agricultural labour;

5   Possibly a social crisis in the West as expressed by the student unrest in France in March 1994 or the hate against foreigners in

other European countries expressed during the 1994 elections.

The challenge of the 1990s for Europe and the US seems to be to keep up with the competition coming from South and East Asia and to seek complementarity.[3] Rapid industrial transformation implies shifts in skill requirements to which the labour force cannot easily adjust. The political consensus recognizes that labour market problems are fundamentally structural in origin. According to the OECD they are expressions of persistent difficulties in adjusting rapidly and smoothly to structural changes in demography, technology, trading patterns and consumer tastes.[4]

On a world scale the following factors influence the competitiveness of the different countries or economic blocs:

1 The implementation of the GATT and its follow-up: are we moving towards the elimination of tariff and non-tariff barriers, or are green and labour protection policies taking the lead?

2 Are European countries introducing a move of taxation away from labour and to capital and (non-renewable) resources (to promote the use of more labour and to promote the environment)?

3 The cost of communication: if taxes on kerosene were to be introduced (required for environmental and competition purposes) the importance of air traffic would decline. Tourism and trade with Africa (flowers and vegetables) would suffer particularly;

4 Political stability at the world level; this can be achieved by the development of a tri-polar world system (East Asia, Europe and the US), rather than a system with only one superpower;

5 The development of the quality and price of labour in the different parts of the world.

The factors influencing success in the field of employment in the OECD countries seem to be:

1 Clustering of economic activities;[5]

2 Flexibility of labour;

3 Continuous structural adjustment and good labour adjustment policies.

Flexibility of labour

The OECD notes that during the recession of the 1990s unemployment in OECD countries affected a broader spectrum of occupations than previous recessions, causing proportionally higher job losses in services and white-collar occupations than previously:

> Many of Western Europe's roughly 132 million civilian jobs also face extinction as old ways of doing things are overtaken by ruthless international price competition. Thousands of clerical and middle-management jobs are being phased out as companies aim for leaner structures. Workers are becoming redundant as manufacturers reorganize production, emphasizing higher skills and more flexible workers who can perform more than one function.[6]

The OECD countries have developed and implemented labour policies to mitigate the negative effects of adjustment for labour.[7] In different degrees governments, enterprises and individual workers contribute to a better functioning of the labour market. For the government the objective is to keep unemployment low.

Van Dijk argues that there are not just three models (the US, Japan and Europe).[8] Within Europe there are several different approaches, if we compare the Scandinavian model (which emphasizes training for the unemployed) to the rest, or the British model (briefly summarized as the Maastricht Treaty, but without the social paragraph) to the social democratic model in some of the Western European countries.

The three conventional models describe the functioning of the labour markets and are summarized in the OECD's report.[9] In Japan, large firms offer their core labour force much training and strong employment protection (the two are related; the firms want to keep employees when they have invested in them); in turn, the firms expect the employees to remain internally mobile and adaptable to an extent which is unknown elsewhere. A principal element of flexibility is provided by the use of subcontractors, either to do work during peak times, or to take over from employees in times of crisis.

In the US, employers rely largely on external labour markets, finding it relatively easy to react to changes in demand by varying employment levels. In addition, the country is characterized by traditionally high levels of geographical mobility and voluntary changes by employees (quitting, relocating, changing employers, etc.). On the other hand, labour-management relations, at least in unionized sectors, are characterized by extensive work rules and seniority arrangements. The type of flexibility American employers seek most is therefore the freedom to deploy labour within the enterprise without union interference and contractual constraints. A worker must move if he loses his job and if necessary he must accept lower wages. Moreover, many of the new jobs created in the US in the 1980s are low-skill, low-paid, service sector jobs. The OECD report notes also that among the new jobs created in the OECD countries in the same period a high proportion are in non-standard or typical forms of employment, such as temporary jobs.[10]

The recent IMF *World Economic Outlook* recommends:[11]

1 Less generous unemployment insurance fees;

2 Wider earnings dispersions;

3 Lower levels of unionization and less centralized wage bargaining;

4 Less government intervention in the wage bargaining process;

5 Fewer restrictions on hiring or firing employees;

6 Lower non-wage labour costs, such as payroll taxes and the amount of paid vacation; and

7 Lower relative incidence of long-term unemployment.

Western European countries have, since the Second World War, strengthened state control over employment relationships and made dismissals more cumbersome and costly. Enterprises are required to care about employment security. Sometimes it is made difficult to close a factory, or advance notice and compensation to the employees are necessary. Functional flexibility in enterprises has generally been high; employer demands for flexibility have, accordingly, centred on loosening employment protection legislation and opening possibilities for non-standard work contracts.

The preceding summaries point to the importance of using the flexibility concept in analysing the functioning of labour markets. Standing distinguishes four forms of labour mobility (what we call flexibility): geographical, employment (or inter-firm), job (intra-firm) and skill mobility.[12] The term flexibility refers to the ability of individuals and institutions in the economy to abandon established ways and adapt to new circumstances. In a broad sense more flexibility is required because of structural adjustment, technological breakthroughs, and quality-of-life considerations, and because of the new social issues societies are facing in the 1990s. Market 'pull' and technology 'push' factors force industries towards greater flexibility.

According to the OECD, flexibility of labour can take five forms:[13]

1 External numerical flexibility: the number of employees is adjusted to the employer's needs by employing and dismissing people;

2 Externalization: part of the firm's work is put out to other

companies; and employment contracts are replaced by commercial contracts (for example, through subcontracting);

3 Internal numerical flexibility: the number of working hours is adjusted according to the company's needs, but the number of workers remains unchanged (varying the number of hours per day, weeks per year, more days off, shift work, and so on);

4 Functional flexibility: workers' job assignments are modified according to the company's needs: people switch jobs within the company;

5 Wage flexibility: labour costs and thus wages are adjusted, for example to a performance-based system. Collective bargaining has a major impact on the balance struck between profits, wages and other benefits which affect total labour costs.

Geographical flexibility needs to be added to the list, particularly because it is important to understand the contribution of workers to labour adjustment in the US.

Continuous adjustment and labour adjustment policies

A continuous process of structural adjustment and spatial reorganization seems inevitable. Are labour market interventions successful in dealing with the consequences? According to the distortionists, the interventions misallot labour, waste resources through rent-seeking, impair adjustment and deter investment.[14] The alternative is to let the markets work and consider industrialization as a spontaneous process.

The system of mass production has reached its limits.[15] Piore and Sabel[16] and Best[17] have argued convincingly that there are alternatives, however. One alternative is having large numbers of small and micro enterprises producing smaller amounts of specially designed goods of a specific quality for a niche market, which may command a higher price.

Flexible specialization and small enterprise development can be related in different ways. Mendez mentions that in Venezuela the growth of micro enterprises between 1980 and 1988 was part of 'a strategy of cost flexibilization engaged by larger enterprises'.[18] This consisted of transferring the cost of an erratic demand to them. He concludes that informalization of the labour force is one of the ways in which the burden of labour market regulations could be bypassed by larger enterprises.

The development of industrial districts can be encouraged through the following policies:

1 The formulation of national and regional policies;
2 The definition of a role for different levels of government; and
3 The provision of a good infrastructure.

Economic policy should take the lessons from Southeast Asia into consideration, including the potential negative effects of this model. The re-emergence of micro and small enterprises seems to be a fact and the strategy of these entrepreneurs can be described by the new competition and flexible specialization concepts. An industrialization strategy integrating these concepts and experiences with industrial districts could be called creating flexible competitive districts. It embraces policies by different levels of government and promotes a role for private sector institutions.

Active policies

Fretwell *et al.* distinguish between proactive and reactive policies. The latter ameliorate the position of the unemployed through income support, while proactive policies add value to individuals through developing new skills.[19]

PUBLIC EMPLOYMENT SERVICES AND ADMINISTRATION
A large number of services are included in this category, such as placement, counselling and vocational guidance, job search courses, support of geographic mobility and administration costs of labour market agencies at different levels, including unemployment benefit agencies and the administrative costs of other labour market programmes.

LABOUR MARKET TRAINING
This category includes all training measures, except those for youth and the disabled mentioned below. The amounts include course costs and subsistence allowances to trainees, if paid. Subsidies to employers are also included, but not employers' own expenses. Two types of training are distinguished:
1 For unemployed adults and those at risk of losing their jobs, or disadvantaged groups such as the poor;
2 For employed adults, if the training is supported for reasons of labour market policy. Often this includes grants to enterprises for staff training in general.

YOUTH MEASURES
Youth measures, including special programmes for youth in transition from school to work:

1 For unemployed and disadvantaged youth: remedial education, training in work practices to facilitate the transition of disadvantaged youth from school to work;

2 Support of apprenticeship and related forms of general youth training in enterprises.

SUBSIDIZED EMPLOYMENT

1 Subsidies to regular employment in the private sector. Wage subsidies for the recruitment of targeted workers or, in some cases, for continued employment of persons whose jobs are at risk;[20]

2 Support of unemployed persons starting enterprises. This support can consist of unemployment benefits or special grants;

3 Direct job creation (public or non-profit). Temporary work and, in some cases, regular jobs in the public sector or in non-profit organizations, offered to unemployed persons.

MEASURES FOR THE DISABLED

Measures for the disabled include the following (only the special programmes are considered here, not the total policy effort in support of the disabled):

1 Vocational rehabilitation: ability testing, work adjustment measures and training other than ordinary labour market training.

2 Work for the disabled: sheltered work and subsidies to regular employment.

PASSIVE MEASURES

The following can be considered as passive measures:

1 *Unemployment compensation* – all forms of cash benefit to compensate for unemployment, except early retirement;

2 *Early retirement* for labour market reasons – only special schemes in which workers receive retirement pensions because they are out of work or otherwise for reasons of labour market policy.

The OECD provides public expenditures on labour market programmes, according to these categories, as a percentage of the gross domestic product (GDP) for all 24 member countries for each year between 1985 and 1991.[21]

Labour adjustment in OECD countries

The OECD countries differ in the way the costs of labour adjustment are handled and the way these costs are distributed among workers, employers and government. The differences also depend on the sectors of the economy concerned. Restructuring in the steel sector in Europe, for example, already has a long tradition and is a very gradual process. In the computer industry it has been a more recent phenomenon and a very drastic process, with IBM shedding, for example, 100,000 people world-wide since 1985. Of those, 40,000 were laid off only in 1992.[22]

In Japan labour adjustment takes place mainly within companies, through training, or labour transfer. In Europe government programmes are very important and focus mostly on education and training, particularly for unemployed, young and disabled people. In the US the individual person has to make an effort, by getting additional training or by moving to a different place.

Each approach has its own specific history. It requires different institutions, different policies and it is characterized by differently composed labour market programmes. Government policies with respect to industrial restructuring, regional development and employment policies are often interrelated in many ways.

Adjustment and the implied industrial restructuring process have strong regional components. The Ruhr area in Germany has taken a long period to restructure its classical industrial base of coal and steel. In the meantime, the more southern Baden-Württemberg region boomed on the basis of automobile, aircraft and related industries. Recently that region also started to show signs of recession.

The three models of labour markets distinguished by the OECD can be readily identified. In Western Europe much depends on government employment policy, while in Japan the principal actor is the enterprise. Finally, in the North American model the worker plays an important role in preparing himself or herself for new employment and eventually finding it. However, the classification is also a reduction of reality. In Japan as well as in the US, the government does play an important role in the restructuring process: through its labour market policies, but also through its macro-economic policies, its science and technology policies and its trade and investment regimes. Within Europe there is a big difference between Germany and the Netherlands (with their so-called social contract policies), Sweden (where the government plays a very important role in the economy with its full employment policy) and France (where there is close consultation between the government and the private sector through the system of indicative planning).

Conclusions

International competition leads to continuing restructuring and relocation of economic activities. This pushes down wages in developed countries and will create pockets of poverty in countries where welfare payments and unemployment benefits can no longer be afforded at the previous levels. It means that there is a conflict between creating employment in developed countries on one hand and developing countries on the other.

Active labour market policies can address frictional or structural unemployment. Employment services help in the first case, while training policies and employment generation programmes address structural unemployment and compensate for decreasing demand in times of recession.

To be effective, several of the mentioned policy measures need to be taken in combination. Supporting measures like job counselling can be crucial for the success of active labour market policies such as skill development. Particular groups may require a special approach.

In Southeast Asia, government and enterprises have reacted more quickly and decisively to the structural changes of the 1970s and 1980s. Labour suffers less in Japan from these changes and the unemployed are able to find a job more easily.

The question remains, what possibilities exist for a social safety net? In Western Europe, the Christian and social democratic tradition has created a welfare system, which is now trimmed. The challenge, however, is to keep it affordable and effective, without going all the way in the direction indicated by the IMF.

Some creative solutions are being explored in Europe. Labour-intensive technology development is one, suggested by the European Commission (Delors White Paper, December 1993). A minimum income for everybody is a second one, which has not yet gained ground. Taxing capital and raw materials more, and labour less, would certainly change the input mix, but it needs to be done at the European level. Redistributing existing employment and allowing more social activities (with the unemployment fee) is being tried in the Netherlands. Finally, youth employment schemes and priority schemes for minorities and for people on welfare for longer than a specified period are presently under experiment.

The situation remains that there is a conflict of interest. Often more work in the South means less employment in the North. Similarly modern sector employment in the South may drive out existing informal sector employment. Hence there is also a need for labour-intensive technologies in the South.

NOTES
1 See also Chapter 10.
2 Stiglitz, J. E. (1993) 'The Role of the State in Financial Markets', World Bank Development Economics conference.
3 Thurow, L. (1993) *Head to Head: The Coming Battle among Japan, Europe and America*, Warner, New York.
4 OECD (1992) *Employment Outlook*, OECD, Paris.
5 Van Dijk, M. P. (1994) *The Interrelations between Industrial Districts and Technological Capabilities Development*, UNCTAD, Geneva.
6 *Wall Street Journal of Europe*, 19 March 1993.
7 In 'Labour adjustment in OECD Countries', World Bank, Washington, Van Dijk (1993) compares the ways OECD countries go about managing the social cost of economic adjustment for workers. What has been the role and at what cost of active and passive labour market policies? How did these policies help unemployed workers affected by structural adjustment? What can we learn from this experience for Eastern European and Third World countries?
8 *Ibid.*
9 OECD (1989) *Labour Market Flexibility, Trends in Enterprises*, OECD, Paris.
10 Growth in non-standard employment is one of the topics for in-depth analysis in the OECD *Employment Outlook*, 1993.
11 IMF (1994) *World Economic Outlook*, IMF, Washington, May.
12 Standing, G. (1988) *Unemployment and Labour Market Flexibility – Sweden*, ILO, Geneva.
13 The OECD *Employment Outlook* of 1984 already distinguished between manpower and labour cost flexibility. Manpower flexibility refers to occupational and geographical mobility, flexibility of working time and the acquisition of human capital. Labour cost flexibility distinguishes between wage cost and non-wage cost flexibility.
14 Freeman (1992), paper to World Bank Development Economics conference.
15 Storper, M. (1989) 'The transition to flexible specialization in the US film industry', *Cambridge Journal of Economics*, Vol. 13.
16 Piore, M. J. and C. Sabel (1984) *The Second Industrial Divide*, Basic Books, New York.
17 Best, M. H. (1990) *The New Competition*, Harvard, Cambridge.
18 Mendez-Rivero, D. (1991) 'Informalization of the Venezuelan labour force', Institute of Social Studies, The Hague, unpublished PhD thesis.
19 Fretwell, D. H., M. Lovell and R. W. Bednarzik (1991) *Employment Dimensions of Economic Restructuring*, IBRD, Washington.
20 Grants aiming primarily to cover enterprises' capital costs are not included, nor are general employment subsidies paid for all workers in certain regions.
21 OECD (1992) *Employment Outlook*, OECD, Paris.
22 *Business Week*, 23 November 1992.

13

Employment and the Internationalization of the Labour Markets

– MIHÁLY SIMAI –

Resources, capabilities, and economic activities have become internationally mobile and have intensified international competition. Global interconnectedness also has a major influence on the trends and patterns of employment, including skills, wages, and labour standards – this despite the fact that the vast majority of the 2.8 billion persons belonging to the global labour force are employed (or unemployed) within national economic frameworks.

Individual governments formulate and implement their employment policies in response to domestic political, social and economic pressures and conditions. Within countries, employment has its specific demographic, technological, macro- and microeconomic, political and institutional dimensions. A macroeconomic category based on a definition of full employment, or the natural rate of unemployment (the relevance of which is a highly debated issue anyway) would make no sense on a global level.

And yet there are many international aspects of employment problems. In an interdependent world, national employment is directly related to changes in the external conditions of demand and supply and also to international competition, especially in those countries which are dependent on foreign trade or which are the main sources and hosts of foreign direct investment. The character of the international trading regimes is also influenced by the employment problems through national attitudes toward international trade policies and agreements. In this system, the capacity to adjust has become a particularly pertinent variable. This is because the labour markets of different countries are today more directly connected in the relatively liberal international trading system through transnational corporations, and marketing and distribution operations. This interconnectedness influences the changes in employment opportunities and in occupational structures. The erosion of national labour market regulations and welfare systems reflects and contributes to this trend.

The future and sustainability of the present, relatively liberal international trading system depends to a large extent on how successfully new employment opportunities can be developed.

The internationalization process of the labour markets: issues and mechanisms

The internationalization of markets, as a process, is usually defined by the degree of liberalization related to the international mobility of the given factor or commodity, and by its actual movements across the frontiers. The degree of internationalization of the labour markets depends first of all on the degree of liberalization of the international mobility of people, especially those in the working-age groups. It is also influenced by the international convergence of labour legislation and by the increasing internationalization of labour standards. In addition, it is influenced by the growing similarity of skill requirements and occupational, educational and training patterns, caused by the postulates of the new technologies and by the internationally integrated production of transnational corporations. The consequences of the internationalization of the labour markets include the establishment of a better international balance of supply and demand of workers and the convergence of labour costs.

The process of internationalization of the national labour markets will probably be faster in regional frameworks as a result of increasing cooperation. Thus far, this process has been important only in Europe within the European Union. The character and the speed of this process are uncertain and will depend on a number of political, social and economic factors, including migration pressures, public attitudes toward foreigners, the degree of social peace, the readiness of national groups to accept the Europeanization of social policies and the future patterns of economic growth.

Labour markets are still much less internationalized than the markets for goods or for capital, for at least two reasons. First of all, the international mobility of people is a highly complex issue and it is influenced by a large number of political, economic, social and cultural factors. There are also much greater constraints limiting the international movement of people, than of capital or goods. Only a rather small part of the labour force could be considered internationally mobile. The institutions which could promote mobility (including those responsible for information flows on demand conditions – for example, on temporary or longer-term labour shortages in certain countries, and on the supplies) are highly specific and much less developed, than for instance, in the case of capital movements.

Second, labour markets are very strongly influenced by national, historical, socio-political, and institutional factors. In the background of these various influences are hard economic realities like the great differences in the levels of development, productivity and incomes. The specific issues related to the internationalization of the labour markets are of a different nature in Europe, North America and the developing regions of the world. The functioning of the labour markets depends on institutions that are often at odds with one another. Some advanced industrial countries are highly unionized and in others the role of trade unions is very limited. From among the industrial countries, for example, the union coverage of bargaining is about 18 per cent in the US and 95 per cent in Sweden. The role of government regulations in the labour markets is also substantially different, as are labour conditions and the incentives offered to labour. In some countries, the larger proportion of remuneration depends on bonuses, while in others wages are more important. There is great variety among unemployment compensation programmes, training and retraining mechanisms, and immigration regulations.

SOME PERSPECTIVES OF INTERNATIONAL MIGRATION

The single most important factor in the internationalization of the labour markets is international migration, and especially the migration of people in the labour force. According to UN estimates, the number of people living in the country in which they were not born is between 50 and 80 million. This is a relatively very small, practically negligible proportion of the global population. The importance of international migration in the internationalization of the labour markets must be analysed through its consequences in influencing economic disparities between countries by reducing wage differentials, contributing to productivity increases, and increasing demand for goods and services (by the consumption of the immigrants or in the sending countries, through remittances). Both push and pull factors are important in the process.

In this context, internal migration may also have important international consequences, especially the movement from rural areas to urban centres, which, according to the empirical evidence, increases the push factors. In the early twentieth century, the world was still very much inhabited by a rural population. Then, only about 14 per cent of the inhabitants lived in urban settlements. By the end of the century, half of the earth's population will be urban.

Seventy-eight per cent of the population of developed countries and 40 per cent of the developing countries will be living in cities. United Nations projections indicated that, in the year 2000, some 77 per cent of the population of Latin America, 41 per cent of Africa, and 35 per cent of Asia will live in urban settlements. In the developing world, most of the urban growth is taking place in already large urban settlements – in 24 megacities – with populations already or soon to be greater than 10 million. In those agglomerations, the creation of new jobs and the capability of municipalities to keep up with the demand for infrastructure and services have already been outpaced. The spread of urban slums (without proper housing, roads, health care, educational facilities, safe drinking water and sanitation) is only one of the grave future dangers. There is a rapid increase in the number of unemployed, underemployed and uneducated people as a result of urbanization in many developing countries.

According to abstract macroeconomic theory, wages are determined, in a smoothly functioning labour market, by the balance of labour supply and demand. If there is a relative scarcity of workers in one market, wages will be high, while in the case of relative abundance in another market, wages will be low. Migration represents an equilibrating mechanism. The consequences of the process would not only be the increasing international equalization of labour compensation, but the elimination of the relative advantages employees gained from labour cost differences in different countries, and in the final analysis, the disappearance of international differences in labour costs as incentives for foreign direct investment. Wage differences, however, are not providing either sufficient justification or the only incentive for international migration. It is a result of a number of socio-economic and political factors, including the constraints on the mobility of the labour force. In the literature on migration, conditions are usually grouped according to their push or pull effects on people: the push effect includes demographic pressures, poor living conditions, civil wars, ethnic tensions and many other adverse problems of the sending countries; the pull effect includes higher wages, faster growth, and better labour standards, social services, human rights records, and so on.

Of course international migration has other incentives besides the search for employment opportunities. The movements of populations have been important components and factors which have formed human history. Entire continents have been depopulated and repopulated. There have been historical waves of migration for demographic reasons, because of changing climatic conditions, or in response to political and economic pressures (or incentives). In the period after the Second World War, the process of international migration had two separate components: one represented by dislocated peoples and refugees, the other by those who were economically motivated to improve their quality of life.

The modern history of international migration has usually been divided into four periods. In the first period, between the sixteenth and nineteenth centuries, the immigration patterns were connected with the process of colonization and mercantilist economic growth in Europe, increasingly based on raw materials from the colonies. The second period started with the post-Napoleonic war era. It was characterized by a massive outflow of people from Europe to North America, certain countries of Latin America, Australia and New Zealand. This period ended with the First World War. In the third period, between the two world wars, international migration became extremely limited. Strict immigration laws were introduced in all the traditional receiving countries. During the Second World War, there was a massive redeployment of people for slave labour and the hostilities also produced a large number of displaced persons.

The fourth period started after the Second World War and could be characterized as the increasing globalization of international migration. In the early part of this period, most of the great population movements took place as results of political changes. Since 1947, when India and Pakistan became independent, more than 40 million people have moved across the frontiers of these two countries. There has been a major movement of people to and from Palestine, related to the establishment of Israel. Wars, revolutions, and upheavals caused tens of millions of temporary international refugees or permanent emigration in all continents. There has also been a large increase in economically motivated migration all over the world, a result of which has been the emergence of a transnational workforce in a number of countries, beyond the traditional destination of emigrants. Among European countries, Britain, France, Germany, Sweden, Switzerland and the Netherlands became especially important targets for this labour force. Saudi Arabia, Kuwait and the United Arab Emirates also received millions of immigrant workers. In Africa, Côte d'Ivoire, Nigeria and South Africa became especially important centres of immigrants.

We may speak about the beginnings of the fifth period of international migration in the era after the Cold War. It is too early to define the characteristics and implications of this fifth period. On the demand side, it will be increasingly specific and selective. The economically motivated migration will be more organized and influenced by new information technologies. On the supply side, increasing demographic and economic pressures may increase the push factors. The socio-political environment is also changing, which may result in more asylum seekers in certain continents and more resistance against foreign labour in others.

It is impossible, or at least it is very difficult, to predict the future trends in international migration. Migration will be related, on one hand, to demographic pressure, which is predictable for certain parts of the world, and, on the other hand, to expected economic opportunities, and especially to employment. Demographic pressure is accumulating for international migration, especially in the land belt south of the developed industrial world (except, of course, Australia and New Zealand). North America will confront such pressures from Latin America, as will Europe from North Africa, and the Arab-Islamic hinterland and Russia from South Asia and China. It is quite possible that the disintegration of the Soviet Union will further result in a mass migration of people, perhaps of Russian and other ethnic minorities residing in a few of the new independent republics. Emigration in past decades temporarily eased employment problems in certain southern European countries. The time of the guest worker in Western Europe is over. As a result of the changes in Eastern Europe, the list of countries from where political refugees are accepted has been redefined. The increasing public hostility may be as important in curbing immigration as the restrictive legislative measures. Immigration will most probably remain relatively high in the traditional receiving countries (the USA, Canada and Australia).

Can or will emigration moderate the demographic pressure in the developing countries as it did in the past, especially in nineteeth-century Europe? The historical experience of Europe in the field of mass emigration is irrelevant to developing countries today. Most of the European emigrants went into cultural environments not too dissimilar from their own. More importantly, the numbers were different. On one hand, demographic conditions in the developing countries make emigration pressures much greater than they ever were in Europe's past. On the other hand, the needs of those countries receiving immigrants are relatively more limited due to the character of technological and structural changes and to the increasingly knowledge-intensive character of the modern economy. During the years after the Second World War, for example, the Asian countries were able to export less than 0.1 per cent of their labour force increment. Taking into account the current and projected disparities and the increasing economic inequalities, it is more or less certain that the pressure for international migration in different forms will increase and become a key problem in all parts of the world, especially between the developing and the developed industrial countries, and between Central and Eastern Europe and Western Europe.

If the development process is left to the spontaneity of socioeconomic forces, people will be uprooted by poverty and their migration may well become an important source of national and international conflicts and social violence. Thus, international migration will in the coming decades become an important issue on the agenda of regional, international, and global organizations. Indeed, there is a great probability that instead of an 'iron curtain' separating the East from the West as in the past, there will now be a 'golden curtain' drawn between North and South. Seen in one light, this will be an important and controversial human rights and humanitarian issue, as the right of people to move and emigrate is understood as a universal human right. It will be quite necessary to help refugees. In another light, however, the industrial countries will have to protect their own labour markets. Measures for stricter regulation will probably be inevitable, meaning quotas and restrictions in obtaining citizenship, or in acquiring education and property.

Another important future aspect of international migration is the brain drain from the less to the more developed countries. This form of migration from the developing countries will be competing in the future with the outflow of highly skilled professionals from Central and Eastern Europe and the former Soviet Union. While it may become more difficult and selective in the future, the skill level of the emigrants will increase, due to the changing demand patterns in the labour markets of the industrial world.

THE ROLE OF TRANSNATIONAL CORPORATIONS IN EMPLOYMENT AND IN THE INTERNATIONALIZATION OF THE LABOUR MARKETS

Transnational corporations (TNCs) have been important actors in the internationalization of the markets of goods and of capital. Their role has been much more limited in the internationalization of the labour markets and especially in employment creation. (According to UN information, in 1992 there were about 37,000 TNCs with about 200,000 foreign affiliates employing about 29 million people outside their home countries – 17 million in the developed countries, 12 million in the developing countries.) They influence, of course, the international demand for, and the career expectations of, a number of professional groups. They also have direct and indirect influence on the changes in global patterns of employment. Employment policies of transnational corporations are, first of all, sector specific. Within a given sector they have declining flexibility in substituting capital with labour. They are also country specific in the sense that in labour-intensive operations they seek low-cost and low-risk countries. The more recent experiences in some Eastern European countries proved, however, that even in the latter cases, employment was reduced, not increased, in the firms which have been taken over by TNCs. In technologically more sophisticated operations, they increased the skill level. The share of employment by TNCs in the total national employment of the developed industrial countries is about 3 per cent in Western Europe and 4 per cent in the USA. It is much higher, however, in the manufacturing sector (10–20 per cent).

The increase of employment by the TNCs has been concentrated in the low-wage developing countries, where the labour-intensive operations are concentrated. In China, for example, employment by the TNCs more than doubled during the first half of the 1990s. There has also been a relatively quick increase in TNC employment in the export processing zones. Beyond the direct employment effect of TNCs they generate employment opportunities through a system of subcontracting and other linkages.

The TNCs also proved to be very important globally in upgrading the labour force within their system. Because they are concentrated in high-technology sectors, which require higher skills, they have been and probably will also be playing a key role in the future in disseminating new skill requirements and, through this factor, inter-nationalizing skill and educational standards. TNCs are efficient instruments for passing on skills to local staffs through personal contacts, on-the-job training, organized visits to other operations in their international system, and formal training courses. The skill level of employees in firms owned by transnational corporations, in most cases, is higher than the level in domestically owned firms, including the public sector. This also increases the compensation level of employees. It is not in the interest of the TNCs to introduce a converging compensation level in their international system, because of the benefits from lower wages. However, they are offering higher compensation than their local counterparts in most cases because their skill requirements are higher and they are more demanding concerning discipline and productivity. They also often offer better working conditions, especially because of their greater visibility.

The competition of many governments for investments by trans-national corporations may also be promoting the harmonization of employment policies. There are three factors (beyond the direct and indirect costs of labour) which are very important for transnational corporations. The first is the quality of the educational system and the availability and development of skills: to what extent researchers, engineers and other qualified technical staff are available, and the apprenticeship schemes and their quality. The second factor is the transparency and flexibility of the labour markets: the labour legislation, unemployment insurance, and retraining facilities. (TNCs are often criticized by trade unions for being 'too flexible' and for disregarding trade union rights and the national bargaining process, and also in shifting their operations from one country to another with very short notice.) The third factor is the degree of freedom of movement of the labour force, both entering and leaving the country. This is especially important for the mobility of labour within the international system of the TNCs.

REGIONAL INTEGRATION AND THE INTERNATIONALIZATION OF THE LABOUR MARKETS

While, in almost all the regions of the world, regional cooperation institutions have formulated some regional programmes for employment, migration, and migration policies, they are mostly rudimentary and, in most cases, are recommendations for national actions. They lack the common determination for collective measures. The European Union is the only regional integration group which has coordinated policy directives in a number of areas. The action programme of the Social Charter includes directives for employment and remuneration, living and working conditions, freedom of movement, information, consultation and participation, equal treatment, health and safety, and the protection of children and youth. These directives, if implemented, may promote the emergence of a regionally integrated labour market in the future. The directive on transnational posting of workers suggests that they should enjoy the same terms and conditions as local workers in the host country.

What is the degree of internationalization of the labour market of the European Union? The data for the immigrants is incomplete because it does not include the naturalized foreigners. It is still, however, a good indicator. In 1990, about 13 million persons, 4 per cent of the total population, were foreign residents; of the 13 million, 8 million came from outside the Union. According to the same statistics, the proportion of foreigners was the highest in Germany (about 16 per cent). Between 1945 and 1989, however, the Federal Republic of Germany received about 15 million foreigners as refugees or guest workers. This corresponds to about 25 per cent of the population. The proportion of foreigners is much lower in the other member countries (in Spain, 0.7 per cent). Immigration has been regulated so far on the basis of national legislation. The Maastricht Treaty on European Union provides common foundations for a European immigration policy, taking into account also common goals and interests. It also recognizes the need for a constant policy dialogue with the countries which are the sources of immigration.

According to sporadic statistical data, in spite of certain converging trends in the long-term movement of labour costs, the differences in wage levels and in social security benefits are still large. To what extent and by what mechanisms those differences will level off is an important issue for future research. Will there be a supranational synthesis of labour legislation, and if 'yes', when and how?

The integration process could contribute to the internationalization of the labour market through common coordinated policies to increase the quality of the labour force, including its educational and vocational skill levels and structure, as well as its capability to adjust in a flexible and disciplined fashion to changes in demand conditions and new technology. The growing internationalization of the labour markets requires a greater degree of collective approach to emerging problems on the global level in order to avoid potential dangers. One should not forget that the accumulation of social dissatisfaction and frustration of hungry and unemployed millions played a substantial role in helping extremist regimes into power which pushed the world toward the great wars of the twentieth century.

The prospects for transnational human resource development policy in a competitive global system

An important international commitment by all nations, at least by all the members of the UN, directly concerns not only the employment issues but also general human welfare. Through the full employment pledge of the United Nations in its early years, employment and the development of human resources became global issues for the first time in human history. Article 55 of the UN Charter states:

> With a view to the creation of conditions of stability and well-being which is necessary for peaceful and friendly relations among nations, based on respect for the principle of equal rights and self-determination of peoples, the United Nations shall promote: (a) higher standards of living, full employment, and conditions of economic and social progress and development....

In later decades, this commitment was largely forgotten, and in the 1990s it was depicted by some politicians as a leftover from an era of statism or the welfare states. The full employment commitments are rooted in the initiatives of US President F. D. Roosevelt and Sir William Beveridge. Many people feared that the end of the Second World War would be followed by a new Great Depression and mass unemployment. Roosevelt proposed a post-war economic bill of rights based on a fundamental right to a job and fair wages. Beveridge proposed full employment as a fundamental post-war goal for Britain. Both proposals were criticized by important political and business groups and caused major debate. In the meantime, the UN Charter was adopted, with the commitment to full employment in Article 55. In 1948, the Universal Declaration of Human Rights strengthened this commitment. The International Covenant on Economic, Social, and Cultural Rights adopted by the General Assembly in 1966 and in force since 1976 put the right to employment in a central place among economic and social rights. This is, however, the wrong approach, and counterproductive. The overall conditions for success in the international economic system have been changing. Emphasis on the proper management and combination of resources – particularly of techno-economic resources – will increasingly shift to the management of human resources. Emphasis will be put on sustaining and improving the ability to utilize appropriate knowledge; mobilizing the will to work in a competitive and cooperative framework; and maintaining voluntary social discipline. However, this will be a more difficult task for many reasons.

There has been marked improvement in the quality of human resources during the past decades. This has been manifested, first of all, in educational patterns. Several factors have been responsible for favourable changes. One was the decolonization process and the efforts of the new countries to establish strong educational and professional foundations for national existence. Another factor has been the acceleration of technological progress, requiring a much more qualified labour force which has contributed to the changes in skill and employment structures. A third factor has to do with new individual needs and attitudes towards social mobility. Education in the new environment has become an important instrument of social mobility the world over. As a result of economic difficulties and constraints, there has been increasing diversity in the quality of educational services – not only on a global level, but also within countries – that has often resulted in a majority of pupils hardly attaining the level of functional literacy in some school systems, while other school systems have directly prepared students for entering the era of the information revolution, even to the extent of equipping them with computer literacy. By the end of the 1980s, the mean period of schooling of the population over 25 years was almost three times higher in the developed than in the developing countries.

The global number and distribution of the highly skilled portion of the population, those having higher education degrees, are very important components of the qualitative improvement of the labour force. The total number of people in the world with university and other higher education degrees was about 80 million by the end of the 1980s, more than twice the number 30 years earlier. While a large proportion – indeed, more than two thirds – of these people lived and worked in the developed industrial countries and in Central and Eastern Europe, a relatively large concentration of highly skilled people appeared in certain developing countries as a result of national policies for increasing the number of university graduates. In countries like the Republic of Korea, China, India, Egypt, Thailand and Indonesia, their numbers reached the critical mass necessary for creating and sustaining modern industries in the new technological era. The consequences of this improvement were, of course, favourable for the countries. In many developing countries, however, the increase of highly qualified people resulted in an excess supply in the labour market, adding a new dimension to the unutilized or under-utilized segments of the population.

In the developed industrial countries, the relationships between workers and employers and income are changing rapidly. Working patterns are changing. Greater employment flexibility is demanded by many employers to secure business survival in an increasingly competitive world. This endangers the opportunities of individuals and it may degrade employment conditions. A new social judgement is required to define the proper balance between flexibility and employment security. In the developing countries, where rural employment opportunities will remain crucially important and the role of the informal sector as a source of employment and income may be even growing, new needs of human resource development and the efficient use of human resources raise such questions as, how to keep the unemployed and underemployed from the streets? The specific tasks may be quite different in various countries. In certain countries they will have to be combined with demographic policies, health policies, and special policies dealing with the more vulnerable and discriminated parts of the population.

The idea that those issues should be dealt with in a national framework is shared by a number of governments, even though there are differences in the definition of their content and instruments. The Social Charter of the EU has been probably the only comprehensive international document aiming at collective approaches to social policy issues. Even within the EU, the views of countries are still divergent with respect to the interpretation and implementation of the Social Charter. On a global level, the differences are naturally even greater. Some of the approaches stress the role of entrepreneurship in the solution of those issues related to human development and employment, including the role of self-employment as an important component of the human development tasks. It is also recognized, however, that the requirements of achieving greater global security in the coming decades make human resource policies extremely important both on national and international levels. The feasibility of international commitments and the availability of possible collective instruments of those policies are highly debated issues.

The problems related to the internationalization of the labour markets will be very important in the coming decades for the global community. Further research work is needed, however, on the concept itself, about the mechanisms, institutions and the roles of the different actors in it, especially the transnational corporations. More empirical research is also needed about the advantages or disadvantages of internationalization. Is it increasing the welfare and the standard of living of people, or reducing it by downward influences on wages? It is also necessary to analyse the interrelations between the internationalization of the labour markets and of other markets (goods, services, capital). Another important area for research will have to be the influence of the speed and structure of economic growth on the internationalization of the labour markets.

Many issues which require new empirical research are related to the institutional consequences of the increasing interconnectedness and internationalization of the labour markets and to the feasibility and reality of internationally binding social norms and labour standards. This chapter is intended to be only a modest contribution to the discussion of the subject.

14

Employment Creation through International Cooperation: Case Studies in Rural Areas in West Africa

– MOGENS HASDORF –

This chapter deals with some aspects of the employment situation in developing countries on the basis of the author's 30-year experience in development activities in Africa, Asia and Latin America. The global perspective will be supplemented by specific references to West Africa.[1]

International assistance

In absolute terms multilateral and bilateral assistance to developing countries has been considerable, but compared to the need it has been insignificant. Moreover, it has been difficult to identify coherent assistance strategies in most cases. Directly and indirectly, assistance programmes have resulted in the creation of a considerable number of jobs in developing countries over the years. With the introduction of various conditionality clauses it is likely that greater attention will be devoted to the need for consistency in the planning of the assistance and in the regulations and legislation of the receiver countries. As most donor countries and institutions feel that the assistance given so far has not led to the expected results, the volume of assistance has not grown since the mid-1980s.[2]

The elements of the investment policies have not been sufficiently coherent within the private sector. In many countries the governments have had hostile attitudes towards private sector operators. With such attitudes it becomes difficult to attract even the local entrepreneurs to invest in their own countries and it is much more difficult to attract overseas operators and investors. Much capital, which could have provided important employment in developing countries, has been transferred to bank accounts overseas.

We have witnessed how some food aid programmes resulted in bizarre situations leading to bankruptcy and unemployment in the receiver countries, because local producers could not compete with foreign, subsidized producers.[3] Instead of investing in local production of basic food commodities in West Africa, such as rice and poultry, overseas donors shipped large quantities of these commodities free of charge to the receiving governments, which could market the articles at prices lower than the local production price. Several integrated poultry production units in Ghana went into bankruptcy because of food aid. Several of the poultry projects were co-financed by overseas development finance institutions. Consistency in the local regulations and in foreign aid planning was lacking.

Food aid programmes are only meaningful in crisis situations. Otherwise they inevitably lead to unfair competition *vis-à-vis* the local producers. Furthermore, foreign development finance institutions with their collaborating foreign know-how and finance partners from the private sector become very reluctant to back project proposals involving local production of food items. In this way the food aid programmes sometimes hinder future development, including employment.

In this context it would be only fair to mention a very interesting experiment in which the European Union will be testing a new type of food aid programme in West Africa. It will be based upon utilization of local raw materials processed locally in accordance with local taste and tradition. Initially, this project will be a joint venture with the participation of local and European interests, including European development finance institutions and, perhaps, the International Finance Corporation of the World Bank Group.

If this experiment is successful the model should be further developed for utilization in other fields and, thus, may contribute to more employment in Africa and in developing countries elsewhere. Local employment is a very important item for development finance institutions to scrutinize in their feasibility studies. However, first and foremost a project proposal must show viability. If viability can be maintained better through the more labour-intensive procedures than the more capital-intensive solutions, these institutions will normally favour the labour-intensive solution. Furthermore, they try to secure a fair distribution of jobs between female and male labour. To a certain extent, this consideration is also valid for staff employment.

In general, assistance policy still contains elements of structural adjustment and stabilization. As mentioned above, consistency in the programmes and in the local regulations is also being more explicitly required. The consistency concept plays an important role when development finance institutions negotiate with the authorities in developing countries. Investment policies are composed of numerous elements and they depend on input from many ministries and directorates. It is often a delicate matter to combine the elements to make a coherent policy. Nowadays, the authorities in developing countries often require expert assistance – from the United Nations Industrial Development Organization (UNIDO), for example – to solve the problem of consistency. Development finance institutions operating in the area are frequently invited to contribute according to their experience. In some cases in West Africa, they have succeeded in bringing the employment element into the regulations.

As a consequence of a rather new conditionality element in the assistance programmes, the already reduced assistance to some African states such as Togo has temporarily been cut off because of open government violation of basic human rights. The combination of very long periods of strike and the dramatic discontinuation of foreign assistance has terrible consequences for employment. The affected populations sink into still more hopeless poverty. Thanks only to the traditional solidarity system within families, tribes and villages, it has been possible for the unemployed and under-employed to survive.

Ethics of solidarity require increased assistance multilaterally and bilaterally from the wealthier countries to the developing countries. Capital is badly needed in developing countries to create productive jobs for the still-growing masses. Resources for development must be mobilized from joint efforts of the public sector and of capital markets, nationally[4] and internationally.[5]

However, the burning question is when that will happen. A real breakthrough will probably depend on a new concept to ascertain an optimal utilization of the needed funds. Besides the standard elements, the concept must be reasonably flexible in the sense that it must be adjusted to the different circumstances of developing countries. Another condition will probably be the introduction of new, tight follow-up procedures with the participation of both donor and receiver representatives. They must be in place before the commencement of any larger project. This condition is always fulfilled in private-sector joint ventures with the financial participation of development finance institutions. The political motivation to increase global assistance to the developing countries can be restored only if donors can foresee that the effects of their efforts will be positive and visible. Therefore, developing countries must demonstrate their clear intention and political will to produce appropriate economic, social and educational policies able to support the development in general.

A significant change in their budget priorities, including a dramatic reduction of their military spending, will no doubt also be demanded.

During their deliberations on increasing assistance, the wealthier countries should bear in mind the very heavy loan burden of most developing countries. Some arrangements concerning loan burden relief should be considered, possibly in combination with contributions to social sector assistance. Many of the critical loans were, so to say, disseminated by lenders in former happy days without much sense of responsibility on either side. The loans did not always have the background of well-considered development plans. Thus, they were often spent irresponsibly. In 1990 alone the developing countries paid instalments amounting to US$20 billion, more than the total value of loans obtained that year. Concerning the interest payment of the developing countries, in general the annual burden amounts to US$120 billion – or nearly twice the value of the annual assistance. So the net financial situation does not favour employment in the developing countries.

Concerning sub-Saharan Africa particularly, one often hears voices in the industrialized countries advocating a discontinuation of all assistance except catastrophe aid. The discouraging results obtained hitherto are mentioned as the main reasons for this thinking. Although it is correct that the results of more comprehensive assistance have been very far from the expectations, it is obvious that, within a shrinking world, the wealthier countries cannot simply neglect the alarming African situation.[6] Rather, active cooperation and participation in assistance efforts are no less than a must for the rest of the world community. However, African leaders, on their side, must demonstrate increased responsibility for and interest in the global and balanced development of their countries. A good base would be an expanded utilization of the traditional family, tribe and village solidarity of their countries. This process will not be an easy one. It will demand a hitherto unseen amount of personal and political courage from the leaders.

The role of assistance programmes in expanding agricultural employment

First of all one can state that, in general, productivity within the agricultural sector can be increased tremendously if a number of conditions are fulfilled. This is not the proper place to go into each and every condition, but most of them require more capital. Enormous areas fit for agriculture are not being cultivated today. The reasons for this situation are many: lack of infrastructure, split plots, ownership models, lack of irrigation, various natural disasters or sheer lack of inspiration and energy. Employment in the agricultural sector can, without doubt, be increased, but feasibility must first be consulted. Will the project be at all viable with more manpower employed? These remarks refer to the production of cash crops, not products for home consumption.

Agricultural productivity can be increased immensely, but in order to do so it must be considered whether the agricultural products can be brought to the consumers, whether there are suitable store facilities, whether the prices obtained are reasonable, and so on. It is a depressing fact that significant amounts of agricultural production in developing countries get spoilt or eaten by rats, mice or insects because of poor access to the customers and lack of storage facilities.

Increased agricultural productivity in developing countries must be combined with improved delivery of cash crops. This is essential in order to establish viable, integrated, agricultural production such as poultry farms and cattle farms with dairy units. It is also a condition for successful horticulture as in the production of vegetables, green plants and cuttings, or fruit and flowers. If the goods are not ready for shipment at the agreed hour the delay can cause huge losses. A new and very labour-intensive cultivation of cassava for modified starch production is in progress in West African countries. Demand for the products comes from the textile and pharmaceutical industries. One of these projects will give employment to approximately 1500 persons.

If the agricultural and horticultural products can be sold at good and fair prices the increased productivity within the mentioned sectors can, without doubt, attract people to work in these sectors. The quality of life in the rural areas will become more attractive with the growing wealth, improved infrastructure and more leisure time, important particularly to the youth. With the improved quality of life, farmers and casual workers will feel more satisfaction with their work in the countryside. Their improved incomes will normally be spent there. That gives derived employment to merchants, craftsmen, teachers, health and social workers, bankers, bush taxi drivers, and so on.

In promoting rural development, what are the roles of local mobilization and government programmes?

In dealing briefly with this important item one must be aware of the essential differences between the scenarios of the developing countries. Life and living conditions vary considerably from continent to continent, but also within the continents. With these reservations taken into consideration, it is probably correct to demand a joint local and governmental mobilization to strengthen the role of the rural areas in the national economy and as a source of new jobs with interesting earning possibilities. In most developing countries more than half of the population is working in the agricultural sector, frequently in so-called self-employment situations. It is characteristic that most agricultural activities are performed by women, especially in Africa. A mobilization of further manpower for agricultural activities will inevitably include the male population. Local leaders will have to contribute to a change in the negative attitude of the male population towards employment in agriculture. However, just as recent decades have established the irrelevance of sex criteria to employment, so it should be possible to overcome the sex barrier in the agricultural sector.

Mobilization to promote local development factors should preferably come upwards from the local grassroots. The cooperative movement in many countries in Africa has failed partly because it was applied over the heads of the local population. Local mobilization, when it is most efficient, should have its roots in the ethics of solidarity, which are so strong in African cultures at the family, tribe and village levels. If the sense of solidarity cannot be invoked satisfactorily, democratic overruling may be used. Examples of projects needing local mobilization include a more rational distribution of plots for cultivation, irrigation programmes, joint purchase of fertilizer and pesticides, local negotiations on joint contract farming for large-scale integrated agricultural projects, environmental conditions and tasks, joint ownership of equipment and processing units requiring major capital investment, cold stores and fire protection. To this list may be added local initiatives for the formulation of claims to the governmental development programmes.

Development programmes exist in all developing countries. There are also five-year plans in countries without socialist pasts. According to Danish experience, the most efficient programmes seem to be those which have been constructed in consultation with local authorities and councils together with experts from donor countries and institutions. The programmes require the formulation of national requests for bilateral and multilateral assistance. In planning offices today, you will often meet foreign experts with the task of ascertaining the coherence and consistency of development planning.

Like many development banks and institutions in developing

countries, those set up to promote the development of rural areas have often gone into bankruptcy. As little development will take place without the possibility of finance, and as development is a necessity, new ways and means must be found, based upon the unhappy experience of the past, to recreate those rural development banks and institutions.

Mobilization and harmonization of local and governmental initiatives to promote a breakthrough in living conditions in the rural areas of developing countries must go hand in hand with private, local initiatives to obtain the optimal results. Local acceptance of ideas is a prerequisite for their successful implementation.

Internal migration and foreign assistance

Migration problems are very complex and they differ considerably from country to country and from continent to continent, partly because of varying traditions, varying degrees of a sense of solidarity, varying physical surroundings and varying economies of the societies in question. I do not consider here the so-called guest workers, who come back year after year to perform seasonal tasks – at planting and harvest time, for example.

The real problems of rural–urban migration derive from the overwhelming masses who leave the rural areas in order to seek jobs in the informal sector of the already crowded cities. Their expectations are seldom met. The will and opportunity to return to their original villages decrease with time, and the urban areas expand without planning. The slum quarters become threats to the rest of the society in many ways. The infrastructure of the townships cannot meet the increasing demands, public health problems proliferate, and as income possibilities are nearly non-existent, criminality and drug abuse become frequent phenomena. It seems very important that migrant work seekers should be able to maintain their personal identities and self-respect. This is a prerequisite to keep them away from the dangerous slums where personality evaporates within a short period of time. It is my experience that social workers are badly needed in the urban areas to assist newly arrived job seekers. Some NGOs do their best in this respect, but a planned action with well-trained social workers could diminish the problems of the job seekers as well as of the local communities. Many of the job seekers arrive in the cities full of unrealistic dreams. They would often have been safer as underemployed labour at home in their rural area, close to their protecting families, friends and relatives.

Many tragedies might have been prevented with the right kind of social workers in place. They could have given realistic advice, in time, about job prospects, dwelling facilities and social conditions in the urban surroundings so drastically different from the village of the migrant worker. It would be cheaper for the society if the job seekers, after consultation with a social worker, were given a return ticket.

Taking into consideration the extent of the human tragedies for migrant workers and their families who do not obtain any employment in the cities, it must be a serious consideration to include the introduction of or the extension of social worker services to arriving job seekers in the new social development plans to be co-financed by donor countries and institutions. It goes without saying that the problems and tragedies of migrant workers ending up in some city of a foreign country, far from their own, without employment, are still more severe.[7] Although they could get the assistance of social workers, at least in the industrialized countries, they often dare not visit them because they have no work permit. They really belong to a high risk group, where the police are often their first contact with the local society. In such cases it is important that the police are cooperating with social workers in order to find reasonable solutions for the migrant persons.[8]

The following two cases will be mentioned to illustrate non-traditional job creation in the rural areas of countries in West Africa. They have been selected because they are non-traditional and not because they have created the largest source of new employment. They both have large expansion possibilities, however, and quite considerable indirect impact on employment.

HORTICULTURE IN TOGO

In 1986 local entrepreneurs and investors created a joint venture company together with a Danish firm and the Danish Industrialization Fund for Developing Countries (IFU).[9] The intention was to produce horticultural products for export, particularly fine herbs and vegetables for the European market (especially for the European off-season period). The farm is situated in agricultural surroundings only some 20 km away from the international airport of Lomé and 25 kilometres from the container port of Lomé.

The local partners provided land, the Danish firm the financing and technical, managerial and marketing knowledge, and IFU participated with financing and its vast experience from other investments in Africa and elsewhere in developing countries. IFU's regional office for projects in Africa was situated in Lomé.

At the time of establishment, few possibilities for employment existed in the area, where a monetary economy was poorly developed. However, the area had many idle or underemployed persons with good practical knowledge about traditional farming. There were also technicians commuting between their homes and jobs in Lomé.

From the beginning, the project gave employment to about 170 persons, more than half of them women. The experimental period was much longer than foreseen. Additional financing had to be provided. Vegetables were removed from the production plan because of important changes in the import situation in the countries of the European Union which now had access to new vegetable-producing countries in Southern Europe.

Experiments with the processing of tropical fruits bought from local farmers gave much employment, but as this side-project was not viable it was also dropped. In the end, and after heavy additional financing, the partners decided to concentrate on fine herbs and to look for cooperation possibilities with expert companies within this specialized field of business. Early in 1994, an international company took over the company from the Danish partners whereas the local partners continued.

The employment has grown considerably, and in mid-1994 some 700 persons are working for the farm. Approximately 650 of them are casual workers. The rest are staff members. The labourers are organized in a trade union and, as in the beginning, more than half of them are women. All labourers have received on-the-job training. Some of the other employees have received more advanced education, depending on the nature of their tasks. With a direct employment of 700 persons, mainly coming from the surrounding villages, and an additional indirect employment in the area and in Lomé, the farm is one of the most important job creators in the private sector of Togo.

As all the products are exported, the farm obtained free zone status a few years ago. This has resulted in cheaper production costs. It is obvious that the employment at the farm has contributed considerably to the increased wealth of the local society. The workers can now afford to send all their children – and not only their boys – to school. They can afford to pay for school uniforms, paper, pencils, and even for transport to more advanced schools. They can afford to buy fertilizer and pesticides for private plot cultivation. The rational cultivation processes can, to a certain degree, be used at home.

Through this experience women have obtained more self-confidence and self-respect as employees. It always causes problems when married women with children are away from home. In this connection it should be borne in mind that women carry out the large majority of agricultural tasks in Togo, but the African women seem to have an advantage compared to their sisters in the industrialized countries. In Africa there is a large reserve of persons in the compound homes who traditionally offer their services, especially when a woman is employed. It is often the case that grandmothers take care of the children and, together with the young girls, prepare the food.

The employees now have better medical facilities with regular health inspections and daily access to a doctor. Assistance for the purchase of medicine is available. The quality of life has also been improved through purchases of radio and television sets, and bicycles or scooters. The employees seem to be happy with their jobs in familiar, nearby surroundings.

It seems likely that more land will be cultivated in the years to come and that a significant increase in the number of jobs will become a reality. But there exists a constant danger, that the fine herbs can be obtained at lower prices from other producer countries. However, Africa has a favourable export agreement with the European Union, so that the danger is limited. Moreover, better skills, and thus products, are constantly being developed.

QUARRY IN GHANA

In 1991, a local development fund, a Danish firm and IFU established a joint venture project in the southeastern part of Ghana, not far from the frontier of Togo.[10] The intention was to produce stone products from local rock formations for road construction and coast protection barriers. The existing roads of the district were under renovation with assistance from multilateral and bilateral sources. An extension of the road network was in the planning phase. The region has great possibilities to become an important producer of agricultural and horticultural products. The very poor infrastructure has hitherto been an obstacle to an increase in production, and the government has therefore given high priority to the development plans of the region. As the financing, in principle, is in place, the establishment of a quarry in the middle of the region should be beneficial to the road works.

The local development fund provided the land and the Danish firm brought in second-hand but totally renovated equipment together with finance, managerial and marketing knowledge. IFU's contribution was finance and its global project establishment expertise. It was important that IFU's regional office for its projects in Africa was situated in Lomé, only 100 km from the quarry and the office of the regional fund.

The commencement of the project was delayed because of bureaucracy and long-term contracts between the road authorities, a major contractor and a distant quarry. Additional finance was therefore required from the partners. The number of employees was originally fifty. It has later grown to 100 and further growth is possible when the road projects are implemented as foreseen. All local employees come from villages of the area, where employment possibilities practically did not exist before the opening of the quarry. The rocky area had hitherto been used by the local population for leisure activities. So it was also necessary for the project managers to negotiate with the local chiefs in order to arrange for a continuation of the traditional activities within the limits of mutual respect of interests.

The labourers have all undergone on-the-job training. The dynamite expert has attended a long course arranged by the Swedish International Development Authority (SIDA). It is worth mentioning that some of the best educated workers had obtained some technical skills at workshops in bigger cities. Some of them were partly working in the cities when the quarry opened. When good job opportunities occurred next to their villages and families, they preferred to work full time there. A quarry operation is of a rather technical character and it has been a positive surprise to the Danish partner that the operation can be executed with only one expatriate on site.

The opening of the quarry, although still new and small, has already contributed to increasing the wealth of the surrounding villages. As up to ten persons can live from the cash income of one worker it is evident that experience of a monetary economy has changed the style of life. The local shops have obtained a broader variety of commodities, the visits of bush taxis have become more frequent, and more radio and television sets can be found in the homes. This is also possible because of the positive side-effect of the connection of the quarry to the national electricity grid with simultaneous connections to the surrounding villages. The former isolation of these villages has been broken and many new perspectives are available. The establishment of the quarry also means that a connection road from the coast to the regional capital, a road passing the site of the quarry, will be upgraded to modern standards shortly. With this improvement of the infrastructure, new production possibilities with positive sales aspects will be opened for the farmers. Also it will have very positive employment effects for the whole agriculturally rich area.

Contrary to the situation mentioned in the first case study, the products of the quarry are primarily for the domestic market as the transport costs are relatively high for stone products. But some export to the cement block industry of Togo is a possibility. The indirect employment deriving from the quarry operation is relatively smaller than that of the farm project mentioned previously, but the transport of the products gives jobs to many small-scale operators. Practically all employees at the quarry area are men, because of the hard physical labour. Women are employed only in the canteen, as cleaners and in the office.

In connection with the privatization of the local development fund and the foreseen expansion of production, new local investors will contribute to the necessary additional financing together with the Danish partners. The employment prospects thus seem to be promising in this rural area where salaried employment is scarce.

NOTES
1 The responsibility for the contents is solely that of the author and in no way that of the Industrialization Fund for Developing Countries (IFU) or of the World Federation of United Nations Associations (WFUNA).
2 World Summit for Social Development (1994) Backgrounder No. 2 (DPI/1487/SOC/CON-31581, August 1994-30M), p. 4.
3 United Nations (1994) Report of the Secretary-General on the Work of the Organization, September, p. 46.
4 United Nations, Resolution of 31 March 1994, adopted by the UN General Assembly.
5 IBRD, *World Development Report 1990*.
6 World Summit for Social Development (1994) Backgrounder No. 2 (DIP/1487/SOC/CON-31581, August 1994-30M).
7 World Summit for Social Development (1994) UN Fact Sheet No. 1, World Employment (DPI/1538-9427833-July 1994-30M).
8 United Nations (1994) Report of the Secretary-General of the United Nations on the Work of the Organization, September, p. 6.
9 IFU (1993) *Annual Report*, p. 20.
10 *Ibid.*, p. 19.

15

Promoting Employment Creation Projects and Programmes: The Role of SIDA

– ARNE STRÖM –

The Swedish International Development Authority (SIDA) does not have a specific strategy for employment creation. However, a very strong underlying principle in Swedish development cooperation is that employment aspects should be taken into account whenever a new project or programme is conceived.

Employment generation is also closely linked to the Swedish main objectives for development assistance which are:

1 To promote economic and social improvement in poor countries;

2 To promote a more equitable distribution of income and wealth;

3 To promote economic and political independence;

4 To promote democratization; and

5 To promote environmental conservation.

For a long time the UN policies, especially those of the ILO, formed the basic principles for SIDA's support in the area of employment creation. There are three different ways in which employment generation is supported by SIDA. These are broadly:

1 Policy training and research (mainly through multilateral channels);

2 Support of employment-generating projects in poor countries; and

3 Systematic work to develop labour-intensive technology and policies.

Policy training and research

Cooperation with multilateral organizations has been part of the Swedish policy for employment generation in developing countries

255

since the 1960s. The ILO World Employment Programme has been the most frequent partner for SIDA. Special support has been given to the Southern African Team for Employment Promotion (SATEP) and ARTEP in Asia. SATEP has received about US$5 million since 1979–80.

The reason for the Swedish preference for multilateral support of employment generation over bilateral project support has been the belief that employment is a policy issue rather than a project investment issue. Normally, multilateral organizations are better suited than bilateral donors to dialogues with governments on general policy issues.

Another example of cooperation with multilateral organizations is the contribution to the UNU/WIDER conference on the Politics and Economics of Global Employment. SIDA has financed a number of workshops and training opportunities on employment in collaboration with the UN and other organizations.

SIDA is also in the process of financing and participating in poverty assessments carried out in Africa by the World Bank. In these assessments, unemployment and underemployment and the reasons for them are important elements of the analysis.

Direct support of employment-generating projects

Most physical projects financed under an aid programme will generate some employment for some people for a time. That is not the issue, however. It is quite possible to pour foreign currency (or food) into a country, to be used to finance large construction or agricultural schemes with labour-intensive methods and thus employ thousands of people. The proper definition of employment generation in development cooperation must specify sustainable and self-generating employment. We find that this type of employment generation is a lot more difficult, especially in the wake of the economic crises in many developing countries. It is no longer possible to rely on the government and tax revenues to create employment for the increasing number of school leavers and previously unemployed.

Examples of projects which SIDA has financed in order to create sustainable employment are the following:

1 A continuing programme to develop social forestry in Orissa, India since 1981. This programme is focused on the employment of women, on firewood production and on commercial sales of timber.

2 Support of the Grameen Bank in Bangladesh. This well-known

scheme specializes in making credits available to landless and other poor people in the rural areas of Bangladesh. A very large proportion of the borrowers are women. The bank has over half a million members who have been given the possibility to employ themselves through production-oriented small-scale credits.

3 A third example is the financing of a fund within the Interamerican Development Bank, IDB, called the Small Projects Programme. The fund – at present US$6 million – is being used for credits for microenterprises in the poorest countries.

4 Between 1978 and 1994, SIDA has supported the Labour Construction Unit (LCU) within the Ministry of Works in Lesotho, Southern Africa. The objective has been to create employment opportunities, mainly in road construction, for the rural population and the returning migrant workers from South Africa. The programme has been successful in terms of the number of jobs and quality of work, but has probably not achieved the desired sustainability.

5 Another SIDA-supported scheme with labour-based techniques is the Road Construction and Maintenance Scheme in Kenya. This is a pilot scheme including empirical tests on the optimal mix of manual labour, simple tools and mechanized methods in order to make road maintenance cost-effective and employment-generating. It will lead up to a national plan called 'Roads 2000'. Altogether, SIDA is committed to road construction projects with labour-intensive methods in seven countries. In the first year, 1992/93, SIDA disbursed US$10 million to these projects.

6 SIDA has for a long time contributed to a large number of small-scale projects aiming at income generation for women. The contributions are very small and normally used for simple equipment like maize mills or sewing machines.

7 The Rural Employment Sector Programme (RESP) in Bangladesh has been supported by SIDA for four years. The present agreement (1993) is for US$13 million and includes the upgrading of rural feeder roads, tree planting, drainage tunnels and agriculture.

Systematic work to develop labour-intensive technology and policies

Research in labour-intensive technology touches on a number of disciplines from pure technical aspects to management techniques, economics and cultural behaviour. SIDA does support research and experiments in most of these areas, although at a rather limited financial level.

Lessons learnt

In its practical work and as financier of labour research and experiments SIDA has collected some experience that may be of value in formulating a strategy for support of employment generation. Some of the lessons learnt are summarized in the following points.

1 Relying on a government to create and finance employment by means of underbalancing the budget or borrowing from abroad is not sustainable and might just postpone a solution and aggravate the unemployment problem. Therefore structural adjustment is not an obstacle to employment, but may expose the problems of redundant workers and unsustainable budget financing.

2 The so-called informal sector could, if accepted by the government, be an even more important employment factor than it is today. The 'informal sector' is not a sector in itself but rather an unregistered and untaxed part of the economy, involving several areas of production of goods and services. By accepting the informal sector, government should register the actors and facilitate legal requirements such as land deeds, but not necessarily tax them.

3 Poverty alleviation should be related to employment. Poverty has to be attacked not only by maintained and improved social services, but also through better legal rights and better possibilities for work. Such possibilities can sometimes be improved by dismantling obstacles to work, improving access to education and credits, and by subsidizing improvement or introducing labour-intensive techniques (rather than subsidizing employment itself).

4 Donors must think of replicability and sustainability whenever they consider financing an employment project.

5 Donors can assist governments in finding their new role in relation to the hitherto unregistered part of the economy and other small-scale employers. Government can be assisted to change from the concept of being an expanding employer to being a promoter of employment in other institutions. This could be part of public administration support.

16

The Role of the United Nations in Developing Human Security

–ÜNER KIRDAR[1]–

In just five short years the twentieth century will be over, bringing to a close an era in which humanity was subject to two major world-wide armed conflicts and one political war that succeeded in dividing the world for close to 50 years. Together these three conflicts deeply affected the course and destiny of mankind.

The Second World War, in particular, taught us many valuable lessons. The ineffectiveness of the League of Nations in preventing such a devastating disaster from occurring pointed to the necessity of creating an international organization that had a different vision for ensuring international security.

Hence, when the United Nations was established on 24 October 1945, its Charter was formulated to be based explicitly on the notion that international peace can only be ensured if human security is guaranteed for all. It has one major goal: to foster peace through promoting social progress and better standards of living in an environment of freedom.

International peace in the coming century can only be ensured if we make a serious effort to fulfil the objectives of the United Nations Charter. We can do this only if we recognize, as the Charter does, that international security has many components. It involves not only political, but human security, and the two are indivisible. In maintaining international peace and security, the well-being of people is equally as important as national political security. The world cannot become a secure place unless people's security can be ensured in their homes, in their jobs, and in their communities. A better and more peaceful world, as foreseen and inspired by the United Nations Charter, can only be secured through the promotion of higher standards of living, full employment, and social progress, with more freedom for all.

Mankind's experiences during turbulent times prove that global confrontations do not result only in death and devastation. Upon their cessation they provide societies with the opportunity to bring about profound changes in the ways in which they are organized. As history has so often shown, traumatic experiences, such as war or political revolutions, cause people to rethink the premises on which their lives are based, prompting them to envision new ways of addressing societal concerns and thus to address the root causes of inequality or injustice.

The League of Nations, the first experiment, constitutionally was neither empowered nor equipped to deal effectively with economic and social problems and, therefore, was unable to conduct substantive operational assistance activities. The League's system was conceived functionally and institutionally as a centralized one: the ILO, for example, was closely linked to the League. Even at that early stage, attention was drawn to the issue of proliferation of agencies, both in number and fields of activity.

A firm belief existed during the Second World War that the failure of the League to keep the peace was mainly due to its insufficient interest in and ineffective treatment of world economic problems. The concept of a post-war organization was seen, therefore, in terms of improving the overall conduct and objectives of economic and social activities. The first official recognition of this imperative was expressed in the Atlantic Charter of August 1941. On 1 January 1942, 26 nations signed the United Nations Declaration in Washington, DC, pledging themselves for 'common purposes and principles'.

The end of the Second World War witnessed just such a watershed in thinking. For the first time in the history of mankind, there was recognition on the part of some that economic and social problems were universal in nature, transcending national boundaries to affect people all over the world. It is somewhat ironic that it was only towards the mid-twentieth century, at a time when technology was advanced enough to create the means for destroying the world with the atom bomb, that mankind, for the first time in its history, realized that only through joint action could it hope to find solutions to the economic and social problems that collectively threatened it. Born of this realization was a new vision, one of multilateral development cooperation as the most likely way to ensure universal economic and social well-being, and hence world peace. Premised on and guided by this vision, the United Nations and its specialized agencies (including the Bretton Woods institutions) were created, the Marshall Plan was launched, and the European Common Market was initiated.

Most of the articles of the United Nations Charter dealing with economic and social cooperation, the main lines of today's structure of the United Nations system, find their origin in a declaration by the four major powers at Dumbarton Oaks, generated mainly from earlier American proposals. According to available information, conflicting views existed within the United States government on the structure of the United Nations system. Some preferred to adopt a loose and decentralized system, while others wanted to integrate economic activities within the overall organization. Due to these divergent concepts, different plans were worked out, such as the Draft Constitution, Draft Charter, the Economist Draft, and so on.

Urgent needs for post-war reconstruction and relief, enthusiasm for increased international cooperation and the slow progress achieved in founding the global institution resulted in the establishment of several autonomous agencies before the United Nations itself, for example the Food and Agricultural Organization (FAO), the IMF, the World Bank, and the International Civil Aviation Organization (ICAO).

The future plans for the United Nations, such as the tentative proposals of the United States to the Dumbarton Oaks Conference, had to be based on this *de facto* situation. They recommended that the agencies should be brought into relationship with the United Nations and that their activities be coordinated. The United Kingdom's proposal was on the same lines. The Soviet Union, in their proposal, wanted to limit the activities of the United Nations to security enforcement problems. According to the Chinese proposal, the ILO was to be maintained as part of the organization and special offices were to be created for social welfare, cultural relations and other matters. At Dumbarton Oaks the United States' proposals concerning economic and social arrangements and relationships with agencies were adopted nearly in their entirety.

At the San Francisco Conference, though the Dumbarton Oaks proposals were accepted, the structure of economic and social cooperation was reinforced and enlarged: objectives were more clearly defined and functions more explicitly ascertained. Thus, compared with the Covenant of the League, the United Nations Charter brought the cooperation in these fields out of the shadows into the spotlight. In contrast to a single article in the former documents, the latter devoted two whole chapters, with a total of eighteen articles, to the ways and means for such cooperation. The Economic and Social Council (ECOSOC) was listed as a principal organ of the Organization. These improvements were due mainly to the efforts of the delegations of Canada, Australia, and the developing countries of Latin America.

Historical evolution proves that the present decentralized structure of the United Nations system is more contingent, rather than the result of cautious design and certainly not an outcome of an overall policy adopted after a thorough consideration and deliberation by the majority of the members of the United Nations. The San Francisco Conference was confronted with a *de facto* situation. Several autonomous agencies were already established, having their own constitutions, assemblies and governing bodies. Therefore, the Conference had to acknowledge officially the existence of a decentralized system, presented later as 'functional federalism', and to confirm that the working relationship of the system had to depend on voluntary 'coordination' and 'cooperation'. Nevertheless, some countries proposed to incorporate those existing agencies into the United Nations.

The San Francisco Conference considered that the provisions agreed to at Dumbarton Oaks regarding the role and power of the United Nations in guiding and coordinating the activities of the specialized agencies were inadequate and, therefore, it added several new provisions, in order to strengthen them.

Contrary to some beliefs, there is no overlapping jurisdiction between the United Nations and the specialized agencies. The United Nations has global policy-making, guiding and coordination tasks in respect of overall international economic, social, cultural, educational, health and related matters. The responsibilities of each specialized agency are specifically in the field of competence for which it has been created.

The existing division between the subsidiary organs of the United Nations dealing with international economic and social cooperation, and the specialized agencies is more the result of power politics, than an overall organizational policy plan worked out according to functional priorities.

Although assumption of full budgetary control of the agencies by the United Nations, or adoption of a joint consolidated budget for the whole system were considered to be the most effective means for coordination of activities, a limited review of the agencies' administrative budgets by the United Nations has been accepted as an alternative, in order to preclude resistance by agencies against entering into a relationship with the organization.

Over the past half a century, parallel to the growth of the membership of the world community from the original 51 to the present 184, the United Nations system has also developed rapidly. Since the 1960s hardly a year has gone by without the establishment of one or two important new international bodies. Today, the United Nations, with its related 17 operational programmes and organizations, 5 regional economic commissions and 19 specialized agencies, constitutes a very complex system.

The founders of the United Nations had the foresight to forecast the paramount importance which the economic and social foundations of peace would acquire in the past quarter century. They also recognized that the United Nations should cooperate effectively in expanding opportunities for better living conditions for all men and women, and in properly using the mechanism which they have established for that purpose. There are some pertinent questions which deserve serious consideration today by the inheritors of the UN system. To what extent have the governments made effective use of the system which they have created? To what degree have the original hopes and intentions of the UN been fulfilled?

All those individuals involved in the creation of these institutions were undoubtedly guided by the perceptions and visions shaped from their painful memories of the Great Depression and the Second World War. This is made abundantly clear by the fact that post-war economic and social policies, both on the national and international level, were guided by an overwhelming concern for ensuring betterment of human life, full employment, and respect for human rights as a means of securing peace. Even during the war itself, there was an official recognition of the necessity 'to bring about the fullest cooperation between all nations in the economic field with the objective of securing, for all, improved labour standards, economic adjustment, and social security',[2] as a prerequisite for international peace.

Is it any wonder that at the end of the Cold War the world is again, just as it was after the Second World War, struggling to envision ways of ensuring that such a conflict never occurs again, or that it does not manifest itself in an even more dangerous 'hot' war? What is reassuring, now on the eve of the twenty-first century, is that there really is no need for new revolutionary thinking. The vision that the founders of the United Nations had close to fifty years ago is just as valid today as it was then.

World social summit

One encouraging sign is the fact that the United Nations is preparing, in March 1995, a summit-level meeting of Heads of State and Governments in Copenhagen, Denmark, to address the major social development dilemmas facing the world as it approaches the next century. The three core issues to be considered are:

1 The alleviation and reduction of poverty;

2 The expansion of productive employment; and

3 The enhancement of social integration.

It is not without thinking that history's lessons endure that I note the basic assumption that is underlying this meeting, namely that only through collectively addressing these core issues will we move closer to attaining international prosperity and peace.

What remains to be seen is if, in the fifty years since the United Nations was founded, the world has become more ready and willing to address the problems of increasing poverty, unemployment, and social disintegration, awarding them the seriousness that these issues deserve.

Population and employment

At present, there is a striking contrast between the age structure of the populations of developed and developing countries. In the future, all the net growth in the world population of the 20 to 40 age group will take place in the developing countries. By the beginning of the next century, in the industrialized countries, there will be nearly 15 million fewer people in that age group. The workforce will continue to age. Rapidly growing numbers of older and retired persons will escalate increases in health, welfare, and social security expenditures.

Normally, the process of ageing has a considerable impact on the size and structure of the labour force, affecting the capacity and willingness to innovate and to respond to technological change. It may, therefore, have major implications for future economic growth. Young people can acquire new skills more quickly and can adapt intellectually and socially to the required changes faster than older people.

In the developing countries, at least one billion new jobs – more than the current total number of jobs in all industrialized countries – will have to be created by the year 2000 just to accommodate the new entrants into the labour forces. If the present high unemployment rates are taken into account, it seems almost impossible that we will meet such a challenge.

In this context, it should be remembered that in the 1960s a similar situation, but on a much smaller scale, also existed in the industrialized countries. The largest segment of the population was young and, in most parts of the industrialized world, youth was in ferment. There was a seething pool of discontent and revolt among energetic and talented young people as they were reaching maturity without the prospect of satisfactory work opportunities and the hope of making a reasonable living for themselves. All these incidents prompted national and international actions for a new social concern and sense of responsibility, and for improvements in the well-being of these young people. If today a similar course of action is not taken urgently, it is more than probable that the world will see a recurrence of the revolt of young people on a much larger and more dangerous scale. This time it will be in the developing world, and will be caused by frustrations, disappointments, and the fear of a lack of satisfactory work opportunities.

History proves that in most social revolutions, the dynamics that trigger such movements normally build up over time. Once the upheaval occurs, the obvious question which is wrongly asked is why the change came so suddenly – not why it took so long. True political wisdom therefore sees well in advance the formulating dynamics and responds in good time to the needs and frustrations of people.

Employment has multiple dimensions in people's lives. It is not merely an economic means to generate financial resources. Far more importantly, it gives people a sense of dignity and integrates them into their society.

As stated earlier, the painful experiences and memories of the Great Depression, as well as the main economic causes of the Second World War, convinced the founders of the United Nations of the necessity of ensuring full employment as one of the main pillars of international peace, stability and well-being. Its members, therefore, pledged themselves to take both joint and separate action for the achievement of this goal. However, in our day, this important objective of full employment seems to be forgotten. It has progressively disappeared from the agenda of the UN, since the time of its establishment.

Jobless growth is a new and common phenomenon. Elimination of jobs and massive lay-offs are considered effective measures to ensure competitiveness in the global markets. Among the richest countries, therefore, structural unemployment has reached its highest point: in Germany, for example, unemployment is around 3.5 million. In France, it now exceeds 12 per cent. In the US and Japan, firms are contemplating job lay-offs on a scale not seen since the Second World War.

During the 1950s and 1960s in the industrialized countries a 3 to 4 per cent unemployment rate was considered normal. Today this figure exceeds 12 per cent. The current policy makers are not only becoming reconciled to poorly paying jobs, but also to high rates of unemployment.

In a classical economy, voluntary unemployment was always regarded as a temporary phenomenon. There was a conviction that market forces would tend to reduce it. With today's market rules this does not happen any more. At present, for example in the United States, permanent job losses as a percentage of total unemployment are reaching the rate of 45 per cent per annum. As a new recipe for profit-making, job-cutting is becoming as popular as take-overs and mergers were in the 1980s. The new philosophy is: if you can fire workers without affecting your production and your sales, you can thus reduce your costs and increase your profits. New technological advancements are making it possible for companies to produce much more with fewer workers. Thus, businesses are increasing their gains by slicing their labour forces.

The growing impact of job-cutting is becoming more evident also in the national economic statistics. Wages are falling as percentages of national incomes, while corporate profits are rising. Recently, for example, General Electric Company, while reducing its workforce from 400,000 to nearly half its size, 230,000, succeeded in tripling its sales during the same period. The same is also true of other profit-able companies such as Procter and Gamble, AT&T, Johnson and Johnson, and IBM.

As stated earlier, in the industrialized countries of today most of the new jobs are created in the service sector – such as in banking, tourism, insurance, retailing, health care and restaurants – while jobs are being shed in such areas as manufacturing and mining. What is happening in these sectors at present is very similar to what happened to the agricultural sector at the beginning of this century. With the mechanization of farming, most of the farmers were forced to migrate to urban areas, in order to find new jobs in the industrial sector.

The link between full employment and the worry about rising inflation is also a new kind of international concern. According to the economic policy makers of today, if people work more, they may spend more money, which in turn may cause higher inflation. Therefore, a trade-off needs to be made between job growth and low inflation. Or, in other words, a choice has to be made between 'putting people back to work' or 'keeping the prices under control'. In the view of market-oriented economists and policy makers, the safeguarding of the value of currencies and low interest rates is more important than job security and economic growth. As a consequence, in the new economic literature the term 'full employment' is being replaced by 'cut off the fat' or 'job shedding'!

The employment problems of developing countries have some other dimensions. As stated earlier, the number of jobs which must be created to accommodate new entrants into the labour market is reaching the insurmountable figure of nearly one billion. On the other hand, each day the powerful role of the corporate world in the globalization of the world economy and in the channelling of capital, according to their own policies and priorities, is becoming more apparent. Capital and goods are moving freely from one country to another. However, the same freedom does not exist for the labour force. Instead, there are strict regulations governing any movement of workers. Also, the moment that developing countries learn to produce something that is labour-intensive, restrictions are immediately applied on those very products.

In the industrialized countries the largest part of the GNP consists of new jobs created in the modern services sector. Developing countries are not fully aware of this structural change in the world economy, nor are they paying enough attention to the training of their human resources in the use of new technologies. Technological change is the real basis of the new economic and transnational corporate power. In the short run, a great number of developing countries are not equipped to compete with industrialized countries because of lack of skill, technological knowledge and resources. They are increasingly falling behind and from the outset are condemned to be marginalized. A new kind of technological dominance is therefore in process.

Human security

The first and foremost lesson to be learned from the past four decades is that we must ensure a change in the prevailing concept of security. While the concept of peace is easy to grasp, international security is more complex. During the Cold War period, the outlook for security was mostly from a political perspective. The security concept was shaped by the potential for armed conflict between the two adversarial camps of East and West. For too long security has been equated with the threats to the borders of the state, as the UNDP *Human Development Report 1994* indicates. States sought arms, as the primary means of protecting their security. As the threats of the Cold War have ended, the need for a change in this concept becomes an urgent prerequisite.

When one reads the following appraisal nearly half a century later, one can only praise warmly the farsightedness of the founding fathers of the United Nations, especially with respect to the concept of security:

> The battle of peace has to be fought on two fronts. The first is the security front where victory spells freedom from fear. The second is the economic and social front where victory means freedom from want. Only victory on both fronts can assure the world of an enduring peace. If the United Nations cooperate effectively toward an expanding world economy, better living conditions for all men and women, and closer understanding among peoples, they will have gone far toward eliminating in

advance the causes of another world war a generation hence. If they fail, there will be instead widespread depressions and economic warfare which would fatally undermine the world organization. No provision that can be written into the Charter will enable the Security Council to make the world secure from war if men and women have no security in their homes and their jobs.[3]

The Secretary of State, at the end of this report, referred also to the United Nations organization itself and stated:

It promises to be an effective instrument. If properly used, it may well become one of the most powerful means for the creation of an enduring peace among the nations.[4]

How far these hopes and intentions have been fulfilled, and what use has been made of this instrument which its architects created in 1945, are important questions deserving serious consideration by their inheritors. The above makes fascinating reading at a time when we are once again rediscovering the complexity of defining the concept of security. It is clear that the architects of the United Nations gave equal weight to 'human security' and 'political security'.

The main argument of this closing chapter is, therefore, the necessity of returning to the basic aims and objectives of the Charter of the United Nations, as foreseen by its founders, and of implementing them vigorously with new vistas and commitments.

To meet the challenges of the twenty-first century we must be inspired by the farsightedness of the UN Charter provisions. We can no longer fight the battle of tomorrow with the weapons of the Cold War period. The preamble of the Charter starts with, 'We the people'. We must, therefore, put people at the centre of all our concerns for the future. Our ultimate objective must put people and the improvement of their conditions first. Our future policies must aim to be responsive to the social and economic needs of people and to reduce their poverty and misery. We must better use the people's capacities and capabilities. We must encourage the release of human energies in accordance with people's aspirations.

NOTES
1 The views expressed in this chapter are those of the author and do not necessarily reflect those of the UN or UNDP.
2 The fifth principle embodied in the Atlantic Charter, the Joint Declaration made by the President of the United States and the Prime Minister of the United Kingdom, 14 August 1941; US Department of State Bulletin, Vol. 5, pp. 125–6, also UN Yearbook 1946–7, p. 2.
3 Report of the President on the Results of the San Francisco Conference by the Secretary of State, Department of State, Publication 2343, 26 June 1945, p. 109.
4 Ibid., p. 124.

Index

Afghanistan 206, 215
Africa 7, 13, 22, 25, 28n, 61, 74, 77, 82, 85, 102, 111, 114, 124, 189, 201, 207, 215, 219, 221, 233, 256; Horn of 206; North *x*, 111, 113, 115-6, 126-8, 207, 214, 235; Southern 206; sub-Saharan *x*, 56, 58, 60, 68, 113, 124-5, 207, 246; West 243-54
Aga Khan, Sadruddin 207
age 14, 19, 104-5, 149, 156, 159, 264
agriculture 11-12, 15, 19-20, 66, 91, 96-7, 114, 123, 125, 131, 156-7, 169, 177-9, 195, 199, 210, 220, 246-53, 256-7
aid 38-9, 243-54, 255-8
AIDS 102
Albania 57
Algeria 57, 61-2, 127
Amsterdam 210
Angola 206
Arab states 7, 56, 58, 235
Argentina 25, 57-8, 116
Armenia 34
arms race 3
Asia 7, 12, 22, 25, 28n, 60-1, 68, 102, 111, 114-5, 129-30, 137, 167-81, 191-2, 201, 215, 233, 243; East 7, 10, 56, 58, 68, 73, 95, 111, 113, 114, 128-30, 167-8, 171, 175-7, 180, 189, 196, 220-1; South 7, 10, 13, 77, 111, 113, 128-30, 168, 221, 235; Southeast 7-8, 32, 68, 77, 111, 113, 128-30, 167-8, 171, 174-5, 178-80, 220, 225, 228; West 7
AT & T 266
Atlantic Charter 260
Australia 47, 57, 61, 152-3, 205, 234-5, 261
Austria 47, 152, 205
Azerbaijan 215

Bahamas 136
Balkans 215
Baltic states 34, 36
Bangladesh 57, 61, 129, 168, 171, 175, 256-7
banking 35-9, 95, 114, 119, 122, 248-9, 266; *see also* finance
Barbados 124, 136
Barcelona 210
Belgium 44, 47, 50, 57, 61, 119, 141
Benin 124
Beveridge, Sir William 240

biotechnology 11
Bolivia 122
Brazil 25, 82-6, 116, 118, 122, 135
Bulgaria 58, 120-1, 214-15
Burkina Faso 57, 82-5
Burundi 206

California 210
Cameroon 82-5
Canada 47, 56-8, 64, 152, 192, 235, 261
capital 7-8, 23-4, 26, 31-2, 36, 81, 85, 91, 97, 192, 194, 199-200, 208, 219, 220-1, 228, 231-2, 236, 242-3, 245, 248, 266; human capital 36, 42, 48, 50, 53, 63-4, 75, 91, 93, 123, 132, 180, 200-1, *see also* human resources
capitalism 216
Caribbean 56, 111, 113-4, 117, 122-4, 136, 206, 208
Caucasus 206
Central America 206, 208
Chad 57
child care 23, 37, 98, 101, 116, 122-3, 127, 130, 144-6, 159, 165-6n, 169, 177
Chile 135
China 13, 28-9n, 57, 116-7, 128, 130, 137, 167-8, 171, 175, 191-4, 199, 220, 235, 241, 261
CIS 34, 37
civil service 21, 66, 104, 116
civil society 209
civil wars 25, 205, 209, 233
Coimbatore 82-6
Cold War 3, 208-9, 216, 234, 263, 267-8
communism 35, 119
communities 23-4, 73, 76-7, 79, 84, 106, 114-5
comparative advantage 19, 31, 49, 117, 131, 172, 187, 194
competition *xi*, *xiii*, 3, 6, 8, 10, 21-2, 25-7, 31-2, 35, 39, 43, 49, 51, 70, 76, 116, 162, 167, 178, 185-204, 211, 221-2, 228, 230, 241, 265; 'new' 185-203; 'unfair' 25, 186, 198-200
cooperation, international 3-4, 6, 8, 18-19, 24, 27, 30, 231, 243-54, 260-2
cooperatives 120, 248
Copenhagen 214, 263
Costa Rica 135
Côte d'Ivoire 61-2, 234

Council for Mutual Economic Assistance (CMEA) 33, 36
crash (1929) 89-90
credit 30, 125, 179, 257
crime 79
Croatia 121, 205
Czech Republic 33, 35, 37, 40n, 185, 214-15
Czechoslovakia 121, 215

Danish Industrialization Fund for Developing Countries (IFU) 250, 252-3
debt 124, 196, 219
Delhi 118
democracy 3-4, 6, 61, 63, 255
Denmark 44, 47-8, 140-3, 147, 151-2, 154-6, 158, 213, 248, 250, 252, 263
dependency 14, 16, 86-7, 151
depression 35, 41, 46, 90; *see also* Great Depression, recession
deprivation 72-88
deregulation *xii-xiii*, 32, 42, 44, 52, 131
devaluation 196-7, 213
dictatorship 175, 206
disability 5, 46, 79, 105-6, 226-7
discrimination 5, 16, 23, 25, 75, 79-80, 112, 114-15, 120, 122, 125, 127-8, 130; and age 16, 209; and class 112; and disabilities 5, 79; and ethnicity 16, 25, 120, 206, 209; and gender 5, 16, 112, 114-15, 122, 125, 127-8, 130, 209; and race 5, 79, 112
Dominican Republic 122
Dublin Convention 212-13
Dunbarton Oaks Conference 260-2

Eastern bloc 8, 195
economic growth *xi-xiii*, 7, 9-11, 15-18, 25, 32, 35-6, 39, 41-2, 45, 55, 59, 63, 74, 89-90, 113, 124, 126, 128, 132, 167, 175, 177, 179, 192, 196-7, 199-200, 231, 233-4, 242, 264-6; employment-oriented 16-19; 'jobless growth' 10-11, 28n, 60, 265-6
economies, centrally planned 63; market 3-4, 6, 30, 36-7, 39, 63, 119, 179; mixed 4; newly industrialized *xi*, 7, 111, 114, 128-9,